THE EXPANSE
ORIGINS

BOOM!

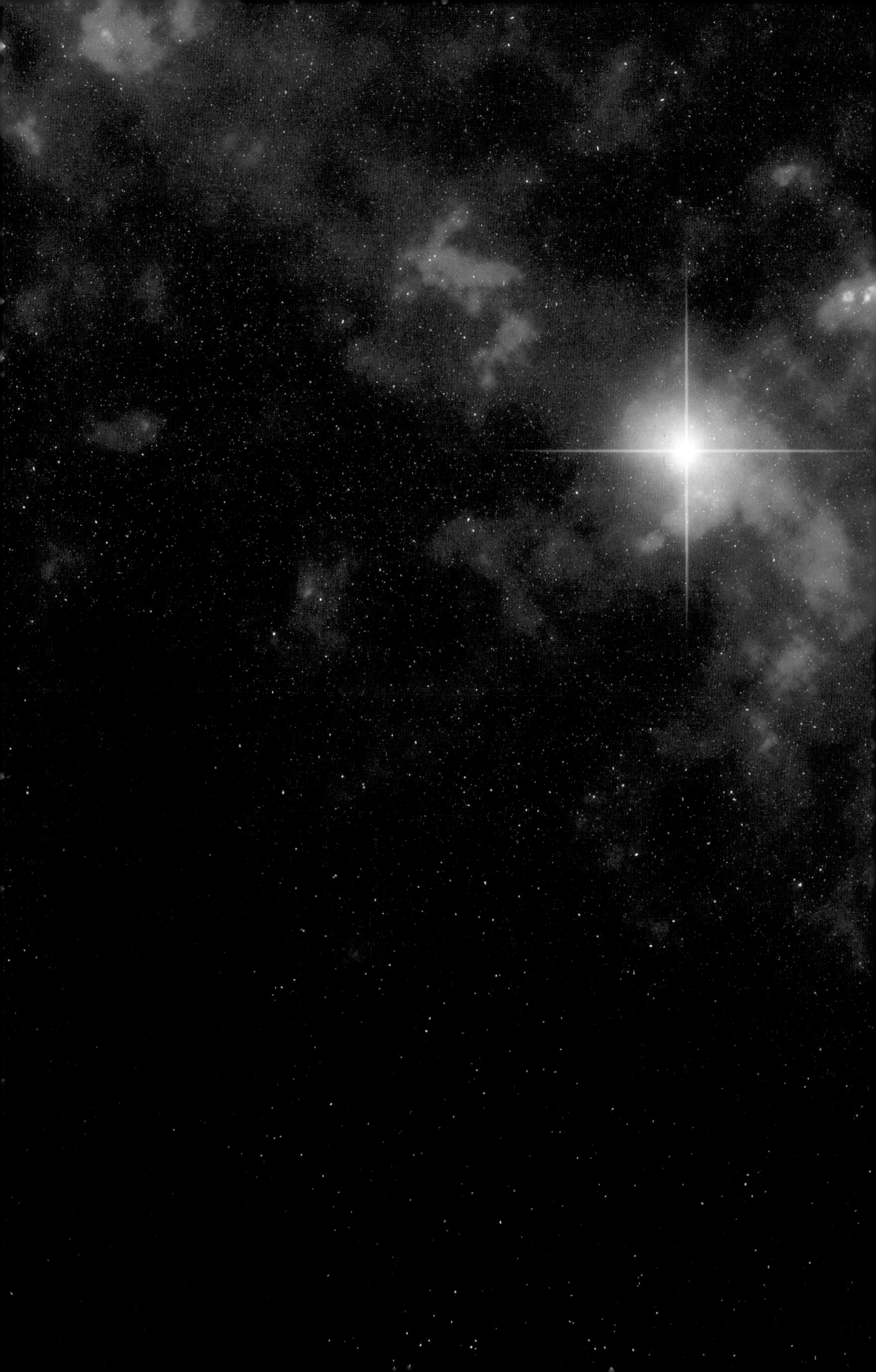

THE
EXPANSE
ORIGINS

BASED ON THE BOOKS BY
JAMES S.A. COREY

STORY BY
JAMES S.A. COREY
HALLIE LAMBERT
GEORGIA LEE

COVER BY **RAHZZAH**

DESIGNER **SCOTT NEWMAN**
EDITORS **CAMERON CHITTOCK** & **ERIC HARBURN**

SPECIAL THANKS TO **ANDREW KOSOVE**, **BRODERICK JOHNSON**, **LAURA LANCASTER**,
BEN ROBERTS, AND THE ENTIRE TEAM AT **ALCON TELEVISION GROUP**

THE EXPANSE: ORIGINS, February 2018. Published by BOOM!
Studios, a division of Boom Entertainment, Inc. The Expanse is ™ &
© Expanding Universe Productions, LLC. All rights reserved. BOOM!
Studios™ and the BOOM! Studios logo are trademarks of Boom
Entertainment, Inc., registered in various countries and categories.
All characters, events, and institutions depicted herein are fictional.
Any similarity between any of the names, characters, persons, events,
and/or institutions in this publication to actual names, characters,
and persons, whether living or dead, events, and/or institutions is
unintended and purely coincidental. BOOM! Studios does not read or
accept unsolicited submissions of ideas, stories, or artwork.

For information regarding the CPSIA on this printed material, call:
(203) 595-3636 and provide reference #RICH is 771249.

BOOM! Studios, 5670 Wilshire Boulevard, Suite 400, Los Angeles,
CA, 90036-5679. Printed in USA. First Printing.

ISBN: 978-1-68415-114-1, eISBN: 978-1-61398-853-4

CHAPTER_001
JAMES HOLDEN

WRITTEN BY **HALLIE LAMBERT** AND **GEORGIA LEE**
ILLUSTRATED BY **HUANG DANLAN**
COLORED BY **TRIONA FARRELL**
LETTERED BY **JIM CAMPBELL**

CHAPTER_002
NAOMI NAGATA

WRITTEN BY **GEORGIA LEE**
ILLUSTRATED BY **HUANG DANLAN**
COLORED BY **TRIONA FARRELL**
LETTERED BY **JIM CAMPBELL**

CHAPTER_003
ALEX KAMAL

WRITTEN BY **HALLIE LAMBERT**
ILLUSTRATED BY **HUANG DANLAN**
COLORED BY **JUAN USECHE**
LETTERED BY **JIM CAMPBELL**

CHAPTER_004
AMOS BURTON

WRITTEN BY **GEORGIA LEE**
ILLUSTRATED BY **HUANG DANLAN**
COLORED BY **JUAN USECHE**
LETTERED BY **JIM CAMPBELL**

CHAPTER_005
JOSEPHUS MILLER

WRITTEN BY **HALLIE LAMBERT**
ILLUSTRATED BY **HUANG DANLAN**
COLORED BY **JUAN USECHE**
LETTERED BY **JIM CAMPBELL**

CHAPTER_001

JAMES HOLDEN

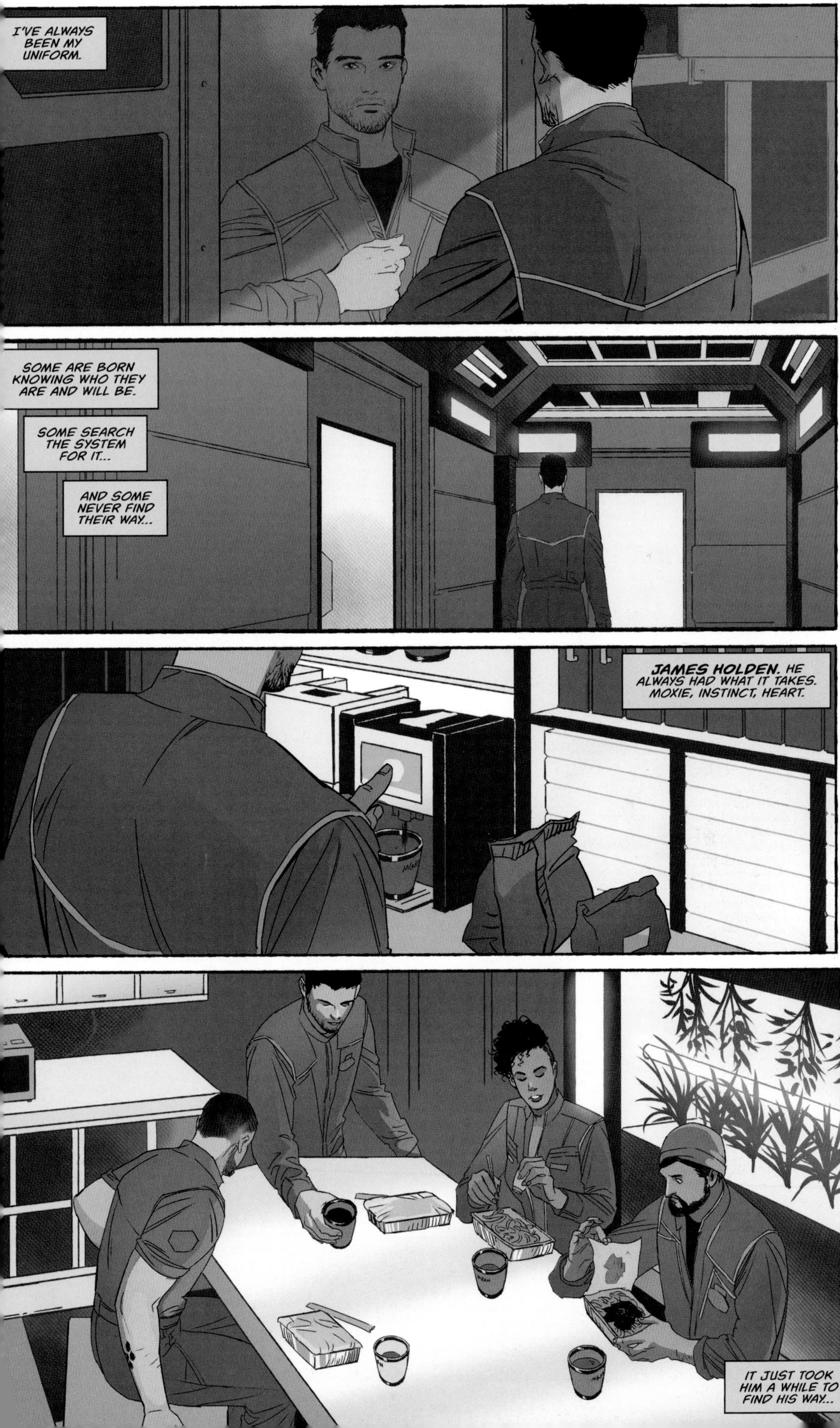
I'VE ALWAYS BEEN MY UNIFORM.
SOME ARE BORN KNOWING WHO THEY ARE AND WILL BE.
SOME SEARCH THE SYSTEM FOR IT...
AND SOME NEVER FIND THEIR WAY...
JAMES HOLDEN. HE ALWAYS HAD WHAT IT TAKES. MOXIE, INSTINCT, HEART.
IT JUST TOOK HIM A WHILE TO FIND HIS WAY...

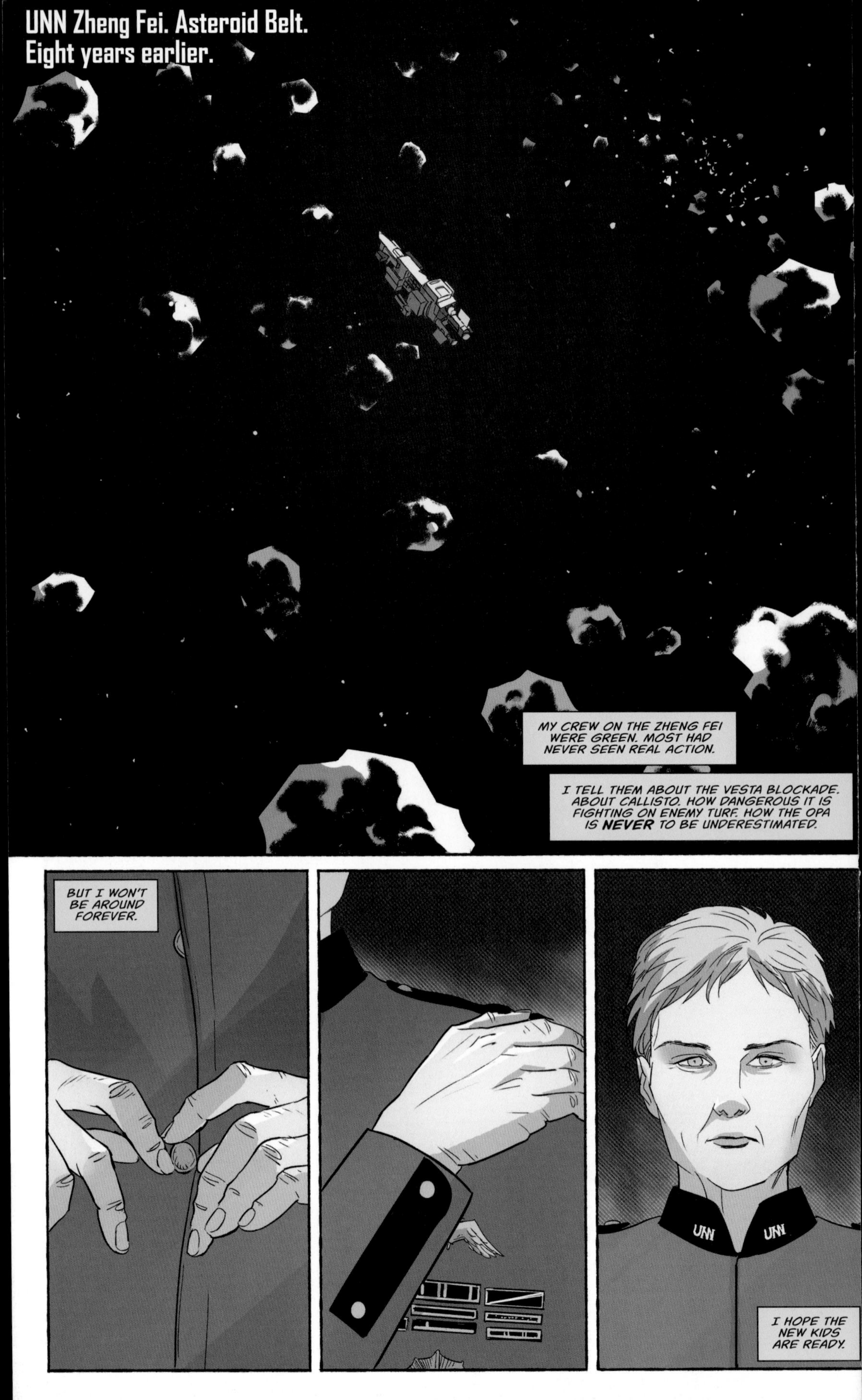
UNN Zheng Fei. Asteroid Belt.
Eight years earlier.
MY CREW ON THE ZHENG FEI WERE GREEN. MOST HAD NEVER SEEN REAL ACTION.
I TELL THEM ABOUT THE VESTA BLOCKADE. ABOUT CALLISTO. HOW DANGEROUS IT IS FIGHTING ON ENEMY TURF. HOW THE OPA IS NEVER TO BE UNDERESTIMATED.
BUT I WON'T BE AROUND FOREVER.
UNN
UNN
I HOPE THE NEW KIDS ARE READY.

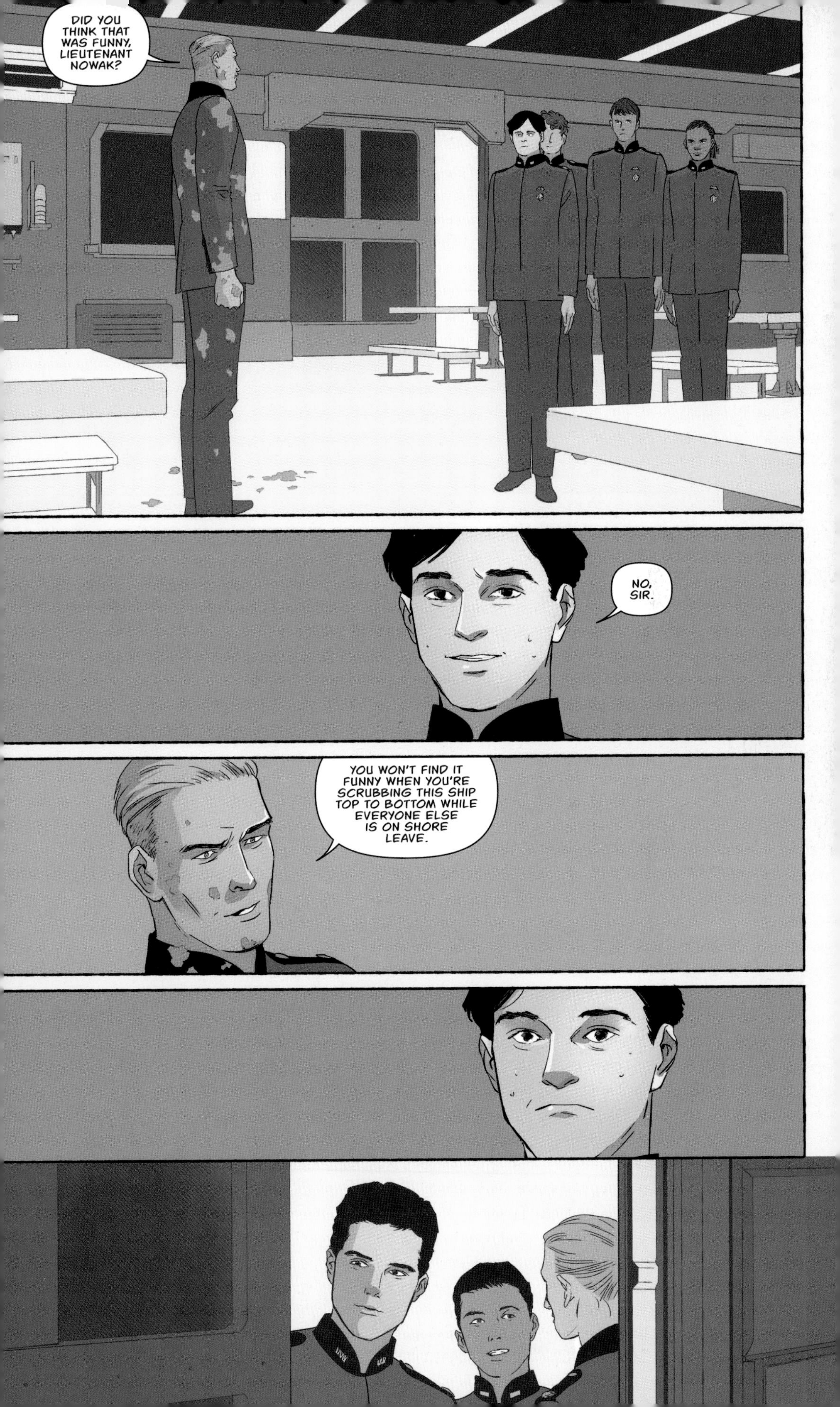
DID YOU THINK THAT WAS FUNNY, LIEUTENANT NOWAK?
NO, SIR.
YOU WON'T FIND IT FUNNY WHEN YOU'RE SCRUBBING THIS SHIP TOP TO BOTTOM WHILE EVERYONE ELSE IS ON SHORE LEAVE.

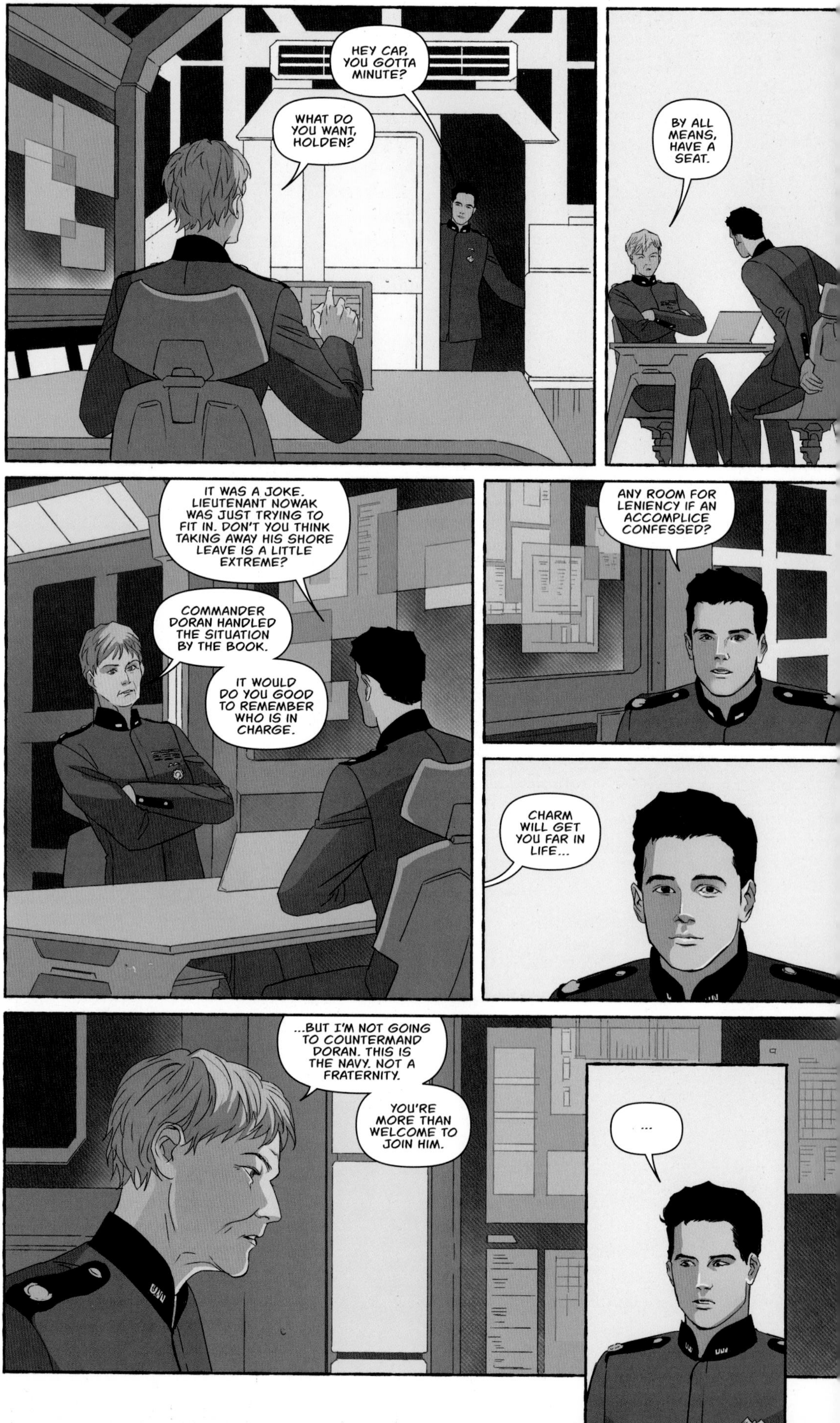
HEY CAP, YOU GOTTA MINUTE?
WHAT DO YOU WANT, HOLDEN?
BY ALL MEANS, HAVE A SEAT.
IT WAS A JOKE. LIEUTENANT NOWAK WAS JUST TRYING TO FIT IN. DON'T YOU THINK TAKING AWAY HIS SHORE LEAVE IS A LITTLE EXTREME?
COMMANDER DORAN HANDLED THE SITUATION BY THE BOOK.
IT WOULD DO YOU GOOD TO REMEMBER WHO IS IN CHARGE.
ANY ROOM FOR LENIENCY IF AN ACCOMPLICE CONFESSED?
CHARM WILL GET YOU FAR IN LIFE...
...BUT I'M NOT GOING TO COUNTERMAND DORAN. THIS IS THE NAVY. NOT A FRATERNITY.
YOU'RE MORE THAN WELCOME TO JOIN HIM.
...

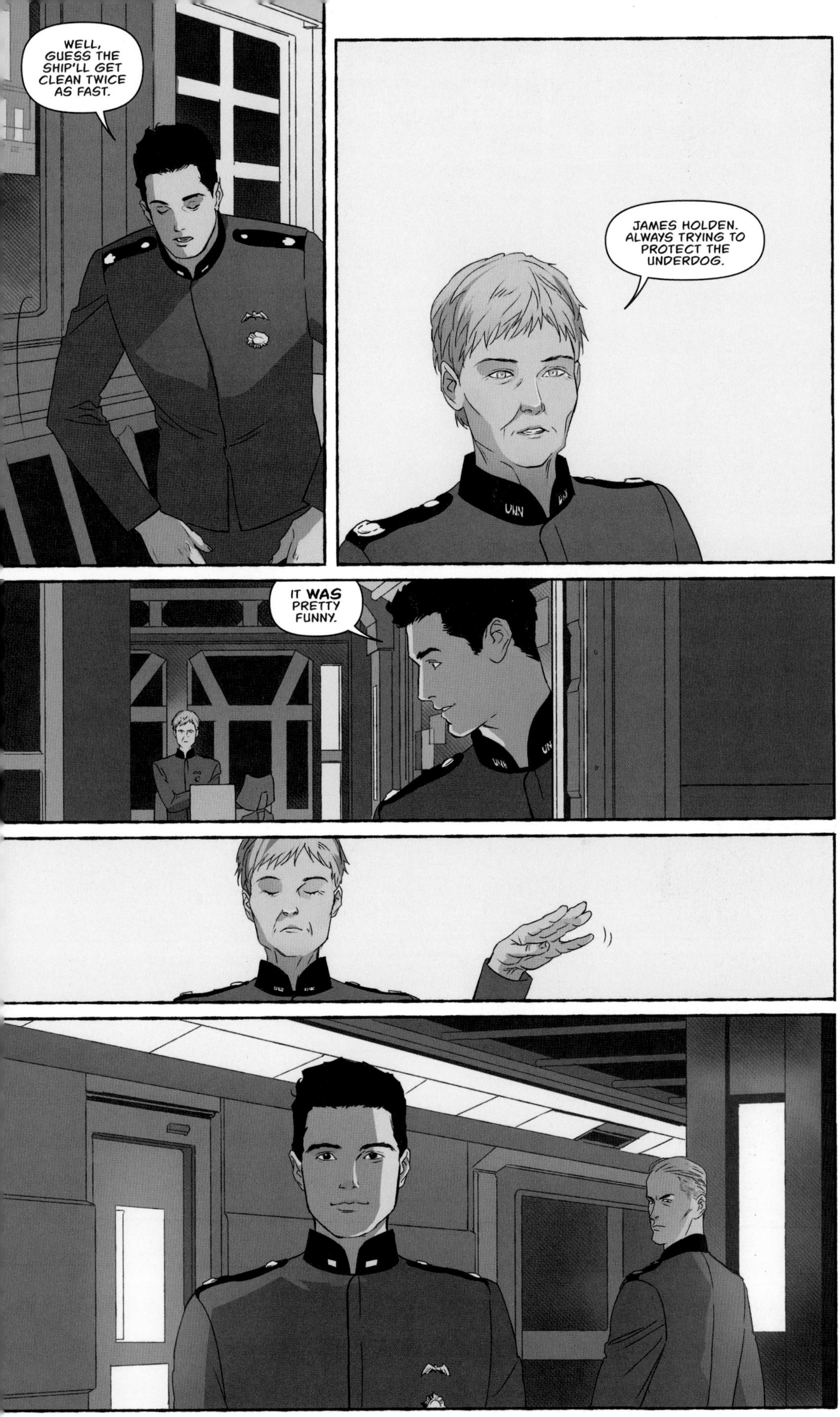
WELL, GUESS THE SHIP'LL GET CLEAN TWICE AS FAST.
JAMES HOLDEN. ALWAYS TRYING TO PROTECT THE UNDERDOG.
IT **WAS** PRETTY FUNNY.

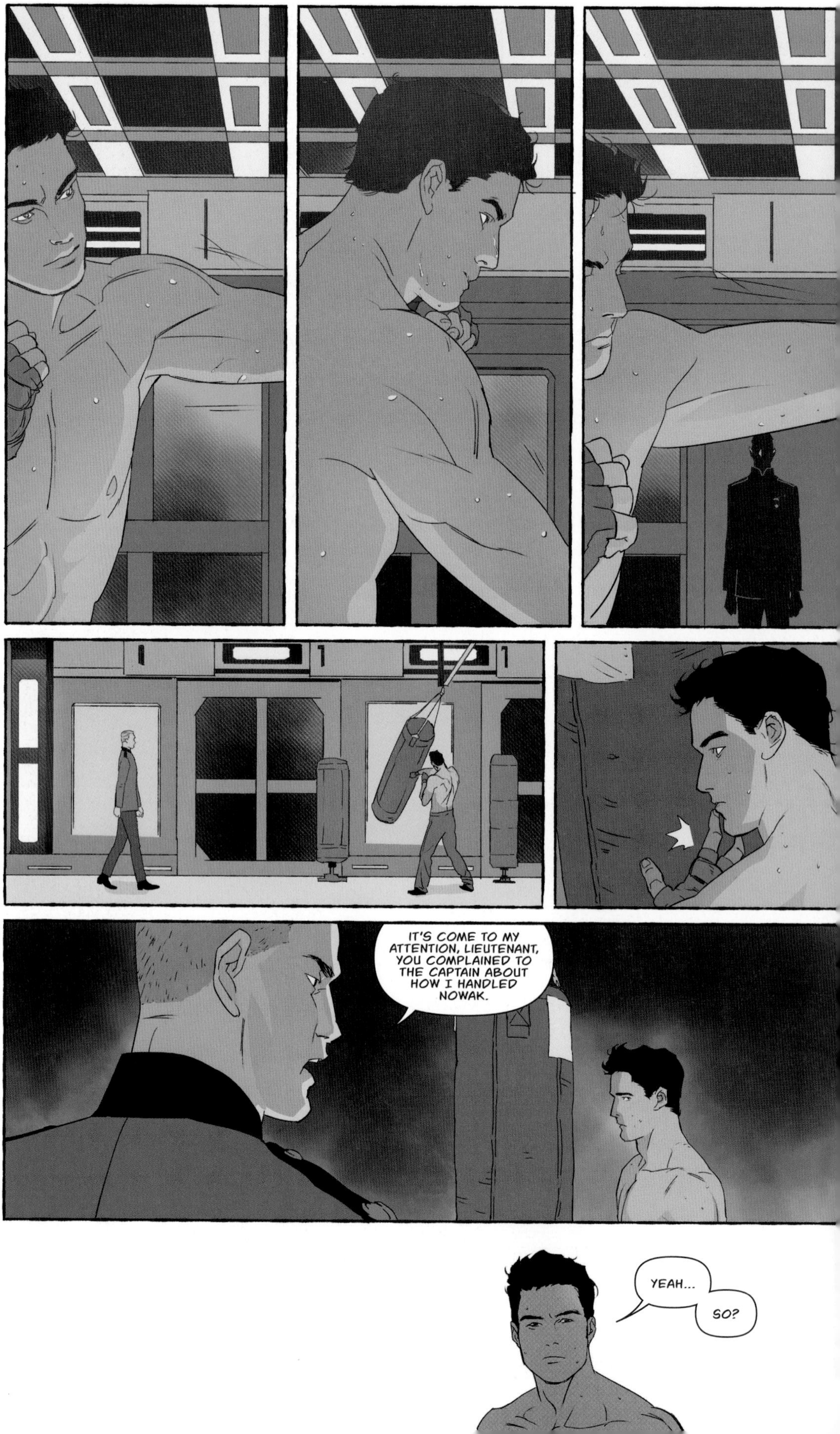
IT'S COME TO MY ATTENTION, LIEUTENANT, YOU COMPLAINED TO THE CAPTAIN ABOUT HOW I HANDLED NOWAK.
YEAH...
SO?

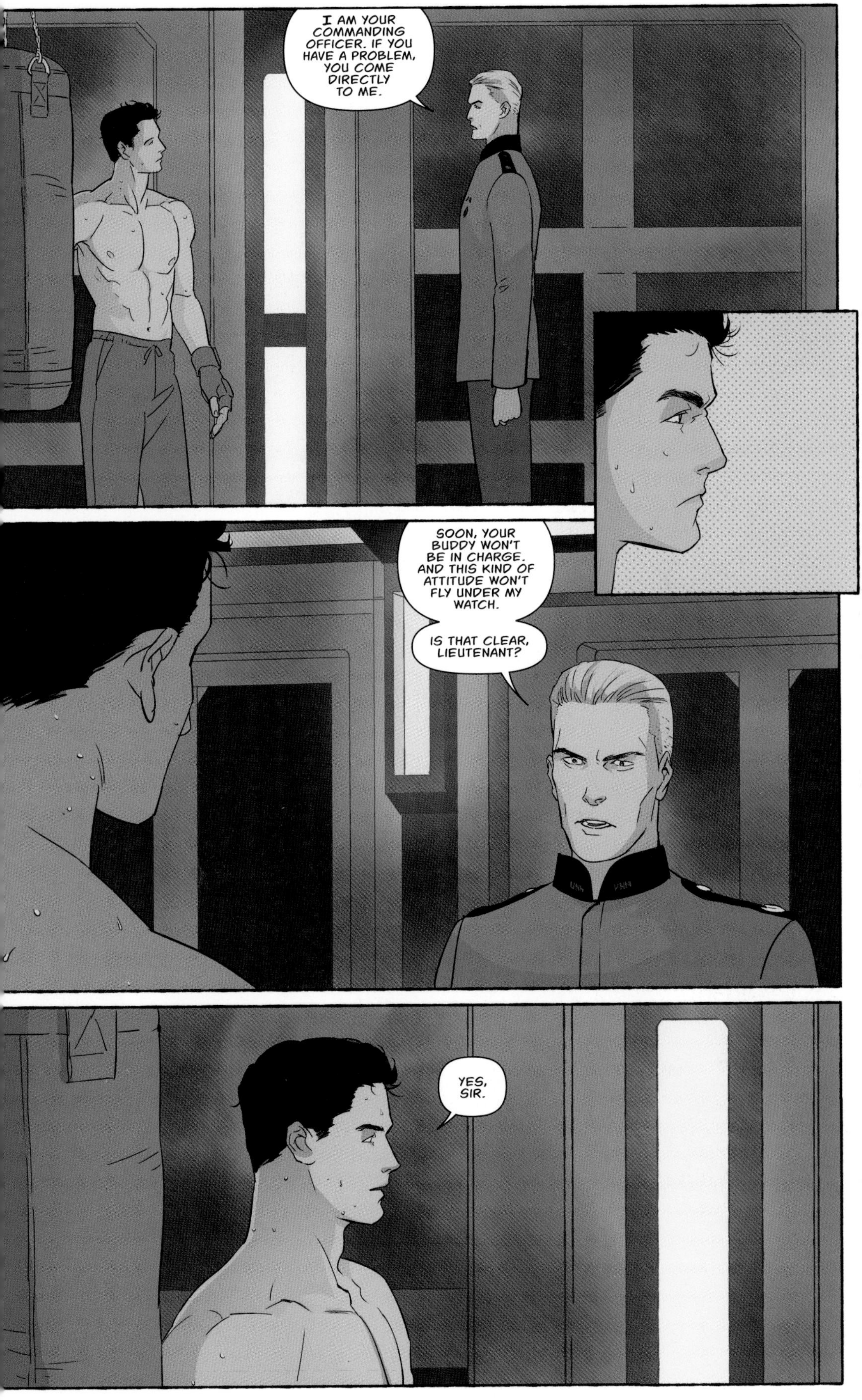
I AM YOUR COMMANDING OFFICER. IF YOU HAVE A PROBLEM, YOU COME DIRECTLY TO ME.
SOON, YOUR BUDDY WON'T BE IN CHARGE. AND THIS KIND OF ATTITUDE WON'T FLY UNDER MY WATCH.
IS THAT CLEAR, LIEUTENANT?
YES, SIR.

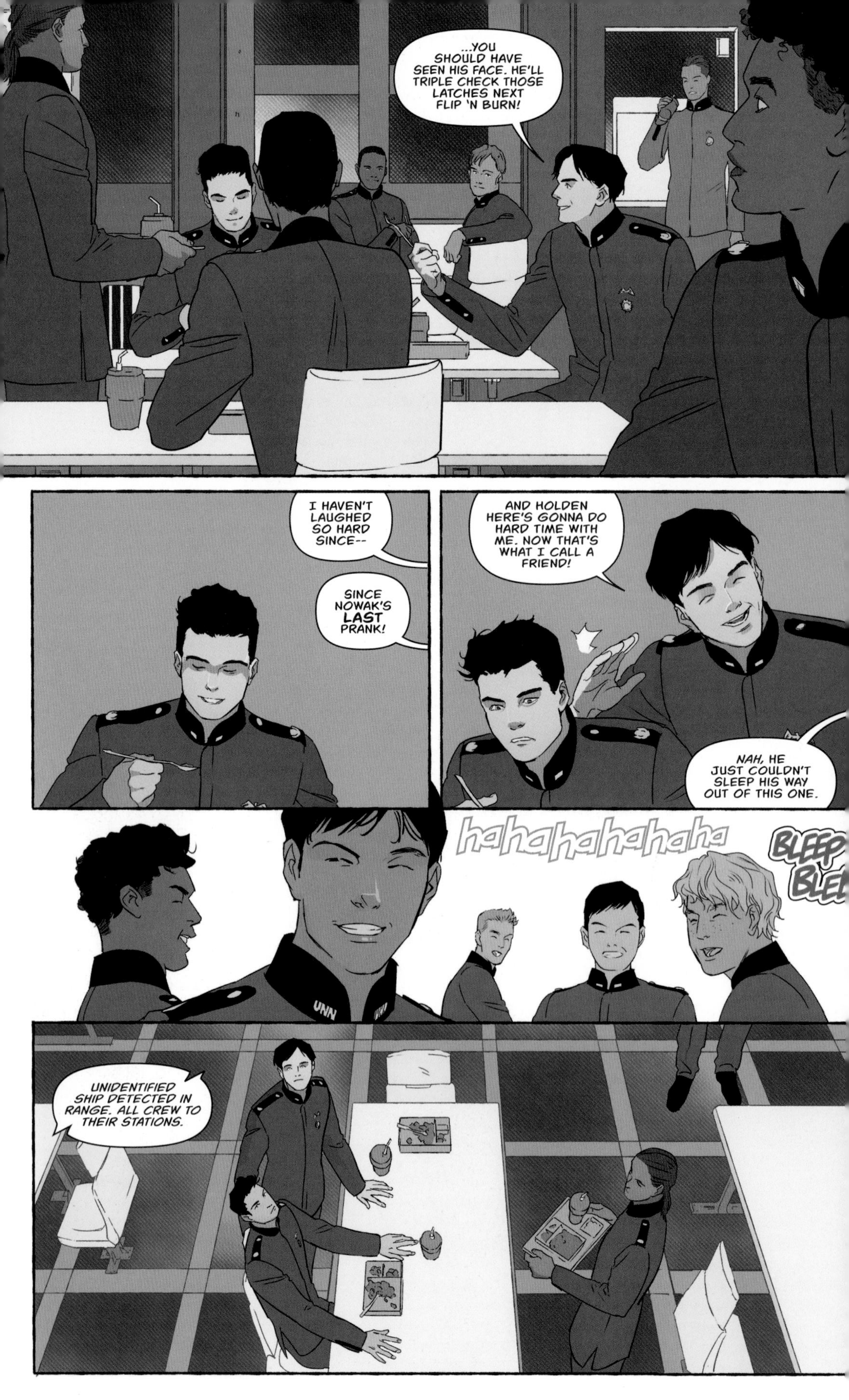
...YOU SHOULD HAVE SEEN HIS FACE. HE'LL TRIPLE CHECK THOSE LATCHES NEXT FLIP 'N BURN!
I HAVEN'T LAUGHED SO HARD SINCE--
SINCE NOWAK'S **LAST** PRANK!
AND HOLDEN HERE'S GONNA DO HARD TIME WITH ME. NOW THAT'S WHAT I CALL A FRIEND!
NAH, HE JUST COULDN'T SLEEP HIS WAY OUT OF THIS ONE.
hahahahahaha
UNN
UNIDENTIFIED SHIP DETECTED IN RANGE. ALL CREW TO THEIR STATIONS.

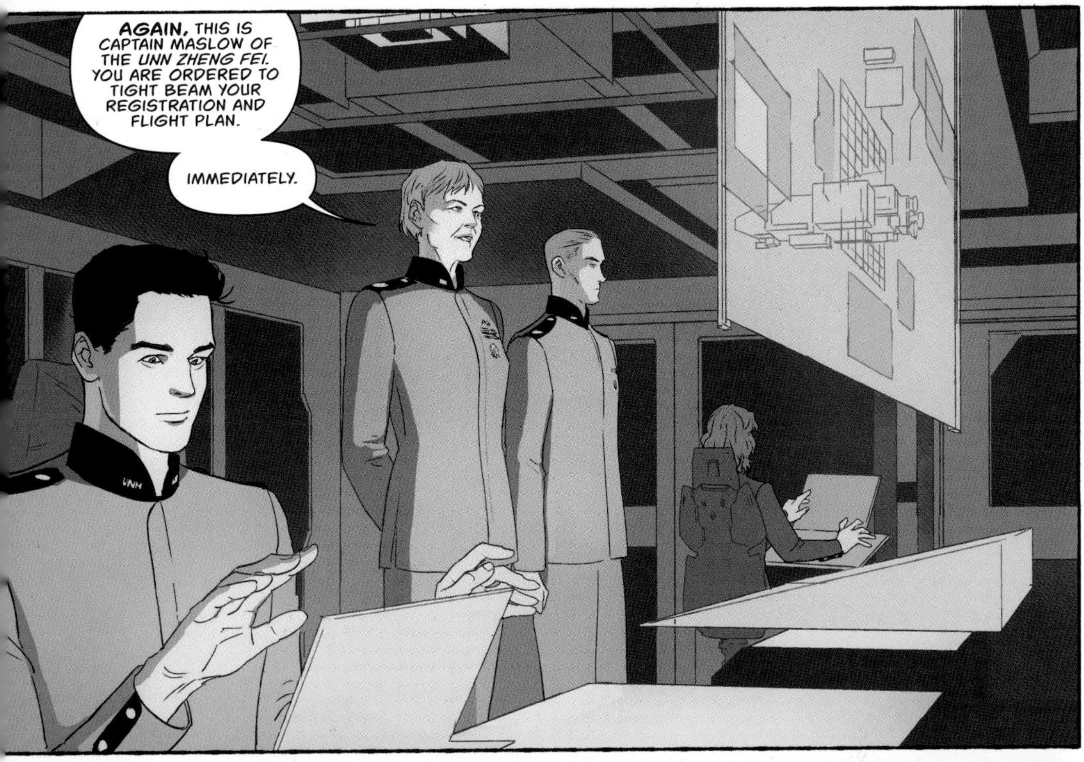
AGAIN, THIS IS CAPTAIN MASLOW OF THE *UNN ZHENG FEI.* YOU ARE ORDERED TO TIGHT BEAM YOUR REGISTRATION AND FLIGHT PLAN.
IMMEDIATELY.
UNN

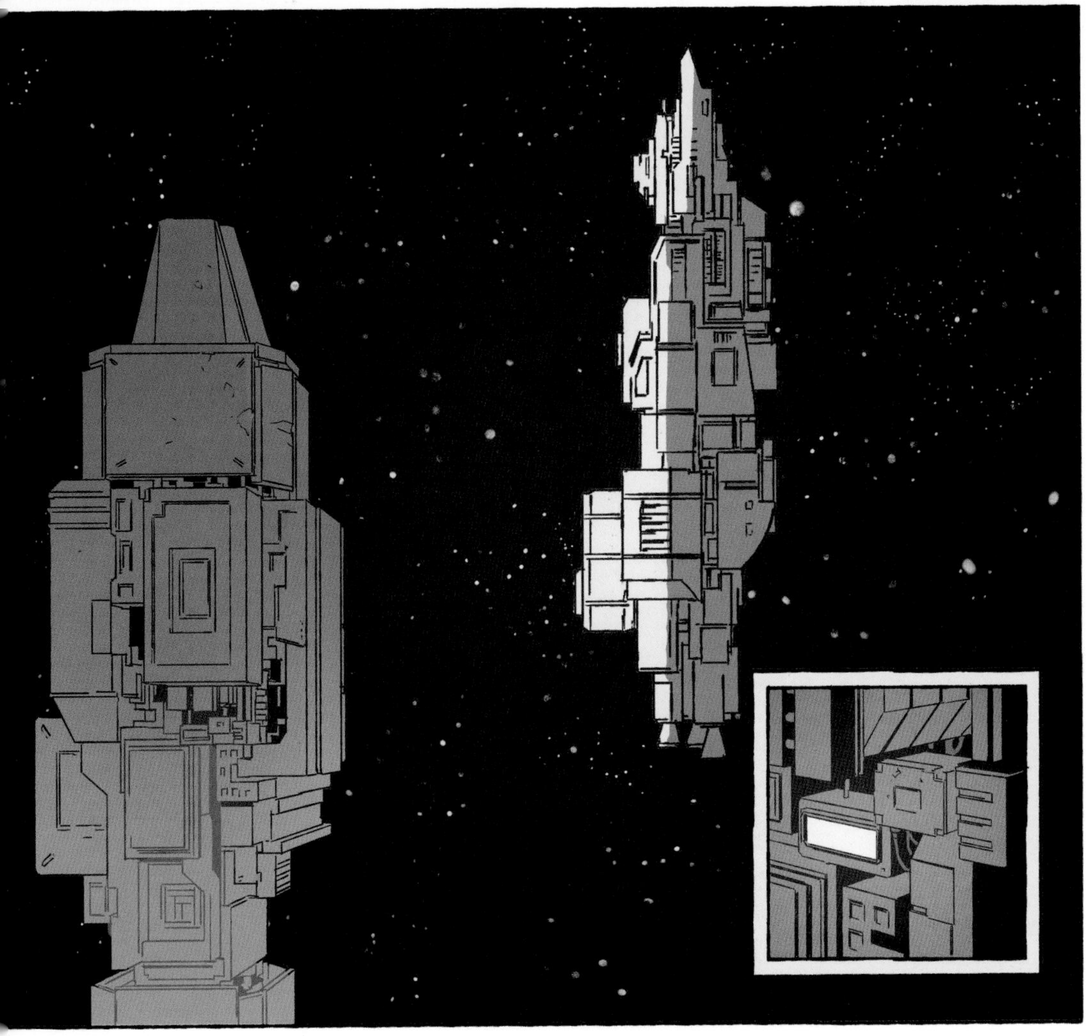

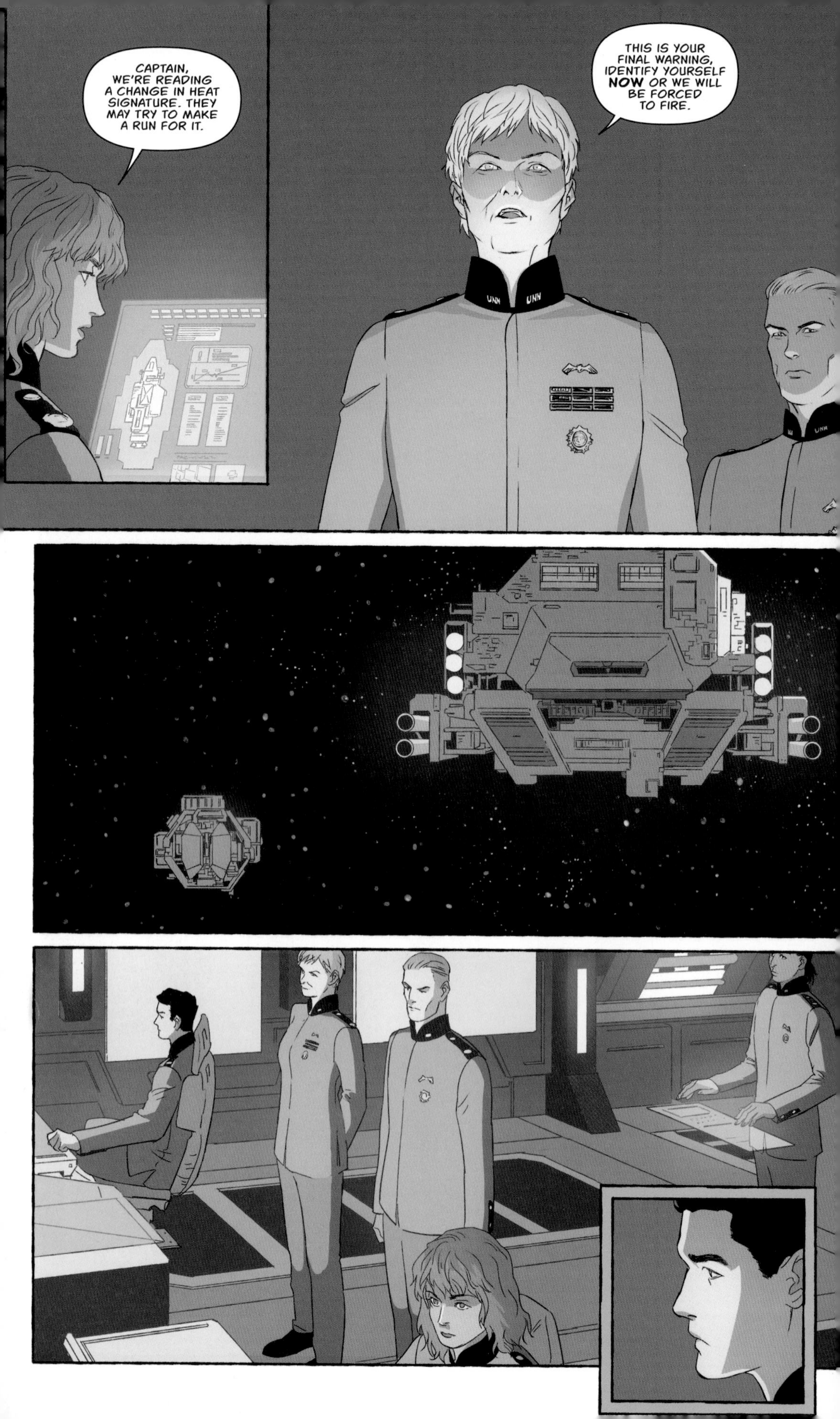
CAPTAIN, WE'RE READING A CHANGE IN HEAT SIGNATURE. THEY MAY TRY TO MAKE A RUN FOR IT.
THIS IS YOUR FINAL WARNING, IDENTIFY YOURSELF NOW OR WE WILL BE FORCED TO FIRE.
UNN
UNN

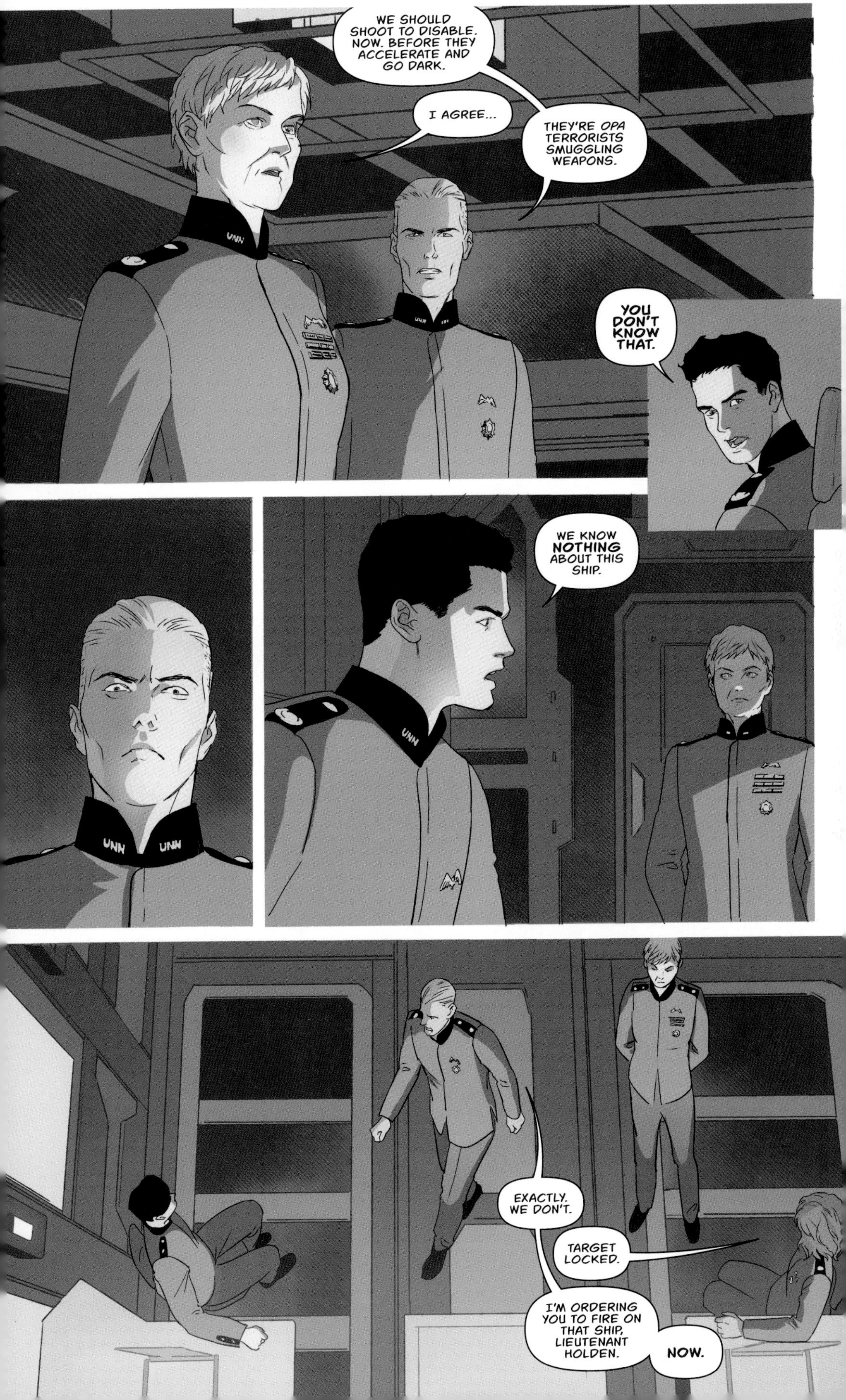
WE SHOULD SHOOT TO DISABLE. NOW. BEFORE THEY ACCELERATE AND GO DARK.
I AGREE...
THEY'RE *OPA* TERRORISTS SMUGGLING WEAPONS.
YOU DON'T KNOW THAT.
WE KNOW **NOTHING** ABOUT THIS SHIP.
EXACTLY. WE DON'T.
TARGET LOCKED.
I'M ORDERING YOU TO FIRE ON THAT SHIP, LIEUTENANT HOLDEN.
NOW.

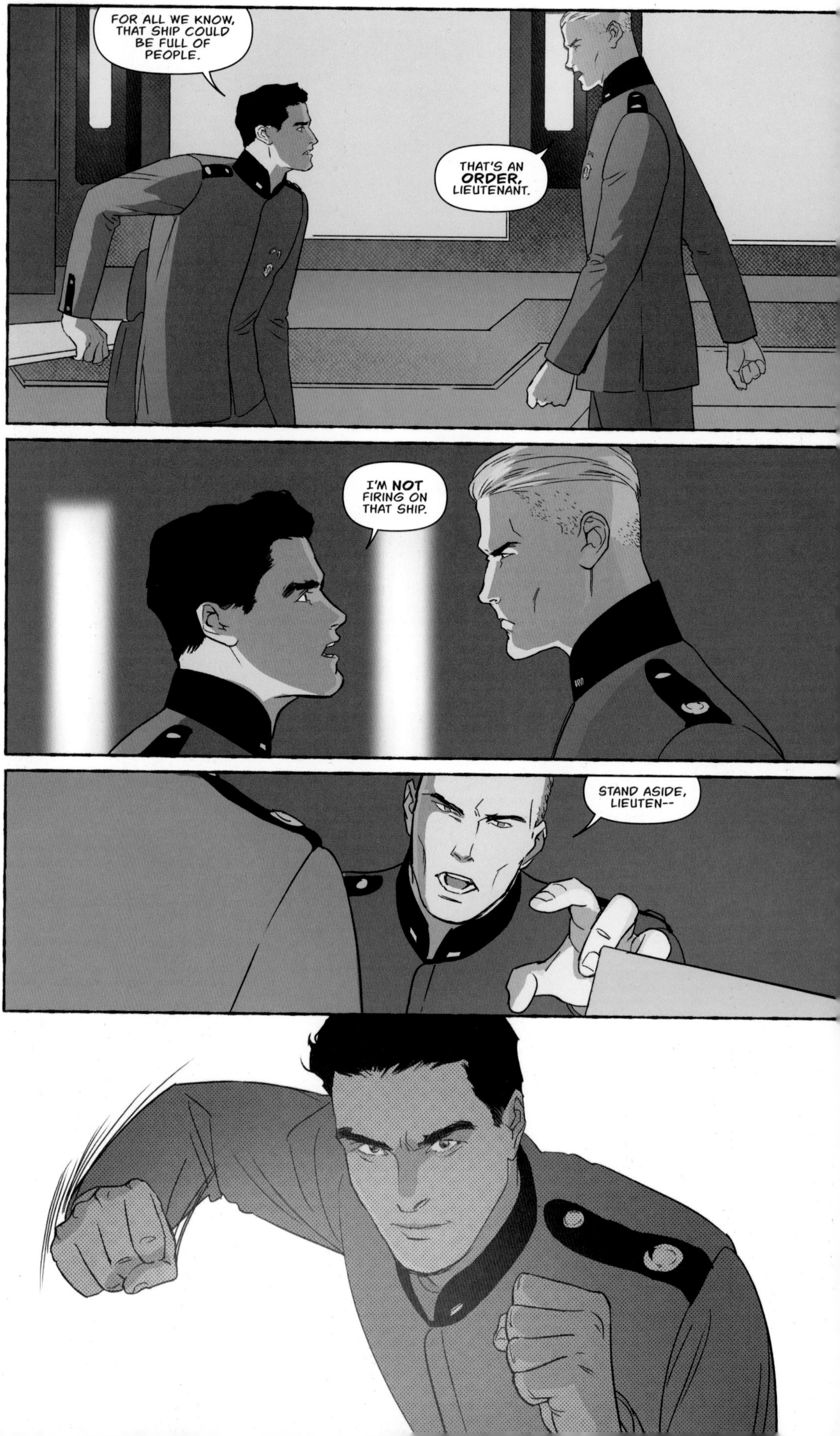
FOR ALL WE KNOW, THAT SHIP COULD BE FULL OF PEOPLE.
THAT'S AN **ORDER,** LIEUTENANT.
I'M **NOT** FIRING ON THAT SHIP.
STAND ASIDE, LIEUTEN--

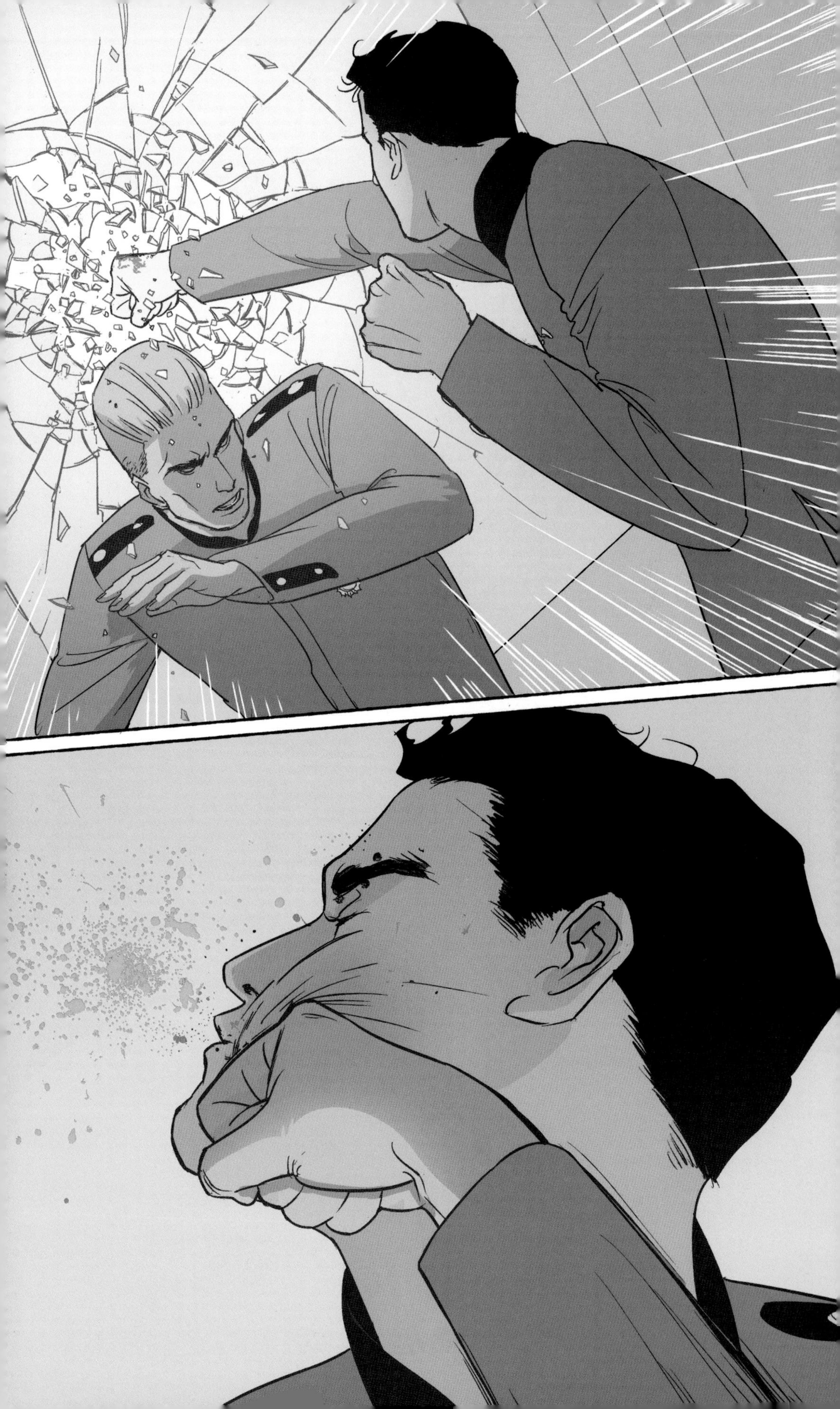

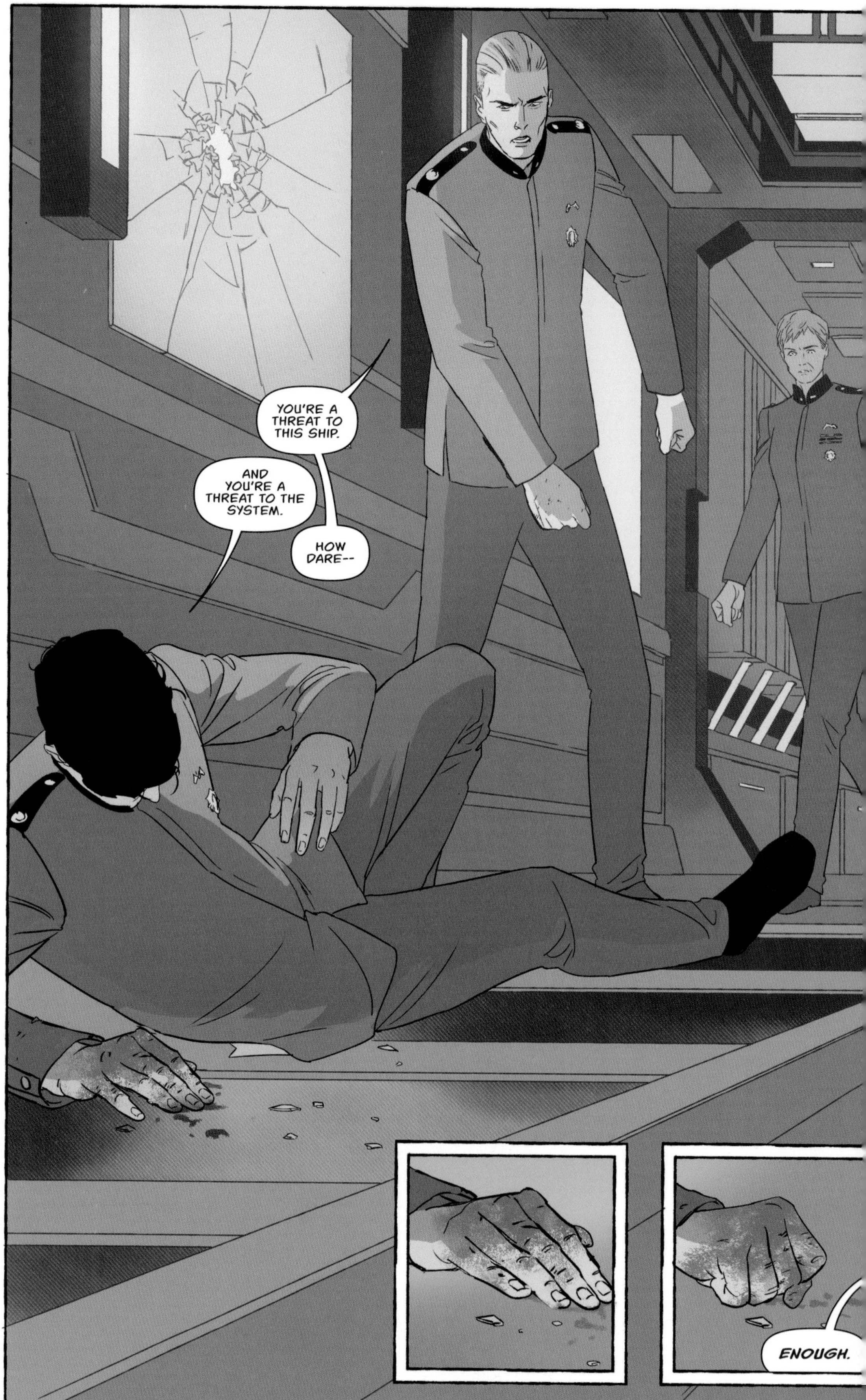
YOU'RE A THREAT TO THIS SHIP.
AND YOU'RE A THREAT TO THE SYSTEM.
HOW DARE--
ENOUGH.

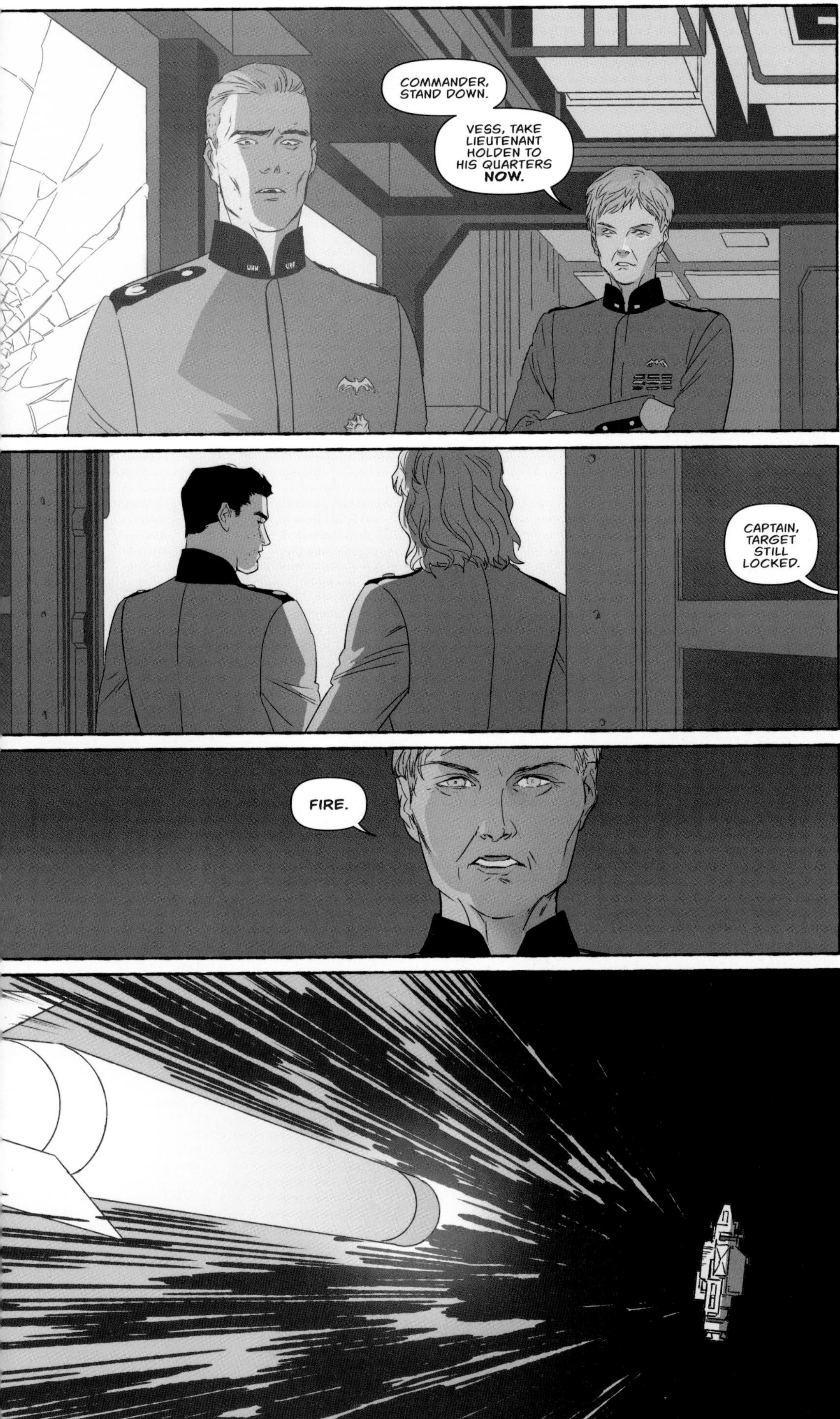
COMMANDER, STAND DOWN.
VESS, TAKE LIEUTENANT HOLDEN TO HIS QUARTERS NOW.
CAPTAIN, TARGET STILL LOCKED.
FIRE.

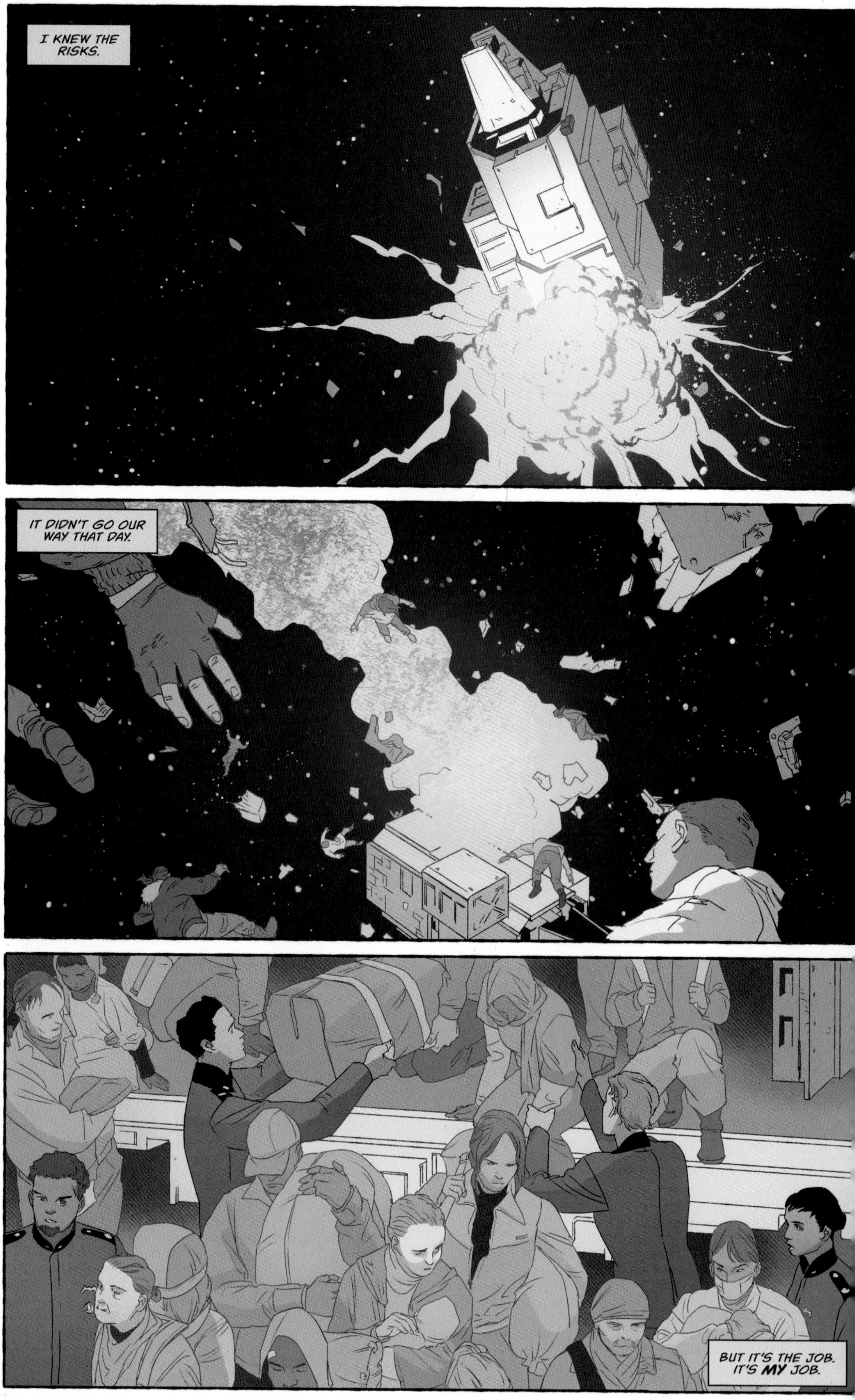
I KNEW THE RISKS.
IT DIDN'T GO OUR WAY THAT DAY.
BUT IT'S THE JOB. IT'S MY JOB.

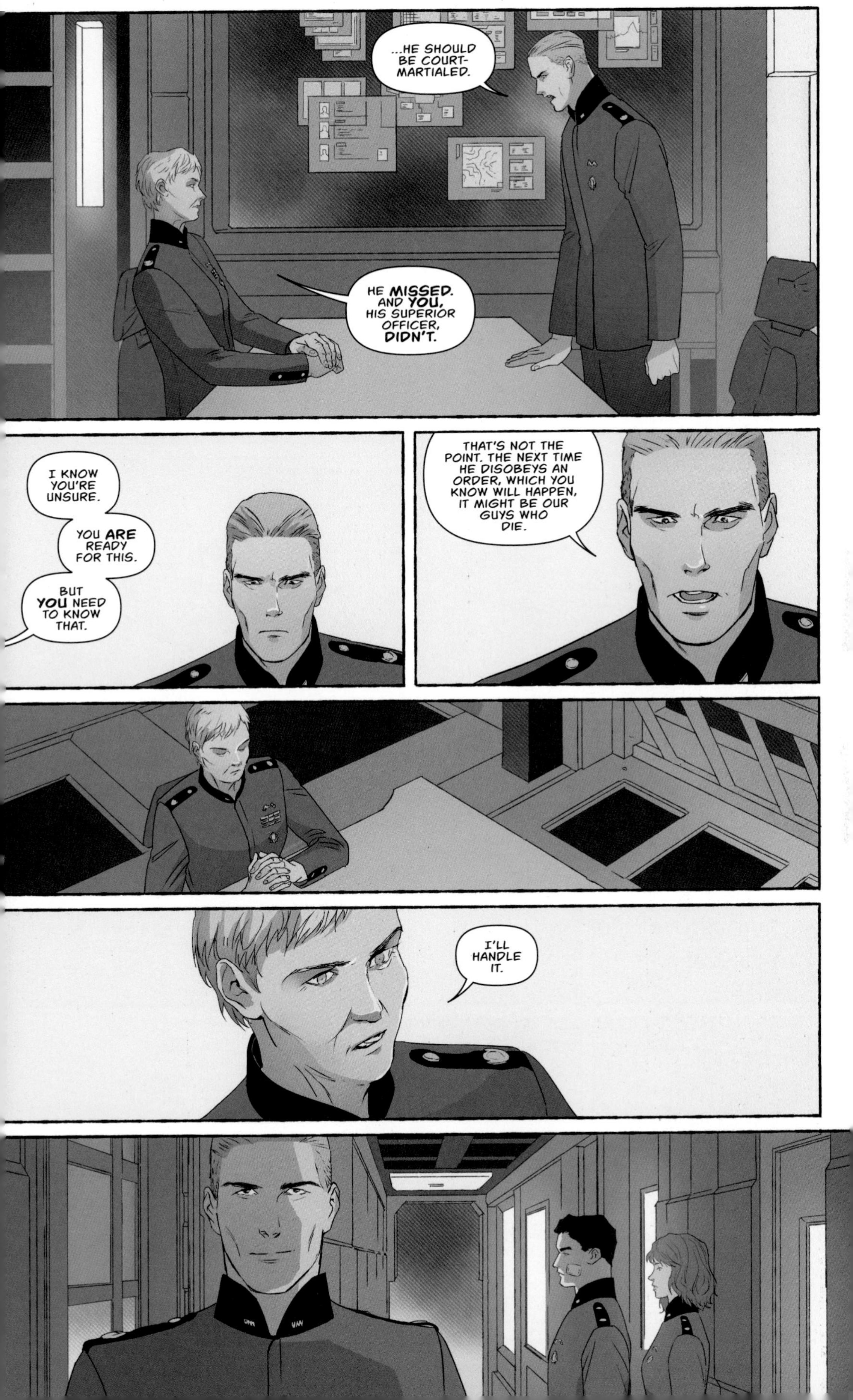
...HE SHOULD BE COURT-MARTIALED.
HE MISSED. AND YOU, HIS SUPERIOR OFFICER, DIDN'T.
I KNOW YOU'RE UNSURE.
YOU ARE READY FOR THIS.
BUT YOU NEED TO KNOW THAT.
THAT'S NOT THE POINT. THE NEXT TIME HE DISOBEYS AN ORDER, WHICH YOU KNOW WILL HAPPEN, IT MIGHT BE OUR GUYS WHO DIE.
I'LL HANDLE IT.

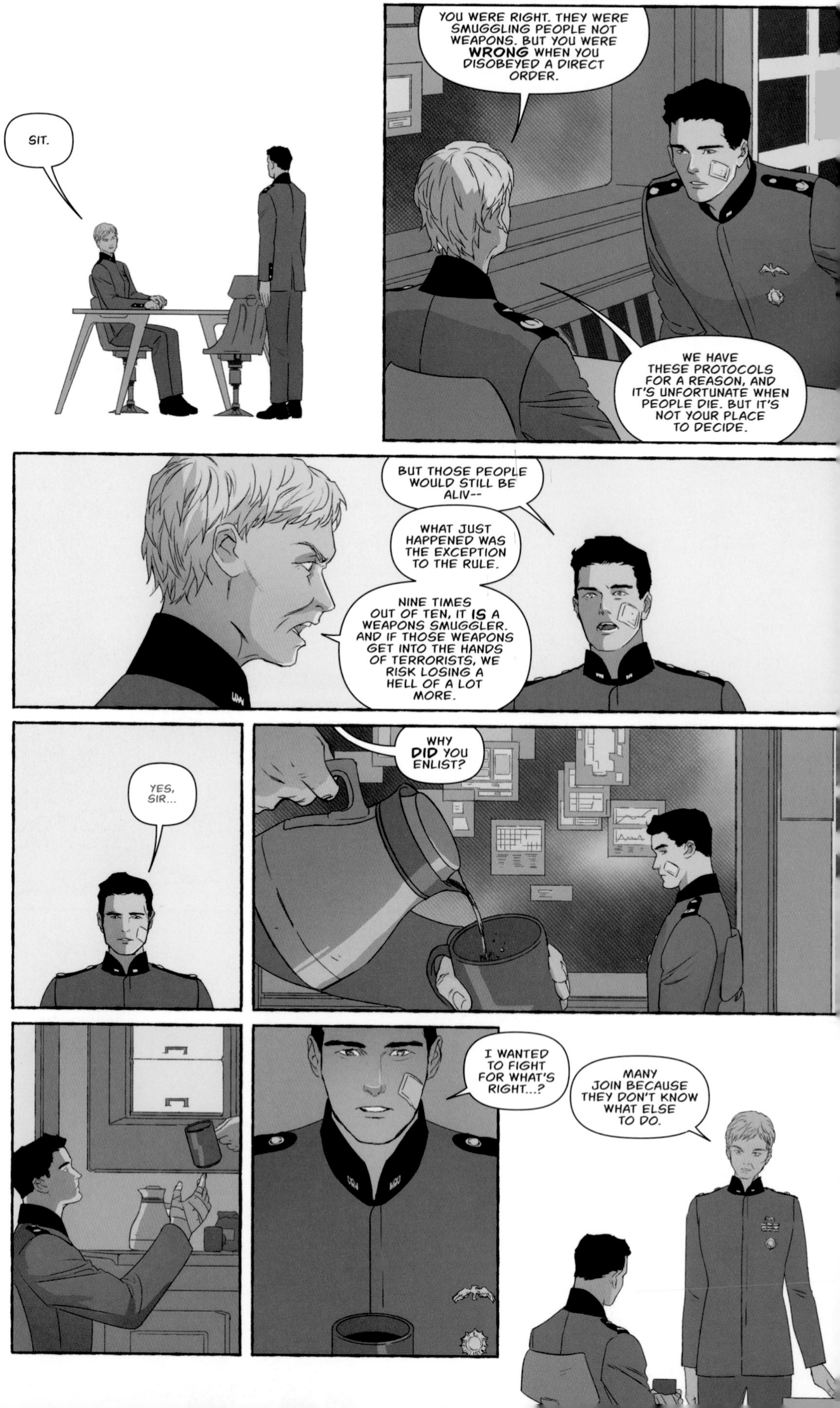

SIT.
YOU WERE RIGHT. THEY WERE SMUGGLING PEOPLE NOT WEAPONS. BUT YOU WERE WRONG WHEN YOU DISOBEYED A DIRECT ORDER.
WE HAVE THESE PROTOCOLS FOR A REASON, AND IT'S UNFORTUNATE WHEN PEOPLE DIE. BUT IT'S NOT YOUR PLACE TO DECIDE.
BUT THOSE PEOPLE WOULD STILL BE ALIV--
WHAT JUST HAPPENED WAS THE EXCEPTION TO THE RULE.
NINE TIMES OUT OF TEN, IT IS A WEAPONS SMUGGLER. AND IF THOSE WEAPONS GET INTO THE HANDS OF TERRORISTS, WE RISK LOSING A HELL OF A LOT MORE.
YES, SIR...
WHY DID YOU ENLIST?
I WANTED TO FIGHT FOR WHAT'S RIGHT...?
MANY JOIN BECAUSE THEY DON'T KNOW WHAT ELSE TO DO.

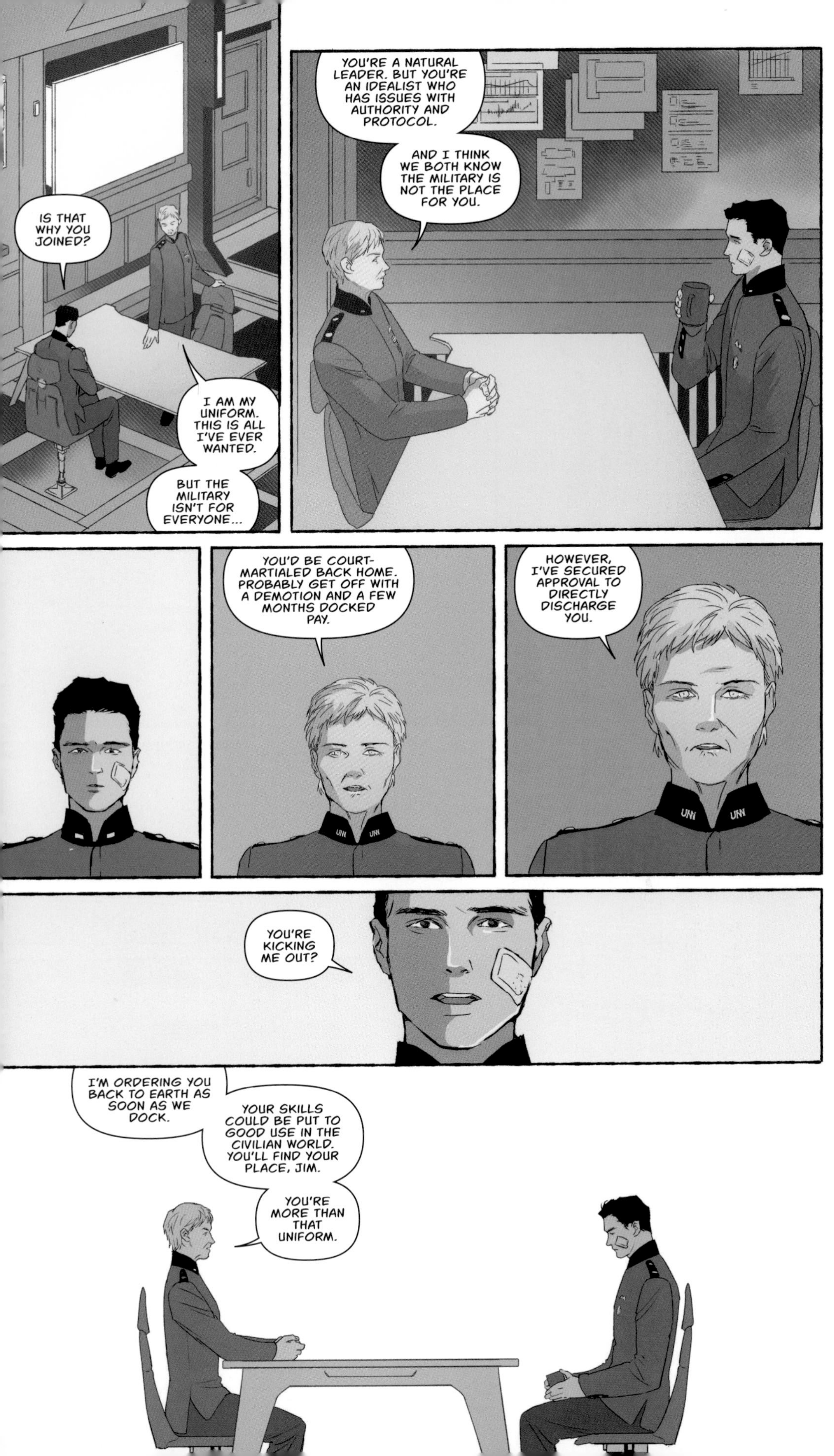
IS THAT WHY YOU JOINED?
I AM MY UNIFORM. THIS IS ALL I'VE EVER WANTED.
BUT THE MILITARY ISN'T FOR EVERYONE...
YOU'RE A NATURAL LEADER. BUT YOU'RE AN IDEALIST WHO HAS ISSUES WITH AUTHORITY AND PROTOCOL.
AND I THINK WE BOTH KNOW THE MILITARY IS NOT THE PLACE FOR YOU.
YOU'D BE COURT-MARTIALED BACK HOME. PROBABLY GET OFF WITH A DEMOTION AND A FEW MONTHS DOCKED PAY.
HOWEVER, I'VE SECURED APPROVAL TO DIRECTLY DISCHARGE YOU.
YOU'RE KICKING ME OUT?
I'M ORDERING YOU BACK TO EARTH AS SOON AS WE DOCK.
YOUR SKILLS COULD BE PUT TO GOOD USE IN THE CIVILIAN WORLD. YOU'LL FIND YOUR PLACE, JIM.
YOU'RE MORE THAN THAT UNIFORM.

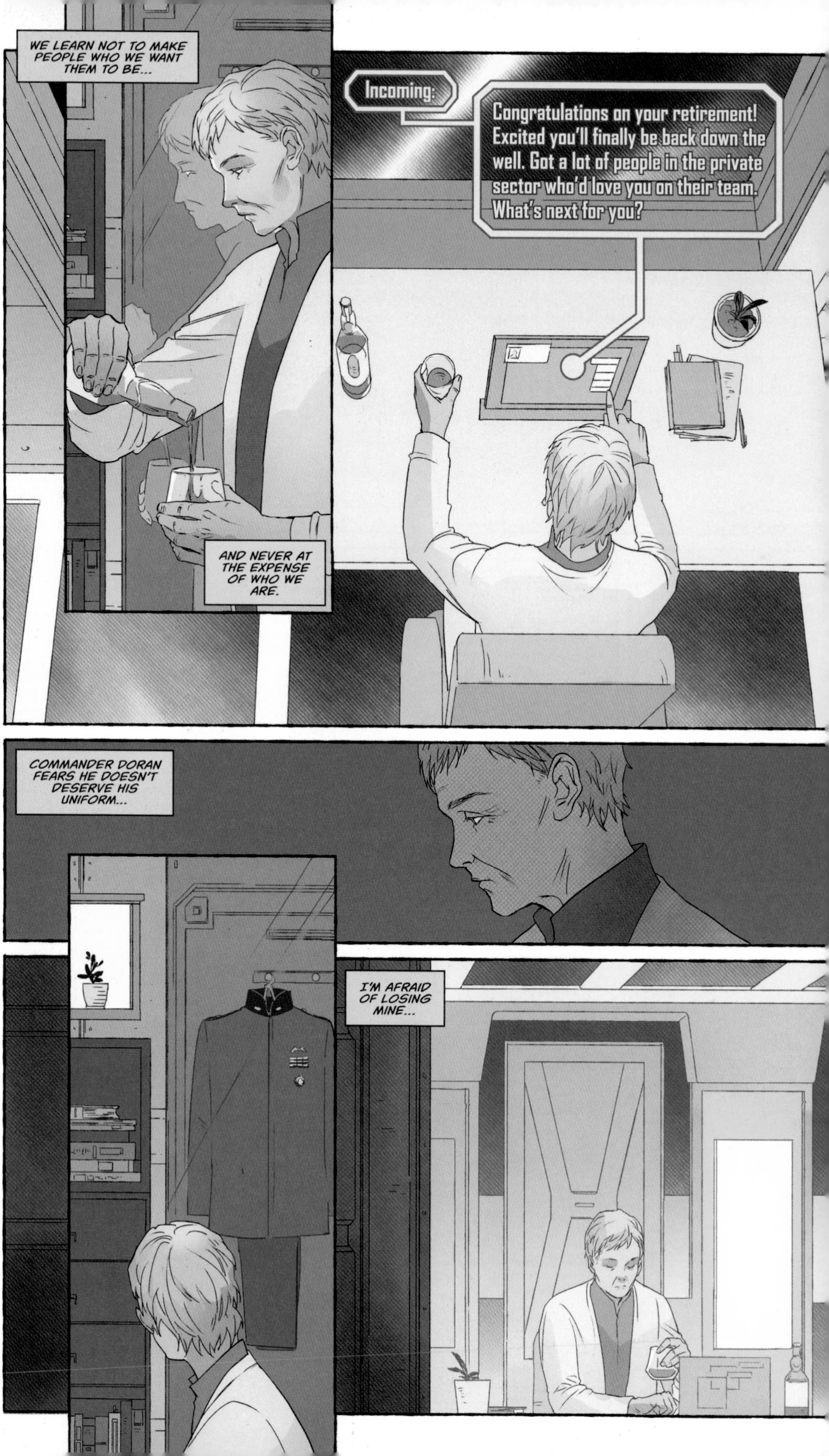
WE LEARN NOT TO MAKE PEOPLE WHO WE WANT THEM TO BE...
AND NEVER AT THE EXPENSE OF WHO WE ARE.
Incoming:
Congratulations on your retirement! Excited you'll finally be back down the well. Got a lot of people in the private sector who'd love you on their team. What's next for you?
COMMANDER DORAN FEARS HE DOESN'T DESERVE HIS UNIFORM...
I'M AFRAID OF LOSING MINE...

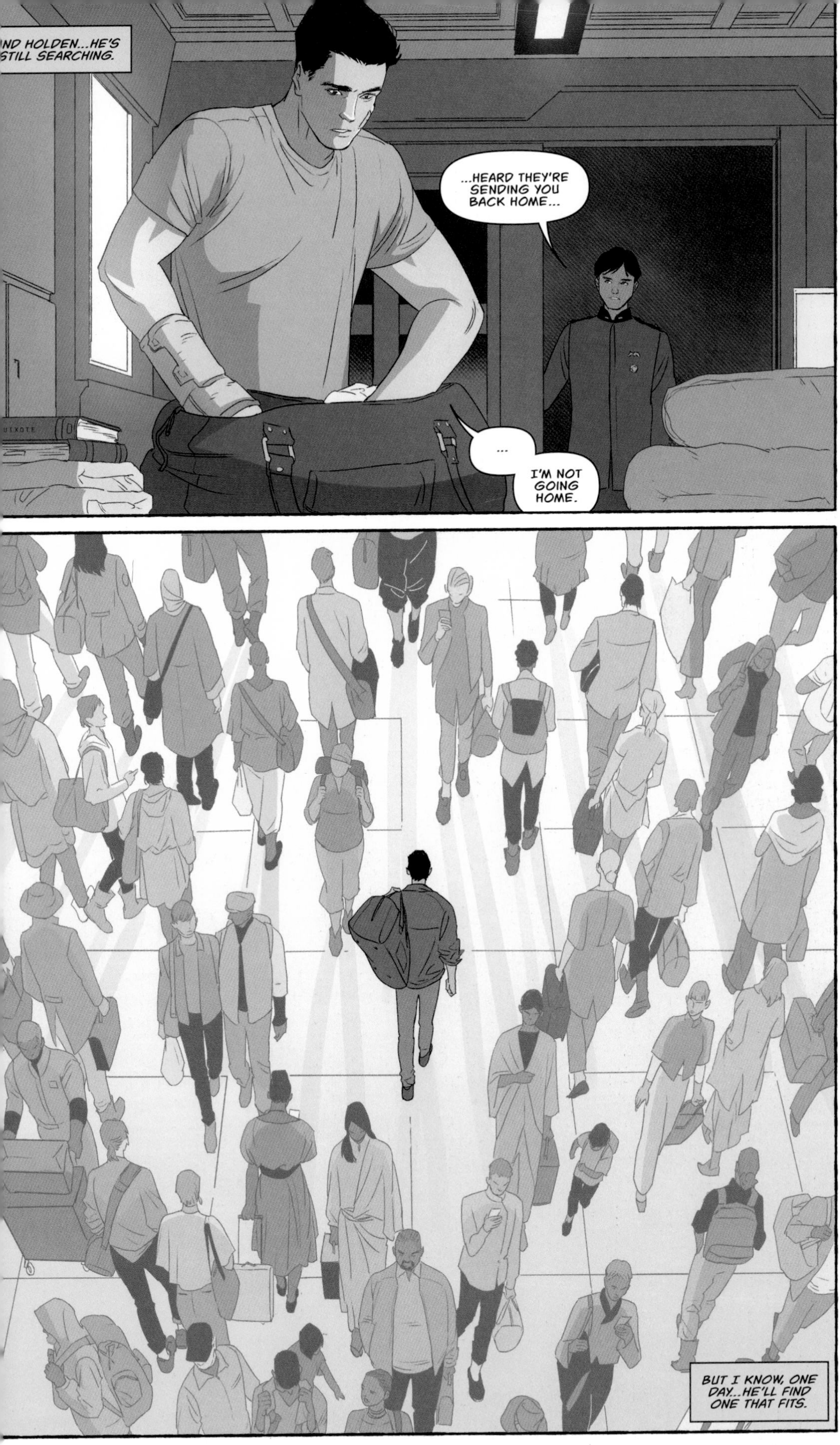
ND HOLDEN...HE'S
STILL SEARCHING.
...HEARD THEY'RE SENDING YOU BACK HOME...
...
I'M NOT GOING HOME.
BUT I KNOW, ONE DAY...HE'LL FIND ONE THAT FITS.

CHAPTER_002
NAOMI NAGATA

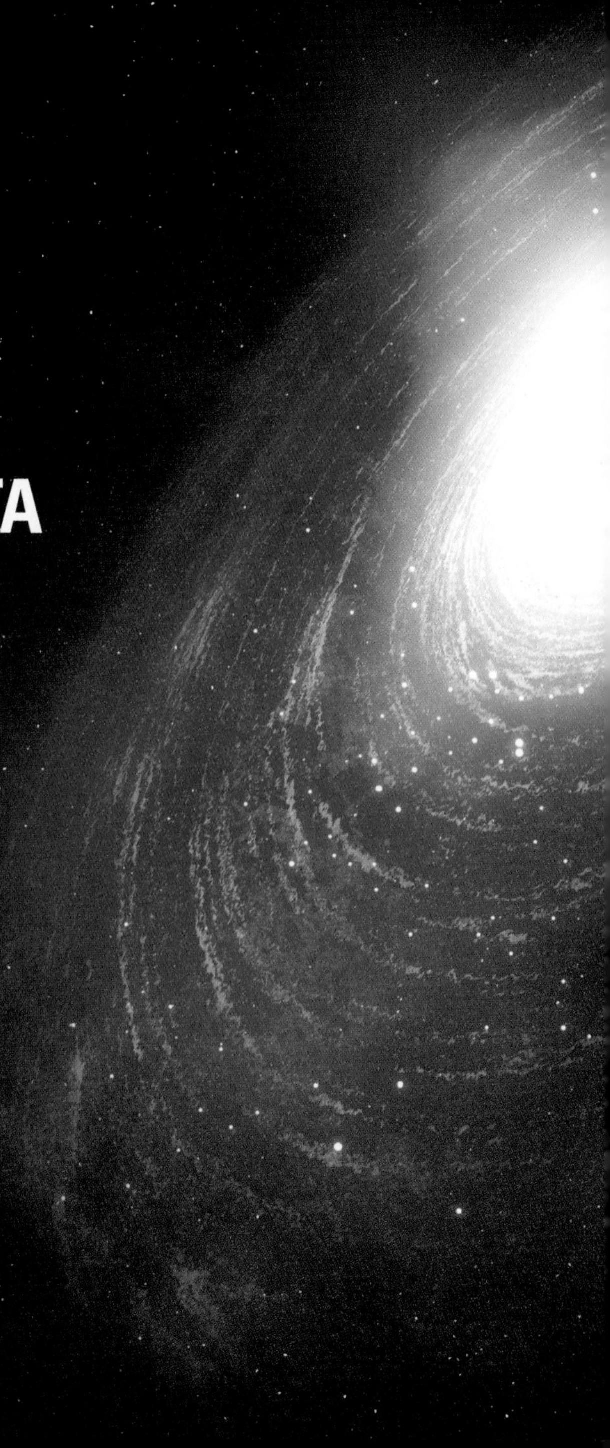

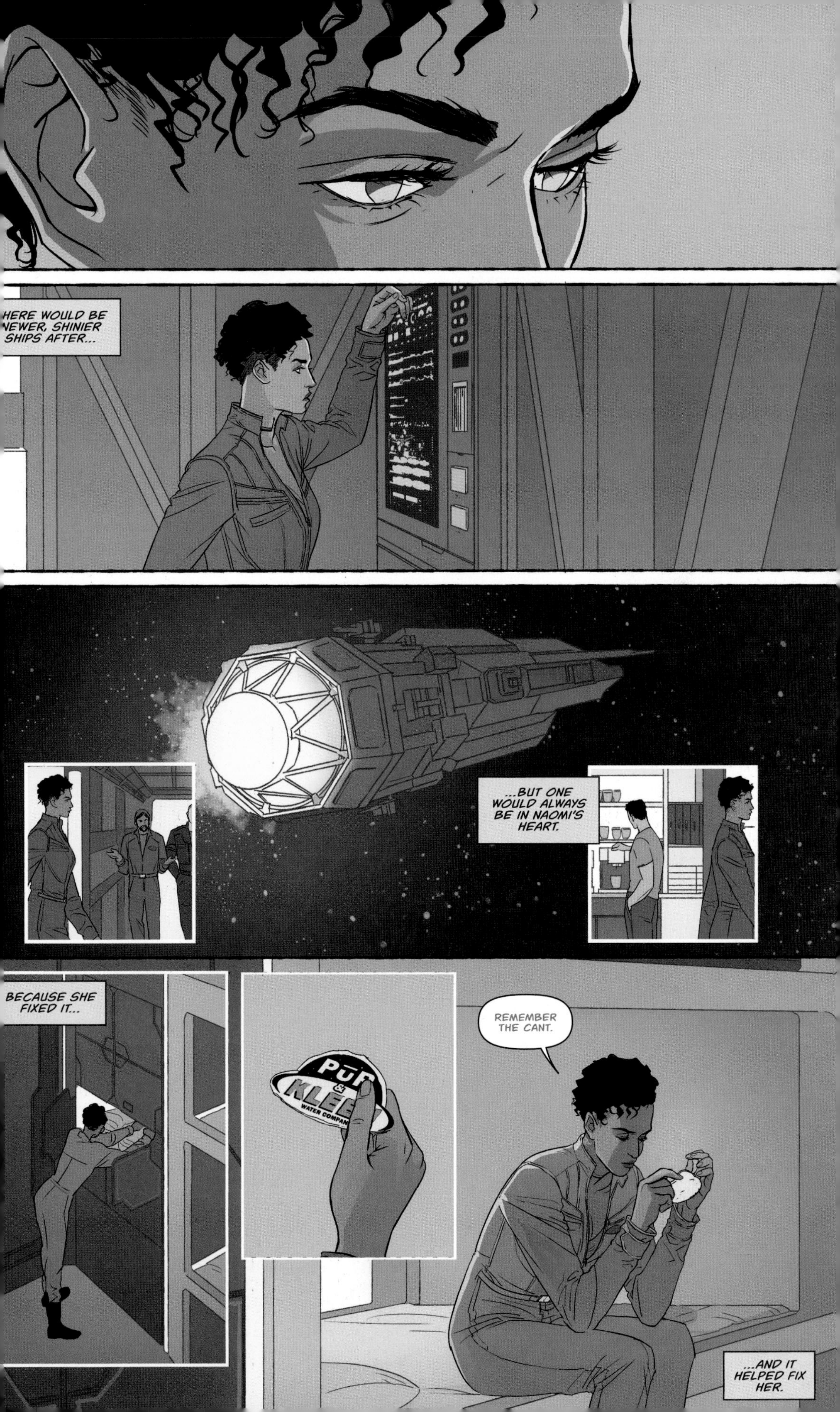
HERE WOULD BE NEWER, SHINIER SHIPS AFTER...
...BUT ONE WOULD ALWAYS BE IN NAOMI'S HEART.
BECAUSE SHE FIXED IT...
PŪR & KLEEN WATER COMPANY
REMEMBER THE CANT.
...AND IT HELPED FIX HER.

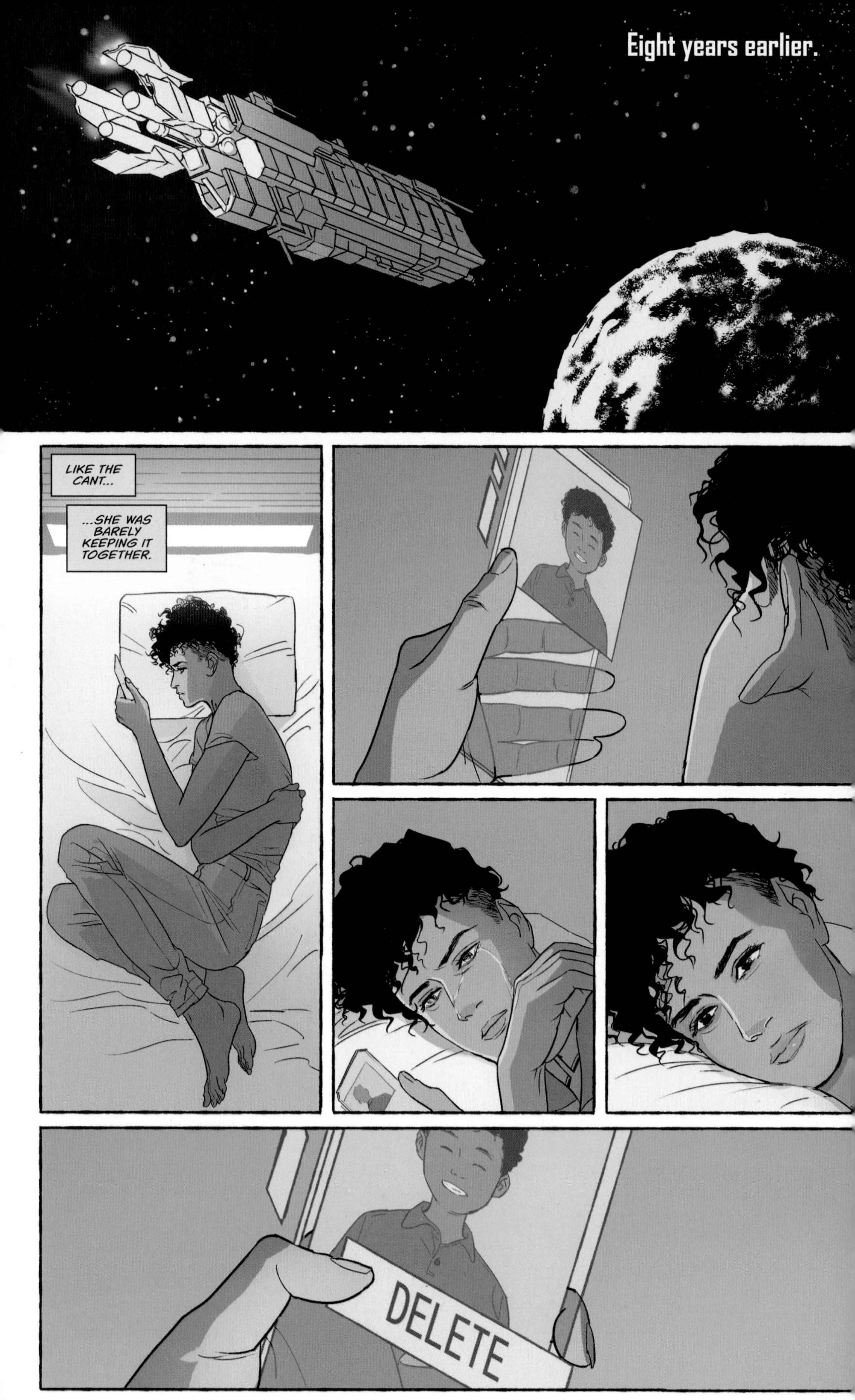

Eight years earlier.
LIKE THE CANT...
...SHE WAS BARELY KEEPING IT TOGETHER.
DELETE

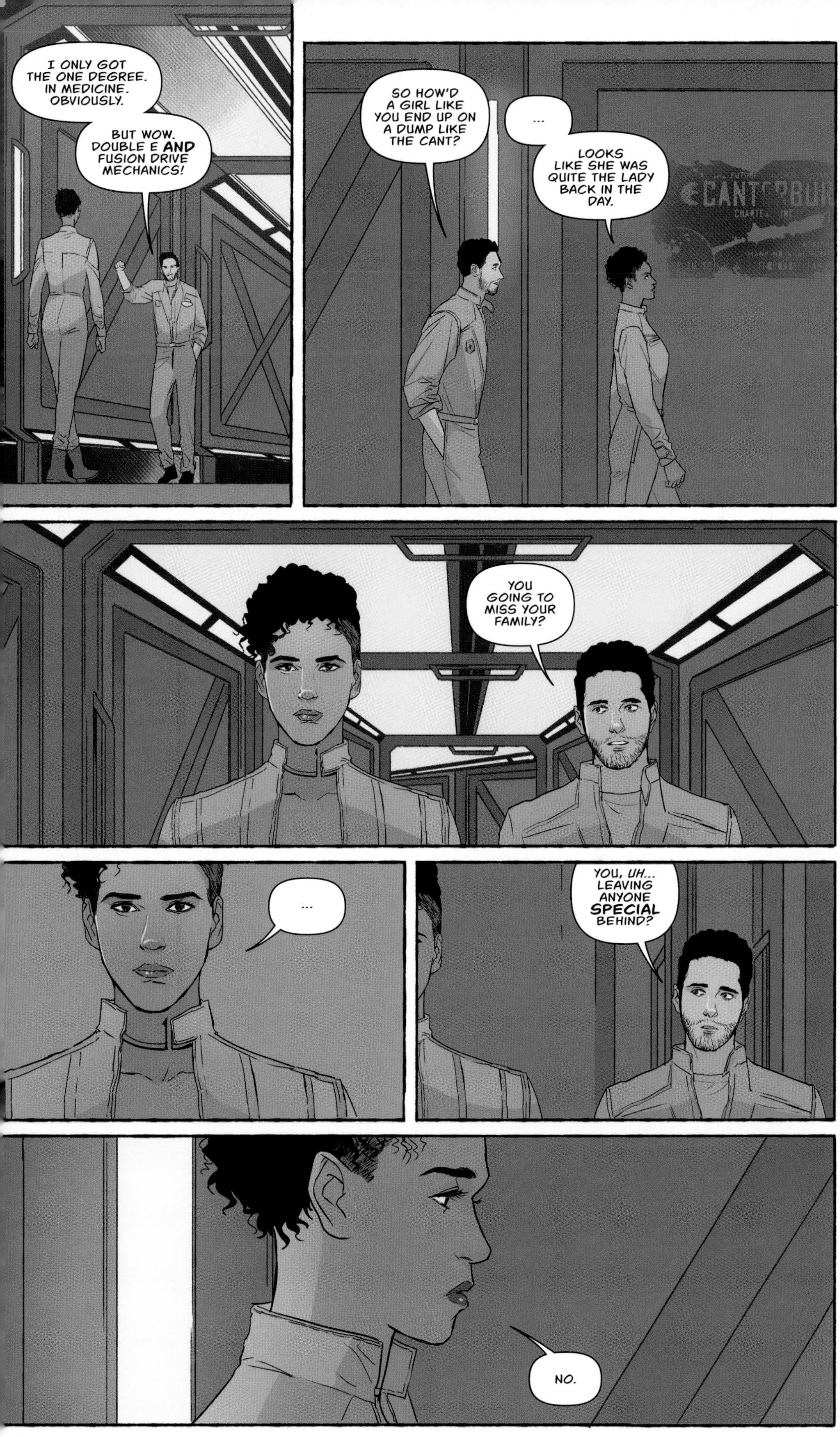
I ONLY GOT THE ONE DEGREE. IN MEDICINE. OBVIOUSLY.
BUT WOW. DOUBLE E **AND** FUSION DRIVE MECHANICS!
SO HOW'D A GIRL LIKE YOU END UP ON A DUMP LIKE THE CANT?
...
LOOKS LIKE SHE WAS QUITE THE LADY BACK IN THE DAY.
YOU GOING TO MISS YOUR FAMILY?
...
YOU, *UH*... LEAVING ANYONE **SPECIAL** BEHIND?
NO.

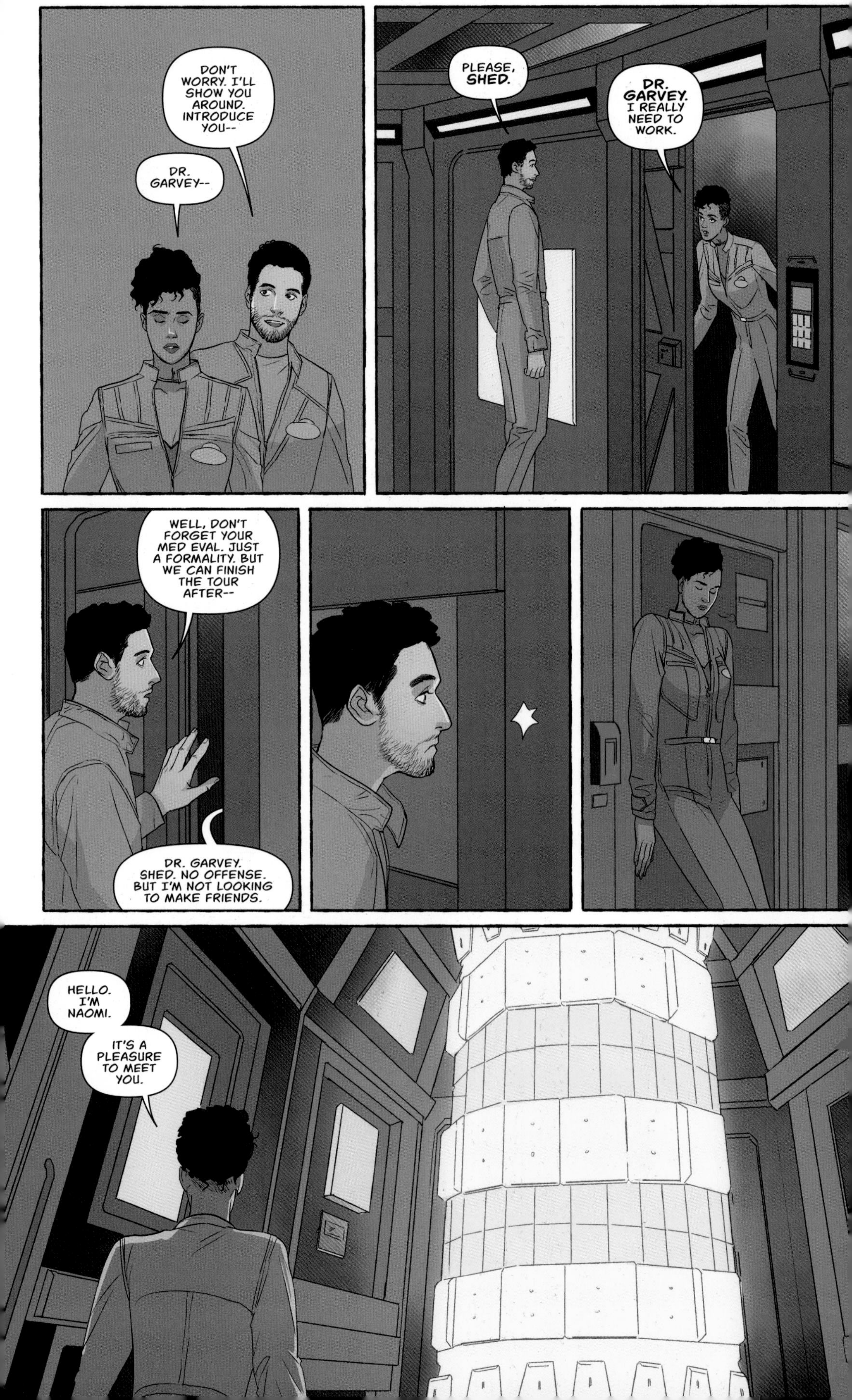
DON'T WORRY. I'LL SHOW YOU AROUND. INTRODUCE YOU--
DR. GARVEY--
PLEASE, SHED.
DR. GARVEY. I REALLY NEED TO WORK.
WELL, DON'T FORGET YOUR MED EVAL. JUST A FORMALITY. BUT WE CAN FINISH THE TOUR AFTER--
DR. GARVEY. SHED. NO OFFENSE. BUT I'M NOT LOOKING TO MAKE FRIENDS.
HELLO. I'M NAOMI.
IT'S A PLEASURE TO MEET YOU.

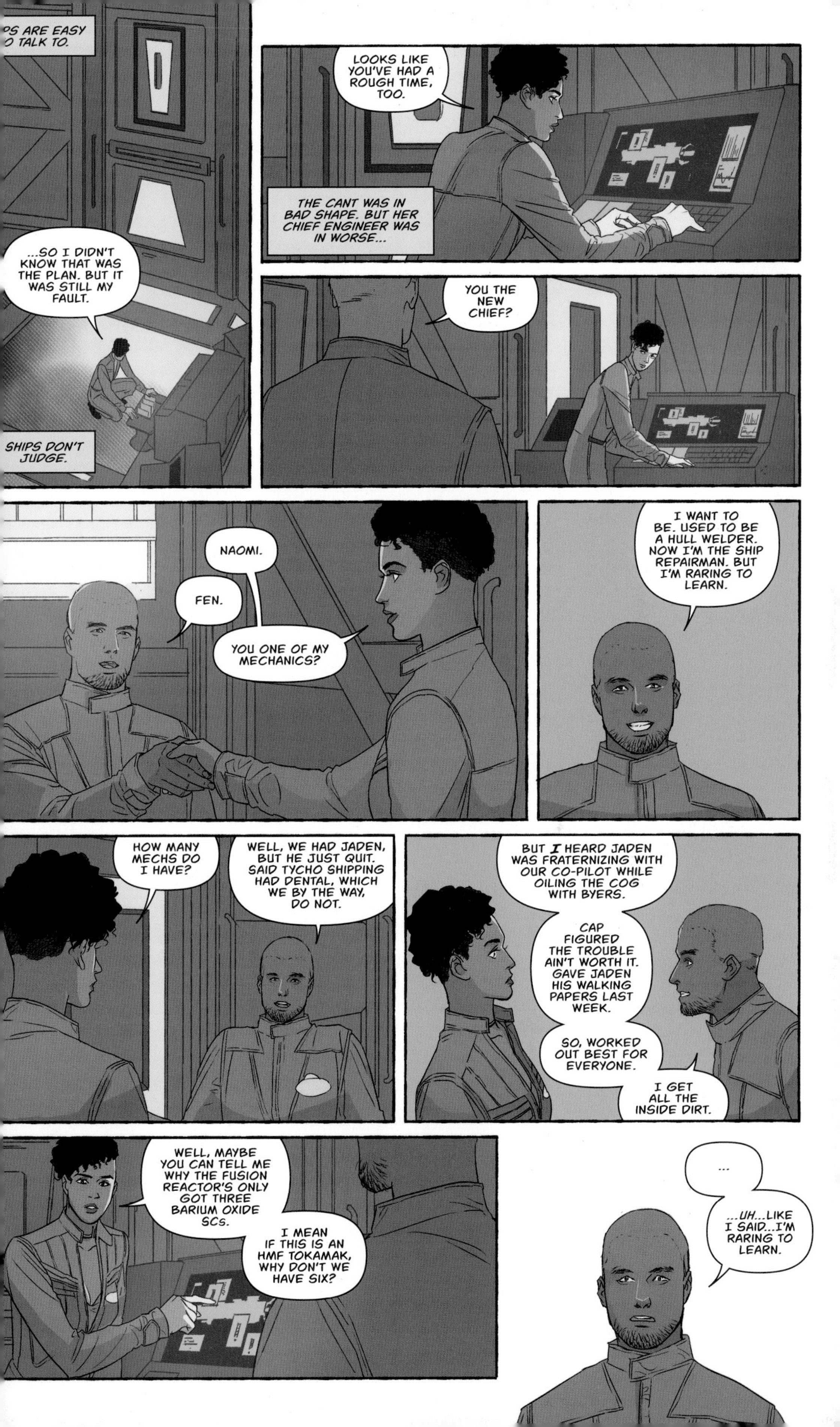
PS ARE EASY
O TALK TO.
...SO I DIDN'T KNOW THAT WAS THE PLAN. BUT IT WAS STILL MY FAULT.
SHIPS DON'T JUDGE.
LOOKS LIKE YOU'VE HAD A ROUGH TIME, TOO.
THE CANT WAS IN BAD SHAPE. BUT HER CHIEF ENGINEER WAS IN WORSE...
YOU THE NEW CHIEF?
NAOMI.
FEN.
YOU ONE OF MY MECHANICS?
I WANT TO BE. USED TO BE A HULL WELDER. NOW I'M THE SHIP REPAIRMAN. BUT I'M RARING TO LEARN.
HOW MANY MECHS DO I HAVE?
WELL, WE HAD JADEN, BUT HE JUST QUIT. SAID TYCHO SHIPPING HAD DENTAL, WHICH WE BY THE WAY, DO NOT.
BUT I HEARD JADEN WAS FRATERNIZING WITH OUR CO-PILOT WHILE OILING THE COG WITH BYERS.
CAP FIGURED THE TROUBLE AIN'T WORTH IT. GAVE JADEN HIS WALKING PAPERS LAST WEEK.
SO, WORKED OUT BEST FOR EVERYONE.
I GET ALL THE INSIDE DIRT.
WELL, MAYBE YOU CAN TELL ME WHY THE FUSION REACTOR'S ONLY GOT THREE BARIUM OXIDE SCs.
I MEAN IF THIS IS AN HMF TOKAMAK, WHY DON'T WE HAVE SIX?
...
...UH...LIKE I SAID...I'M RARING TO LEARN.

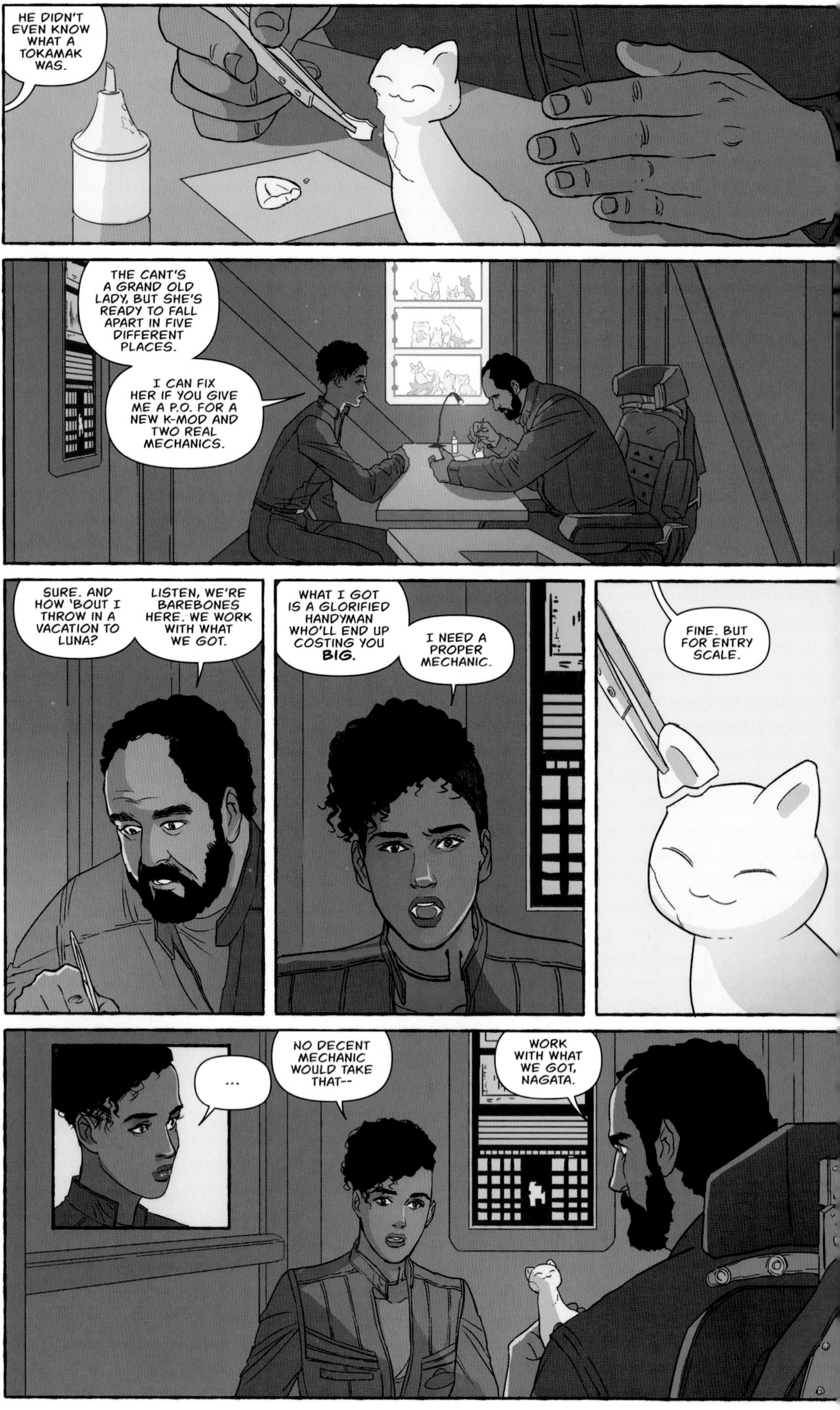
HE DIDN'T EVEN KNOW WHAT A TOKAMAK WAS.
THE CANT'S A GRAND OLD LADY, BUT SHE'S READY TO FALL APART IN FIVE DIFFERENT PLACES.
I CAN FIX HER IF YOU GIVE ME A P.O. FOR A NEW K-MOD AND TWO REAL MECHANICS.
SURE. AND HOW 'BOUT I THROW IN A VACATION TO LUNA?
LISTEN, WE'RE BAREBONES HERE. WE WORK WITH WHAT WE GOT.
WHAT I GOT IS A GLORIFIED HANDYMAN WHO'LL END UP COSTING YOU **BIG.**
I NEED A PROPER MECHANIC.
FINE. BUT FOR ENTRY SCALE.
...
NO DECENT MECHANIC WOULD TAKE THAT--
WORK WITH WHAT WE GOT, NAGATA.

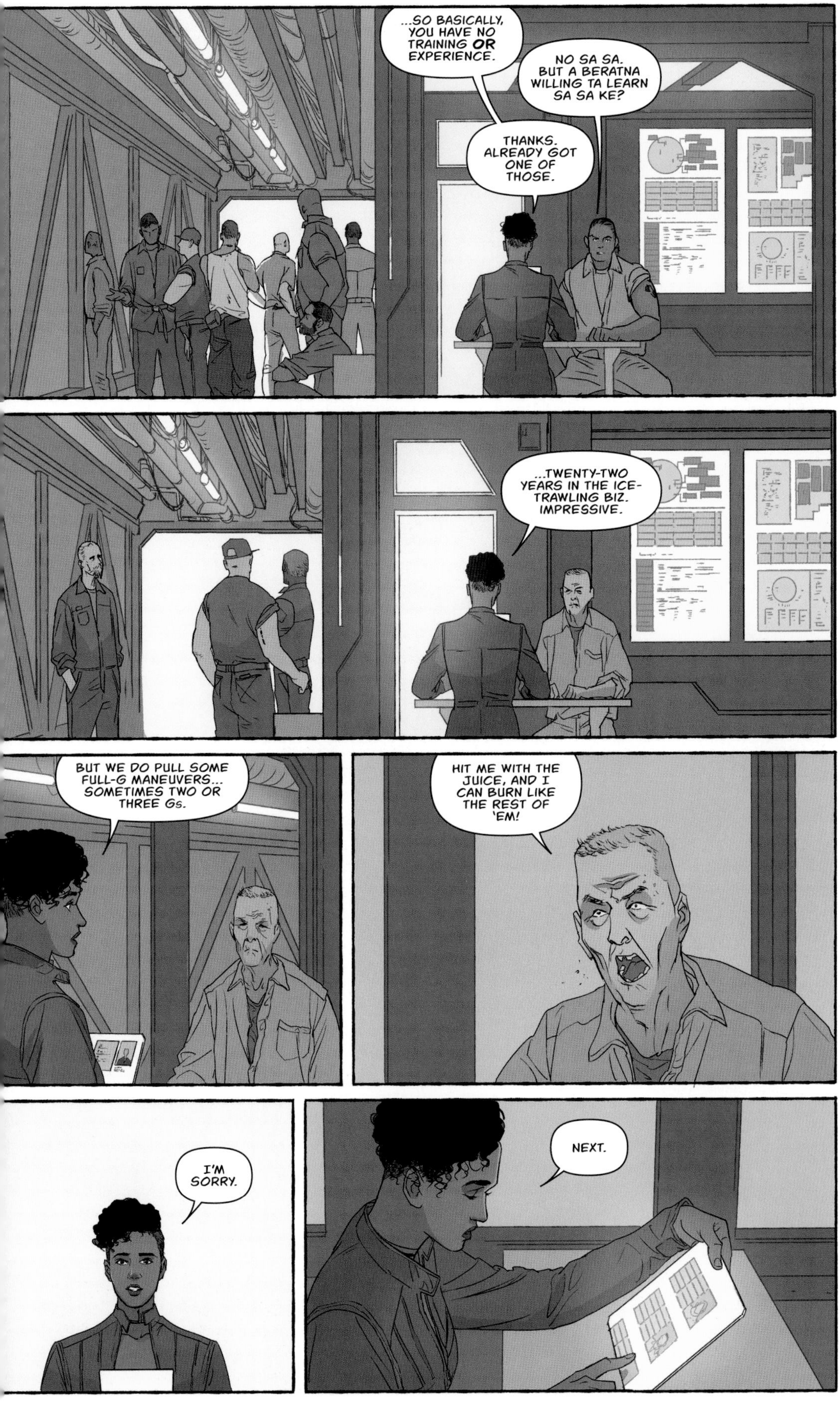
...SO BASICALLY, YOU HAVE NO TRAINING OR EXPERIENCE.
NO SA SA. BUT A BERATNA WILLING TA LEARN SA SA KE?
THANKS. ALREADY GOT ONE OF THOSE.
...TWENTY-TWO YEARS IN THE ICE-TRAWLING BIZ. IMPRESSIVE.
BUT WE DO PULL SOME FULL-G MANEUVERS... SOMETIMES TWO OR THREE Gs.
HIT ME WITH THE JUICE, AND I CAN BURN LIKE THE REST OF 'EM!
I'M SORRY.
NEXT.

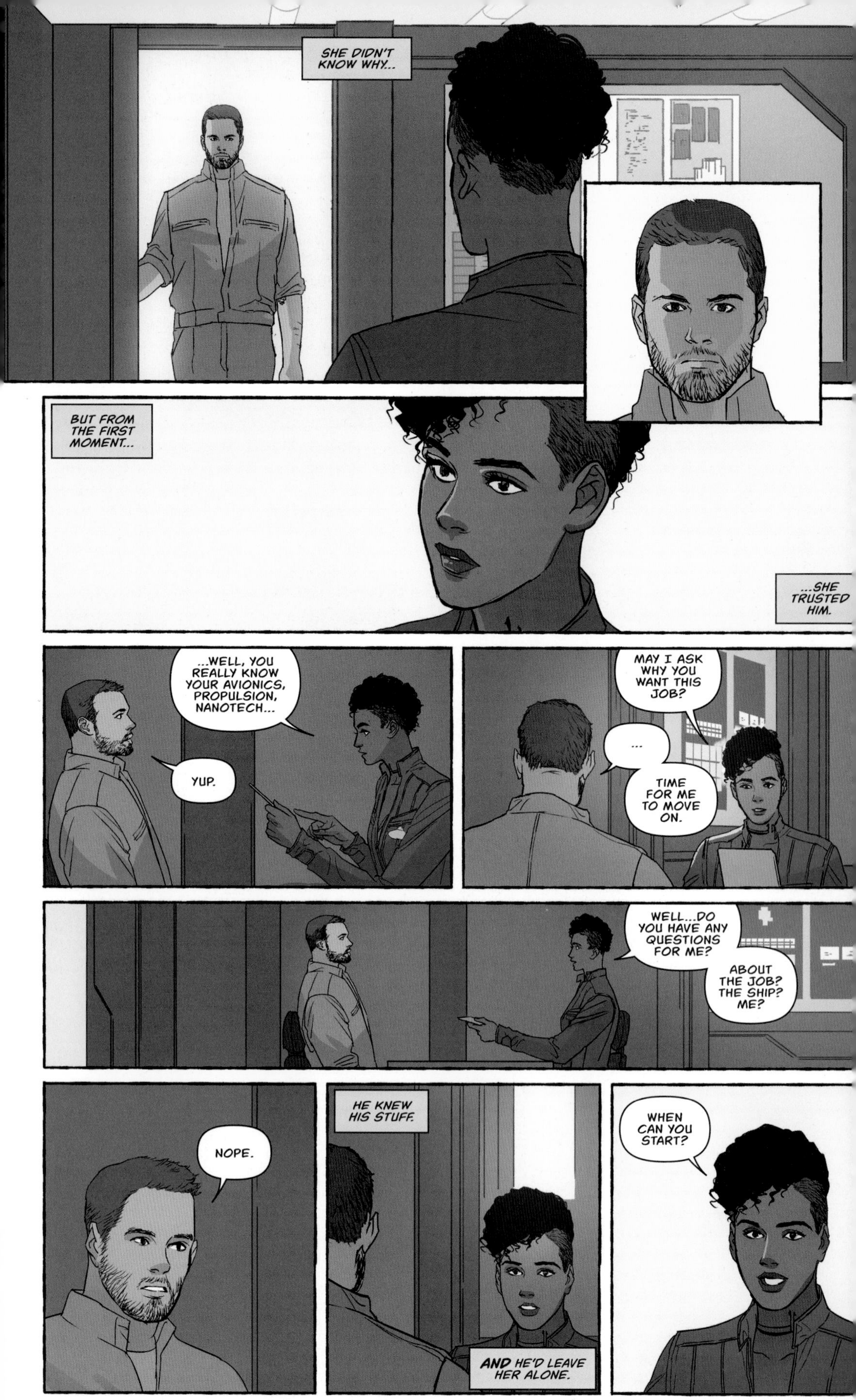

SHE DIDN'T KNOW WHY...
BUT FROM THE FIRST MOMENT...
...SHE TRUSTED HIM.
...WELL, YOU REALLY KNOW YOUR AVIONICS, PROPULSION, NANOTECH...
YUP.
MAY I ASK WHY YOU WANT THIS JOB?
...
TIME FOR ME TO MOVE ON.
WELL...DO YOU HAVE ANY QUESTIONS FOR ME?
ABOUT THE JOB? THE SHIP? ME?
NOPE.
HE KNEW HIS STUFF.
AND HE'D LEAVE HER ALONE.
WHEN CAN YOU START?

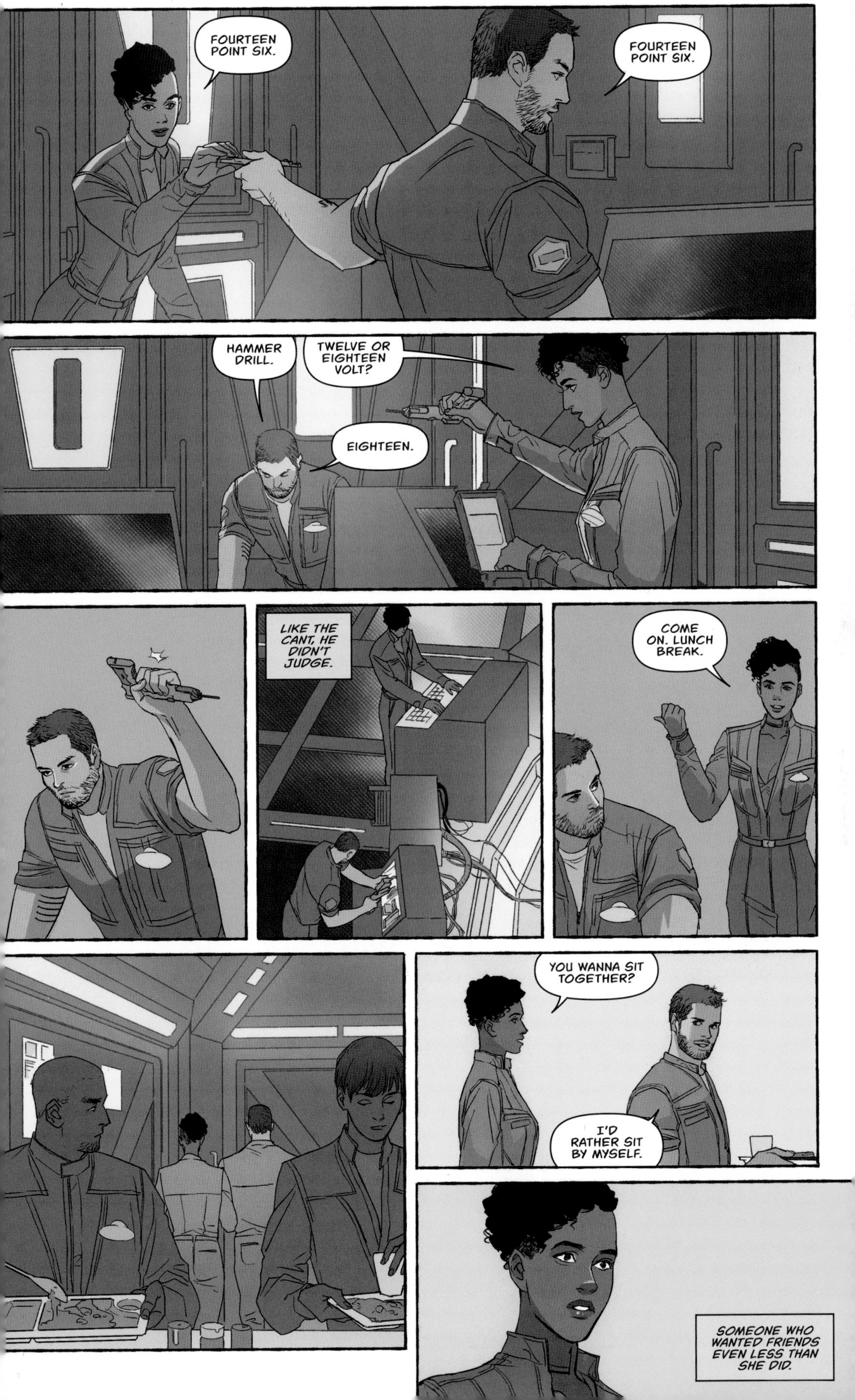
FOURTEEN POINT SIX.
FOURTEEN POINT SIX.
HAMMER DRILL.
TWELVE OR EIGHTEEN VOLT?
EIGHTEEN.
LIKE THE CANT, HE DIDN'T JUDGE.
COME ON. LUNCH BREAK.
YOU WANNA SIT TOGETHER?
I'D RATHER SIT BY MYSELF.
SOMEONE WHO WANTED FRIENDS EVEN LESS THAN SHE DID.

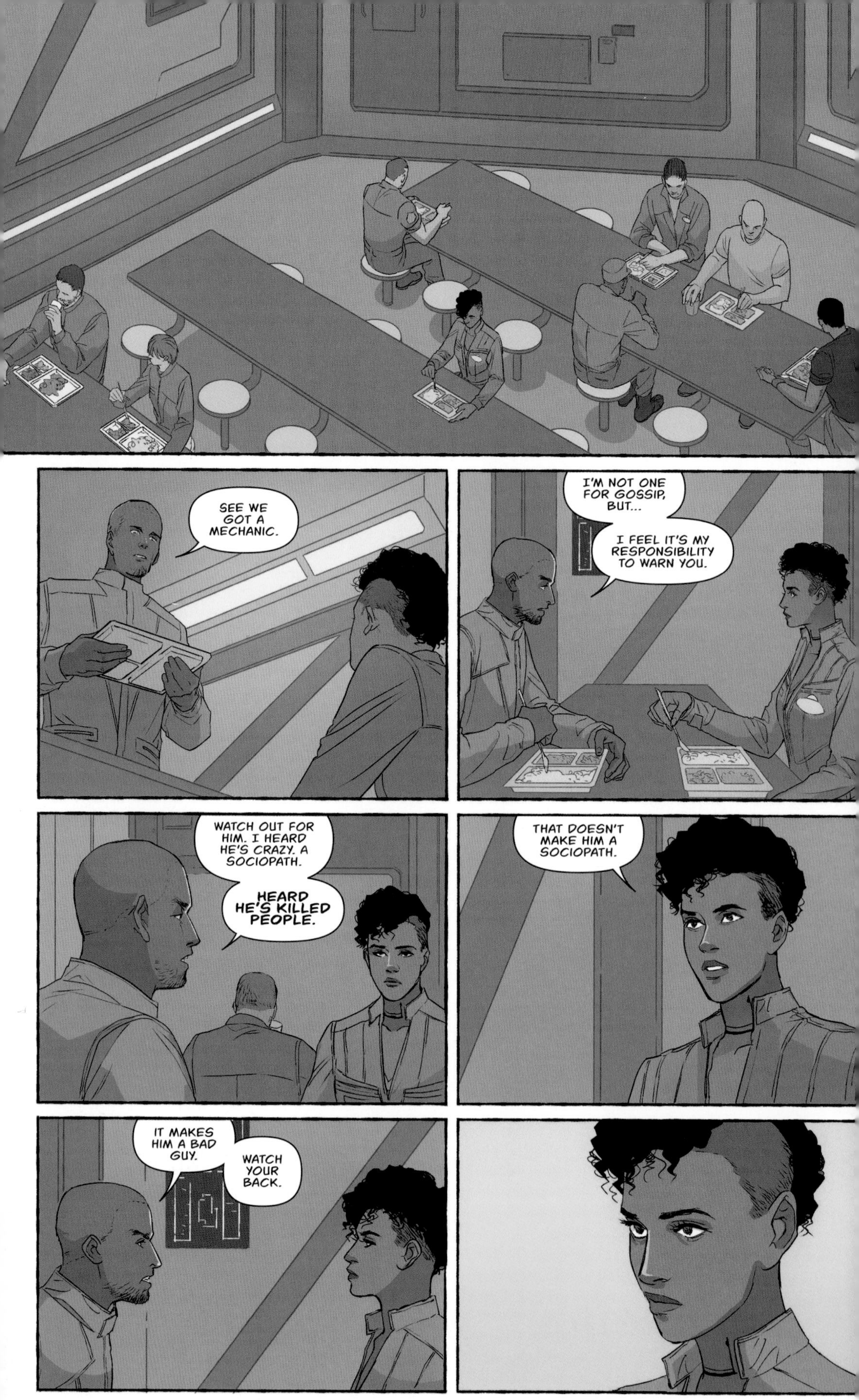
SEE WE GOT A MECHANIC.
I'M NOT ONE FOR GOSSIP, BUT...
I FEEL IT'S MY RESPONSIBILITY TO WARN YOU.
WATCH OUT FOR HIM. I HEARD HE'S CRAZY. A SOCIOPATH.
HEARD HE'S KILLED PEOPLE.
THAT DOESN'T MAKE HIM A SOCIOPATH.
IT MAKES HIM A BAD GUY.
WATCH YOUR BACK.

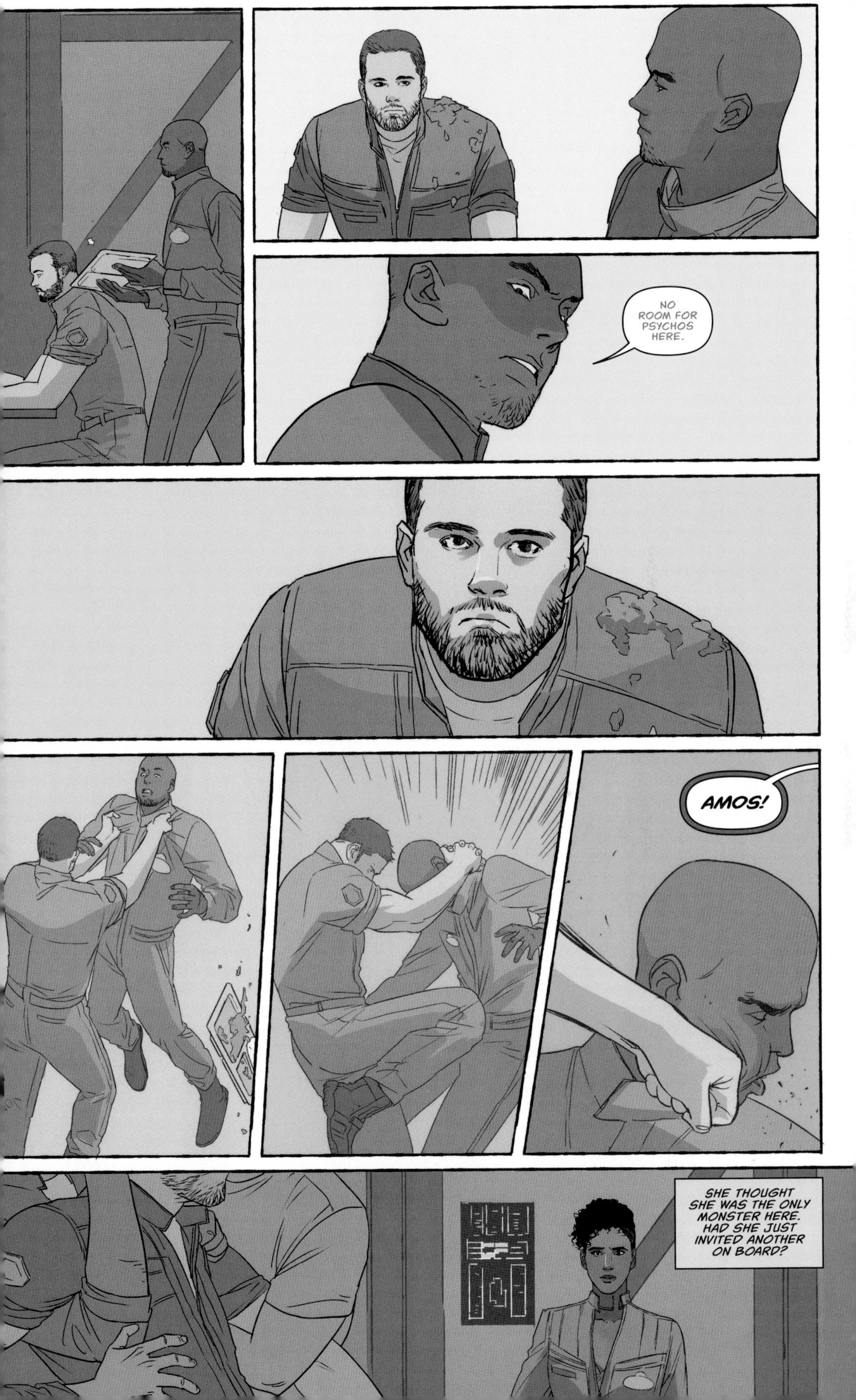
NO ROOM FOR PSYCHOS HERE.
AMOS!
SHE THOUGHT SHE WAS THE ONLY MONSTER HERE. HAD SHE JUST INVITED ANOTHER ON BOARD?

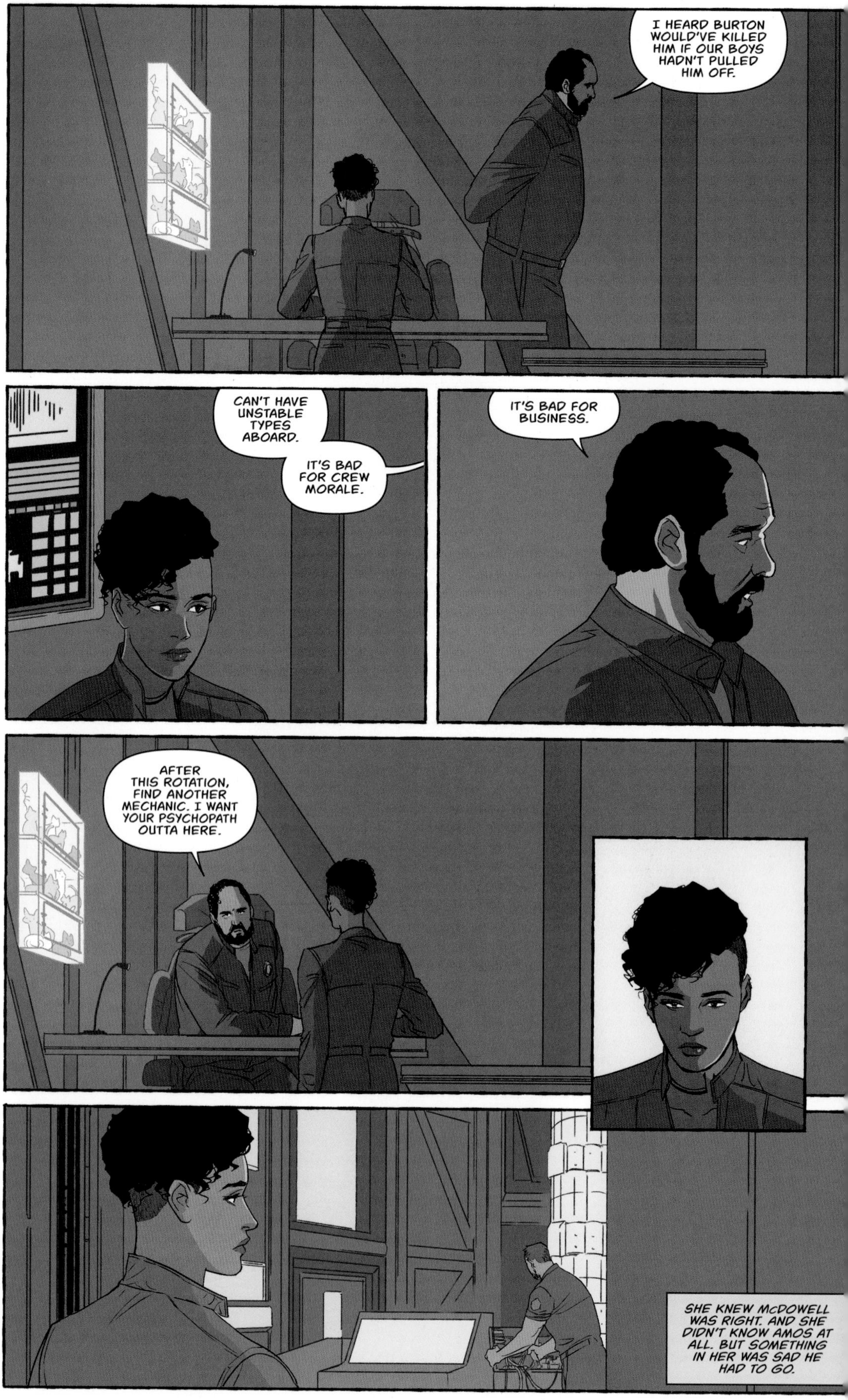
I HEARD BURTON WOULD'VE KILLED HIM IF OUR BOYS HADN'T PULLED HIM OFF.
CAN'T HAVE UNSTABLE TYPES ABOARD.
IT'S BAD FOR CREW MORALE.
IT'S BAD FOR BUSINESS.
AFTER THIS ROTATION, FIND ANOTHER MECHANIC. I WANT YOUR PSYCHOPATH OUTTA HERE.
SHE KNEW McDOWELL WAS RIGHT. AND SHE DIDN'T KNOW AMOS AT ALL. BUT SOMETHING IN HER WAS SAD HE HAD TO GO.

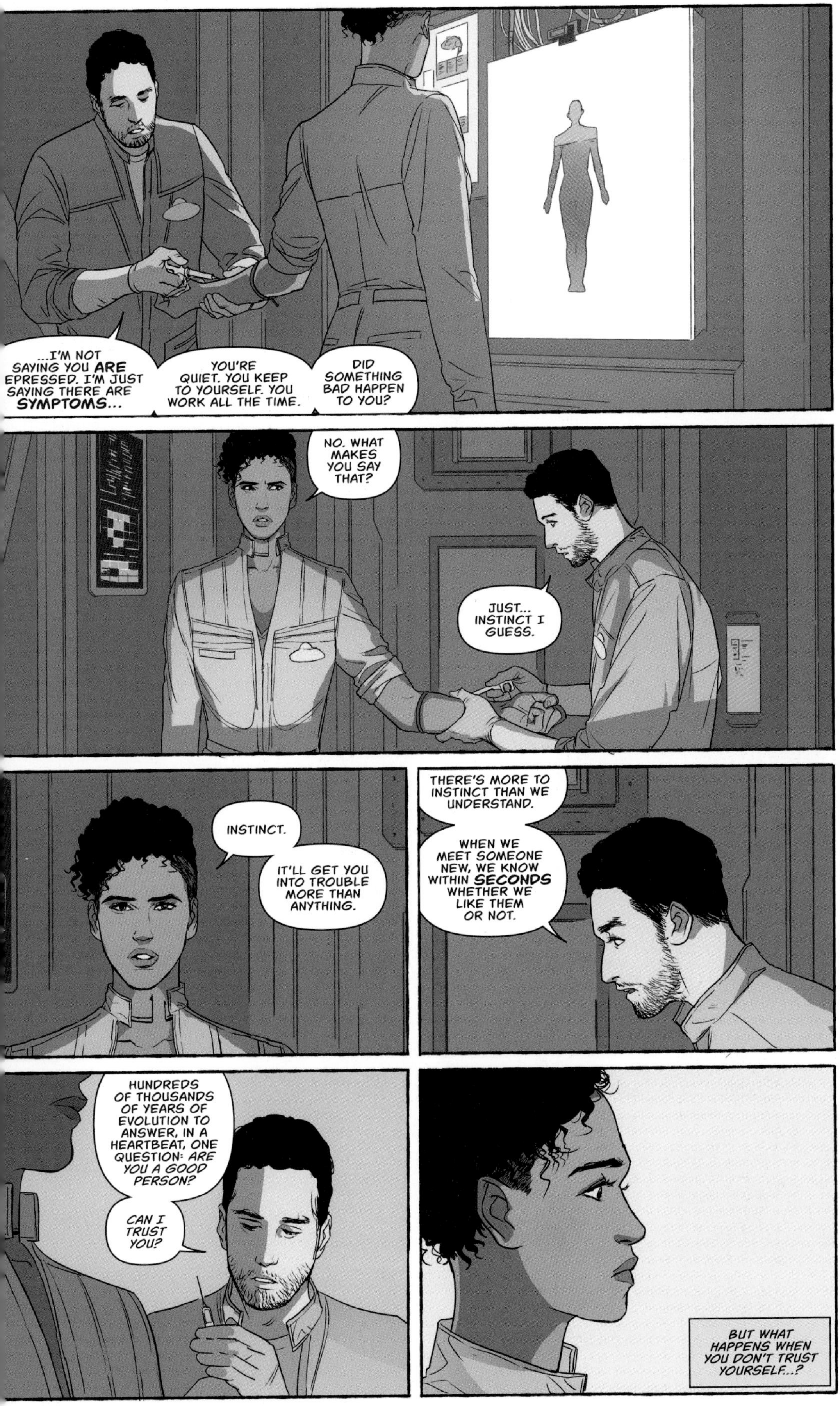
...I'M NOT SAYING YOU ARE EPRESSED. I'M JUST SAYING THERE ARE SYMPTOMS...
YOU'RE QUIET. YOU KEEP TO YOURSELF. YOU WORK ALL THE TIME.
DID SOMETHING BAD HAPPEN TO YOU?
NO. WHAT MAKES YOU SAY THAT?
JUST... INSTINCT I GUESS.
INSTINCT.
IT'LL GET YOU INTO TROUBLE MORE THAN ANYTHING.
THERE'S MORE TO INSTINCT THAN WE UNDERSTAND.
WHEN WE MEET SOMEONE NEW, WE KNOW WITHIN SECONDS WHETHER WE LIKE THEM OR NOT.
HUNDREDS OF THOUSANDS OF YEARS OF EVOLUTION TO ANSWER, IN A HEARTBEAT, ONE QUESTION: ARE YOU A GOOD PERSON?
CAN I TRUST YOU?
BUT WHAT HAPPENS WHEN YOU DON'T TRUST YOURSELF...?

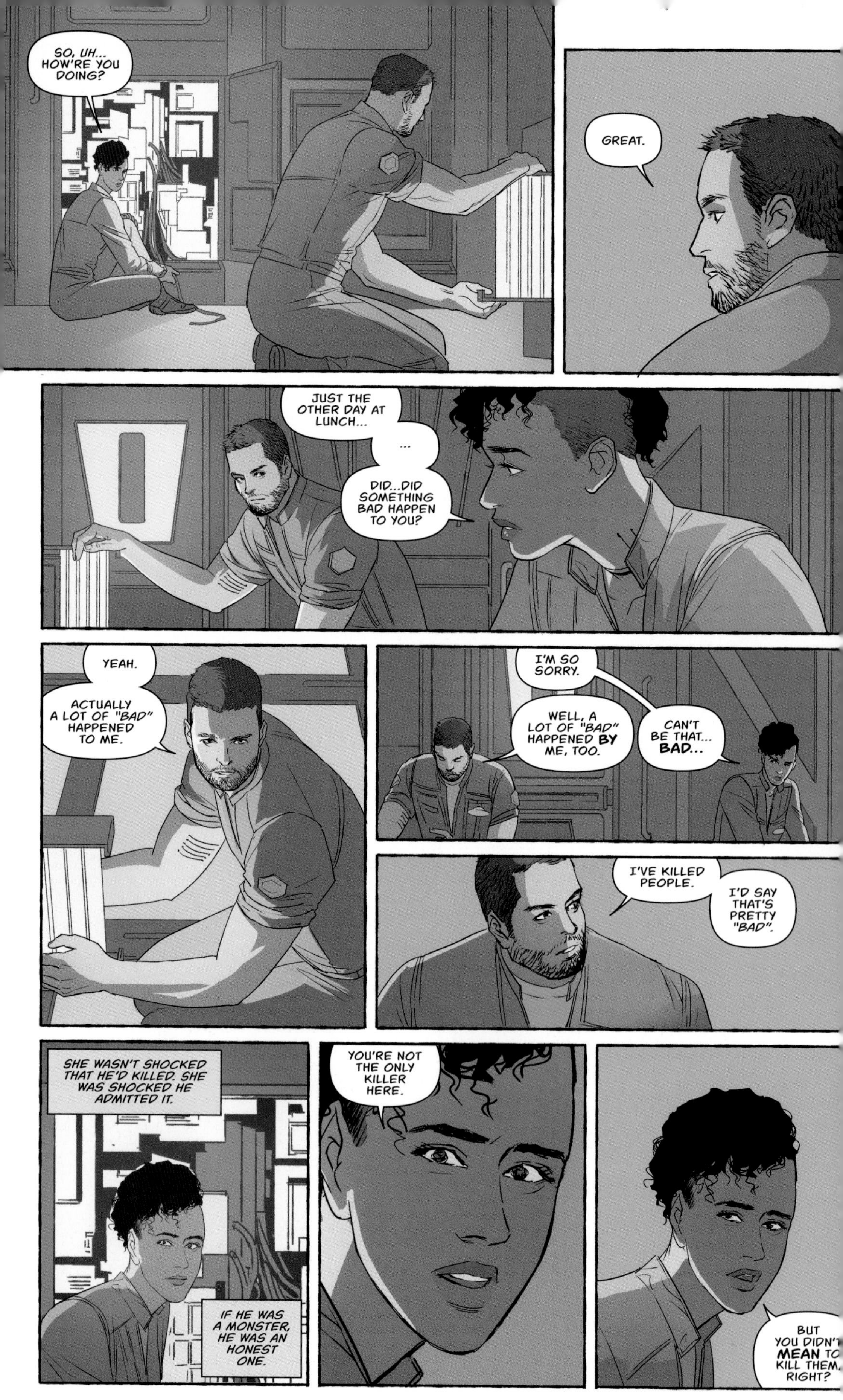
SO, UH... HOW'RE YOU DOING?
GREAT.
JUST THE OTHER DAY AT LUNCH...
...
DID...DID SOMETHING BAD HAPPEN TO YOU?
YEAH.
ACTUALLY A LOT OF "BAD" HAPPENED TO ME.
I'M SO SORRY.
CAN'T BE THAT... BAD...
WELL, A LOT OF "BAD" HAPPENED BY ME, TOO.
I'VE KILLED PEOPLE.
I'D SAY THAT'S PRETTY "BAD".
SHE WASN'T SHOCKED THAT HE'D KILLED. SHE WAS SHOCKED HE ADMITTED IT.
IF HE WAS A MONSTER, HE WAS AN HONEST ONE.
YOU'RE NOT THE ONLY KILLER HERE.
BUT YOU DIDN'T MEAN TO KILL THEM, RIGHT?

NO. I DID.

DID YOU?

NO! NO, OF COURSE NOT!

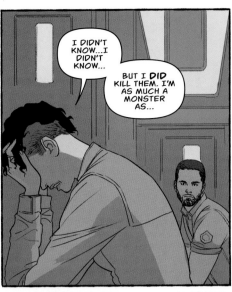

I DIDN'T KNOW...I DIDN'T KNOW...

BUT I **DID** KILL THEM. I'M AS MUCH A MONSTER AS...

I DIDN'T MEAN--

AT LEAST YOU FEEL BAD.

I KNOW LOTS OF FOLKS WHO **GOT OFF** ON HURTING OTHERS.

WHAT ABOUT YOU? DO YOU FEEL BAD?

I DON'T FEEL ANYTHING.

IS THAT WORSE?

RRRR RRRRR

RRRR

RRRRR

DAMMIT. ONE OF THE HELIUM COPVs INSIDE THE LOX TANK FAILED.

IF THE OXYGEN FREEZES, IT'LL IGNITE THE CARBON COMPOSITE IN THE HELIUM TANKS AND...

BOOM.

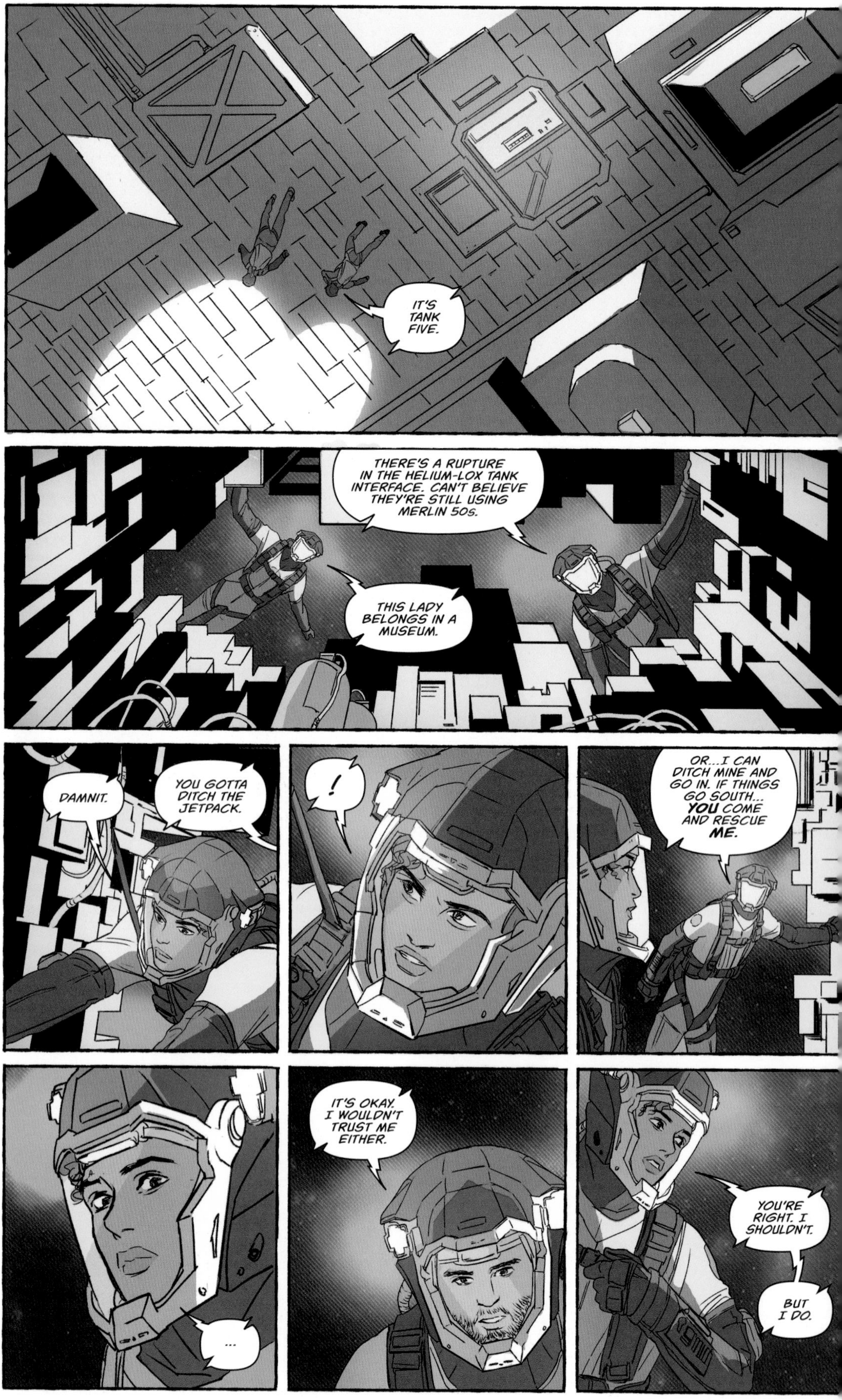
IT'S TANK FIVE.
THERE'S A RUPTURE IN THE HELIUM-LOX TANK INTERFACE. CAN'T BELIEVE THEY'RE STILL USING MERLIN 50s.
THIS LADY BELONGS IN A MUSEUM.
DAMNIT.
YOU GOTTA DITCH THE JETPACK.
!
OR...I CAN DITCH MINE AND GO IN. IF THINGS GO SOUTH... YOU COME AND RESCUE ME.
...
IT'S OKAY. I WOULDN'T TRUST ME EITHER.
YOU'RE RIGHT. I SHOULDN'T.
BUT I DO.

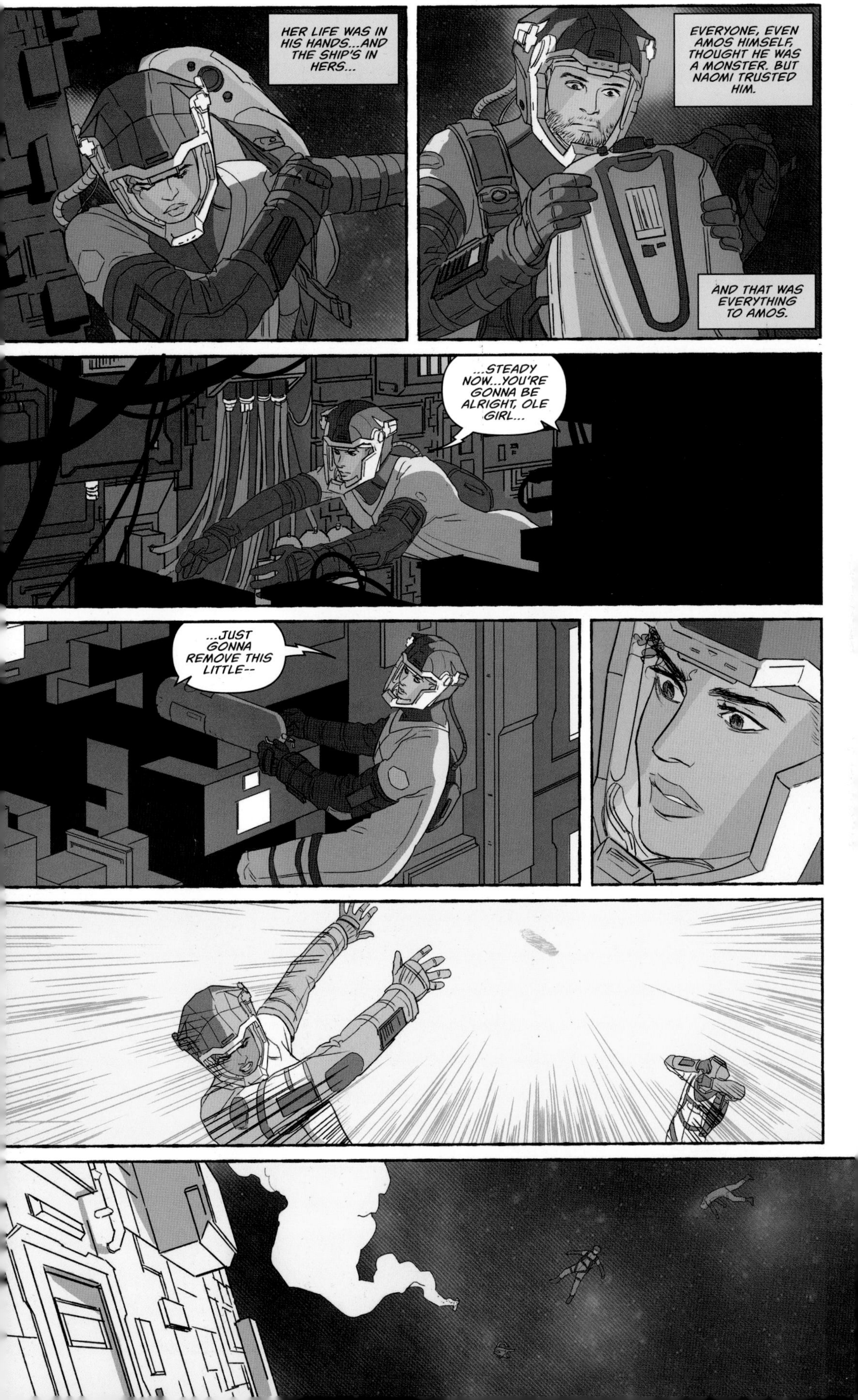
HER LIFE WAS IN HIS HANDS...AND THE SHIP'S IN HERS...
EVERYONE, EVEN AMOS HIMSELF, THOUGHT HE WAS A MONSTER. BUT NAOMI TRUSTED HIM.
AND THAT WAS EVERYTHING TO AMOS.
...STEADY NOW...YOU'RE GONNA BE ALRIGHT, OLE GIRL...
...JUST GONNA REMOVE THIS LITTLE--

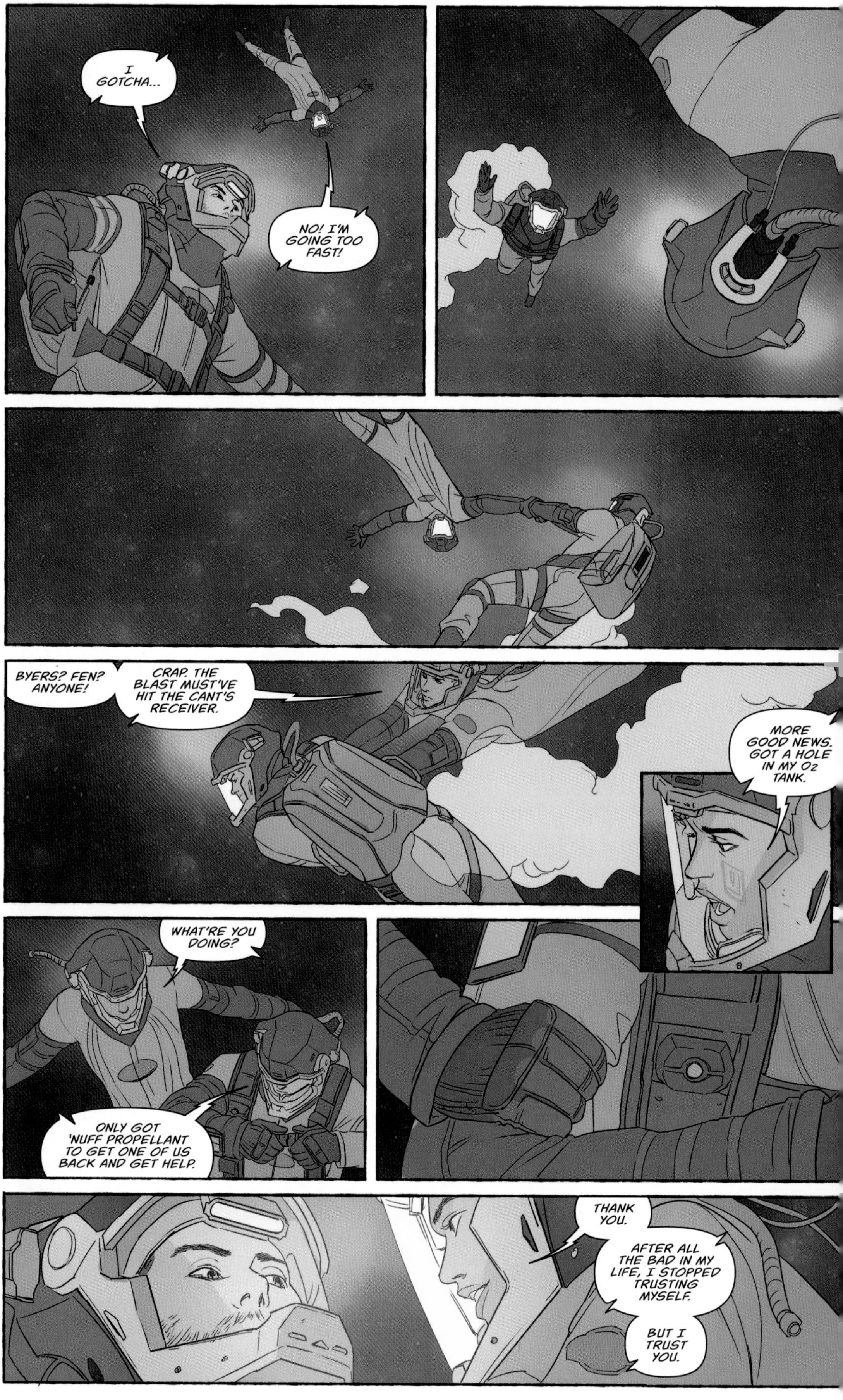

I GOTCHA...
NO! I'M GOING TOO FAST!
BYERS? FEN? ANYONE!
CRAP. THE BLAST MUST'VE HIT THE CANT'S RECEIVER.
MORE GOOD NEWS. GOT A HOLE IN MY O2 TANK.
WHAT'RE YOU DOING?
ONLY GOT 'NUFF PROPELLANT TO GET ONE OF US BACK AND GET HELP.
THANK YOU.
AFTER ALL THE BAD IN MY LIFE, I STOPPED TRUSTING MYSELF.
BUT I TRUST YOU.

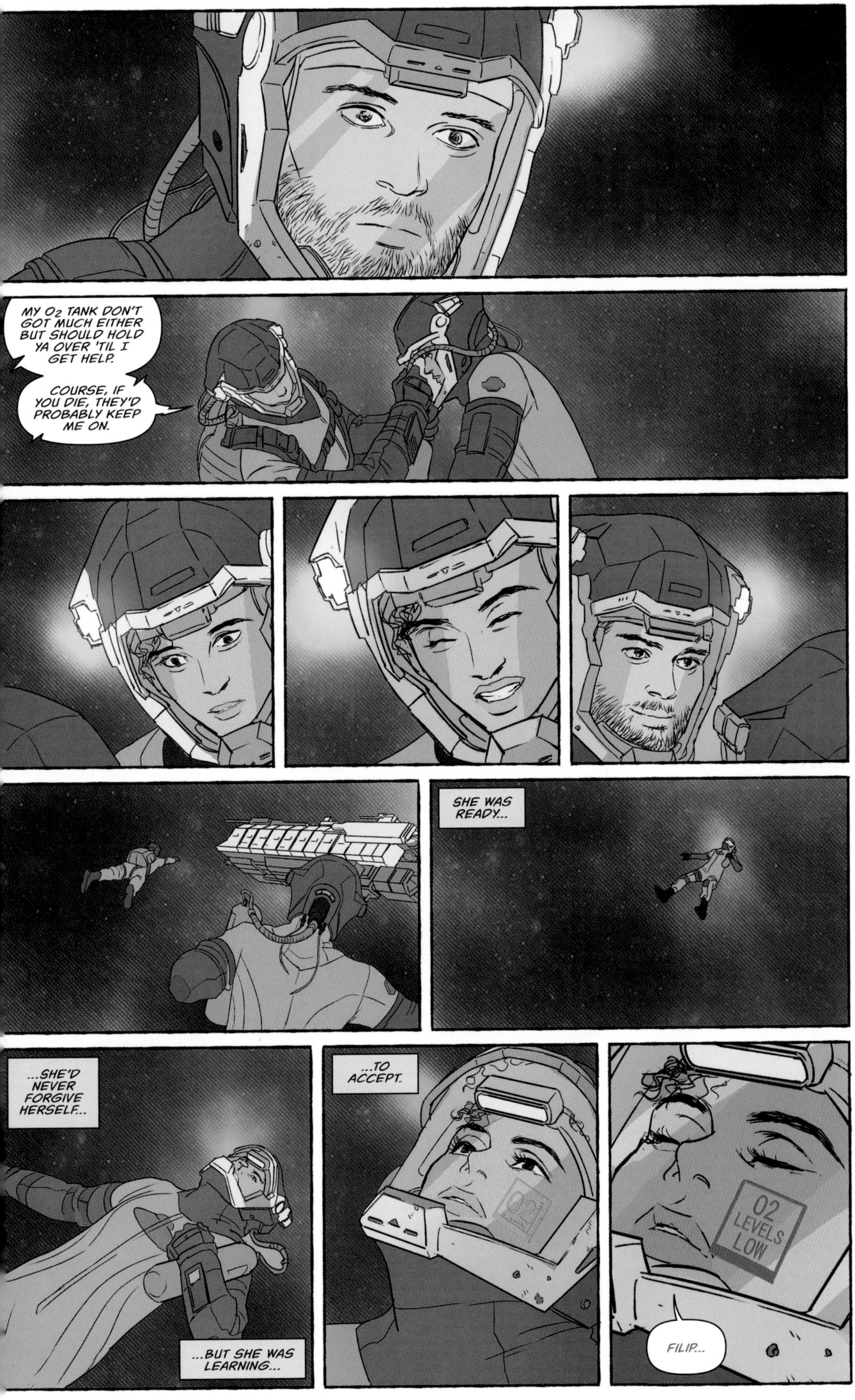
MY O_2 TANK DON'T GOT MUCH EITHER BUT SHOULD HOLD YA OVER 'TIL I GET HELP.
COURSE, IF YOU DIE, THEY'D PROBABLY KEEP ME ON.
SHE WAS READY...
...SHE'D NEVER FORGIVE HERSELF...
...BUT SHE WAS LEARNING...
...TO ACCEPT.
O2
O2 LEVELS LOW
FILIP...

WELCOME BACK.

YOU SAVED THE SHIP.

WHAT HAPPENED TO FEN?

OH. UH... AMOS THOUGHT HE TOOK TOO LONG PREPPING THE RESCUE POD.

HEARD YOU CHANGED THE CAP'S MIND.

LOOKS LIKE WE'RE STUCK TOGETHER.

YOU'RE A GOOD PERSON.

I'M NOT. I'M REALLY NOT.

BAD PEOPLE DON'T FEEL BAD FOR THE THINGS THEY DONE.

I FIGURE, YOU FEEL SO BAD, YOU MUST BE GOOD.

WE'RE ALL A LITTLE BROKEN INSIDE...

BUT WE CAN HELP FIX EACH OTHER.

CHAPTER_003

ALEX KAMAL

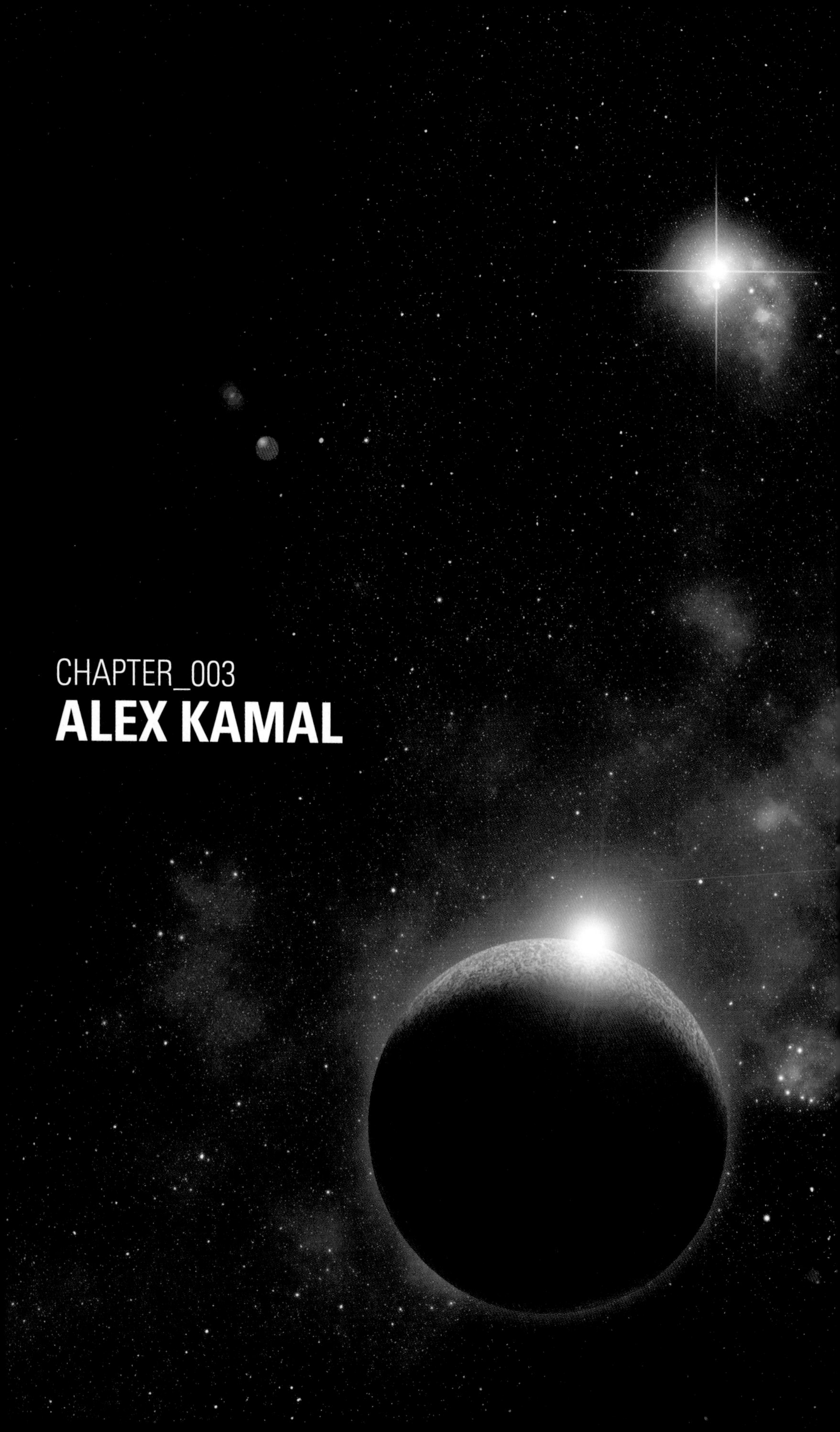

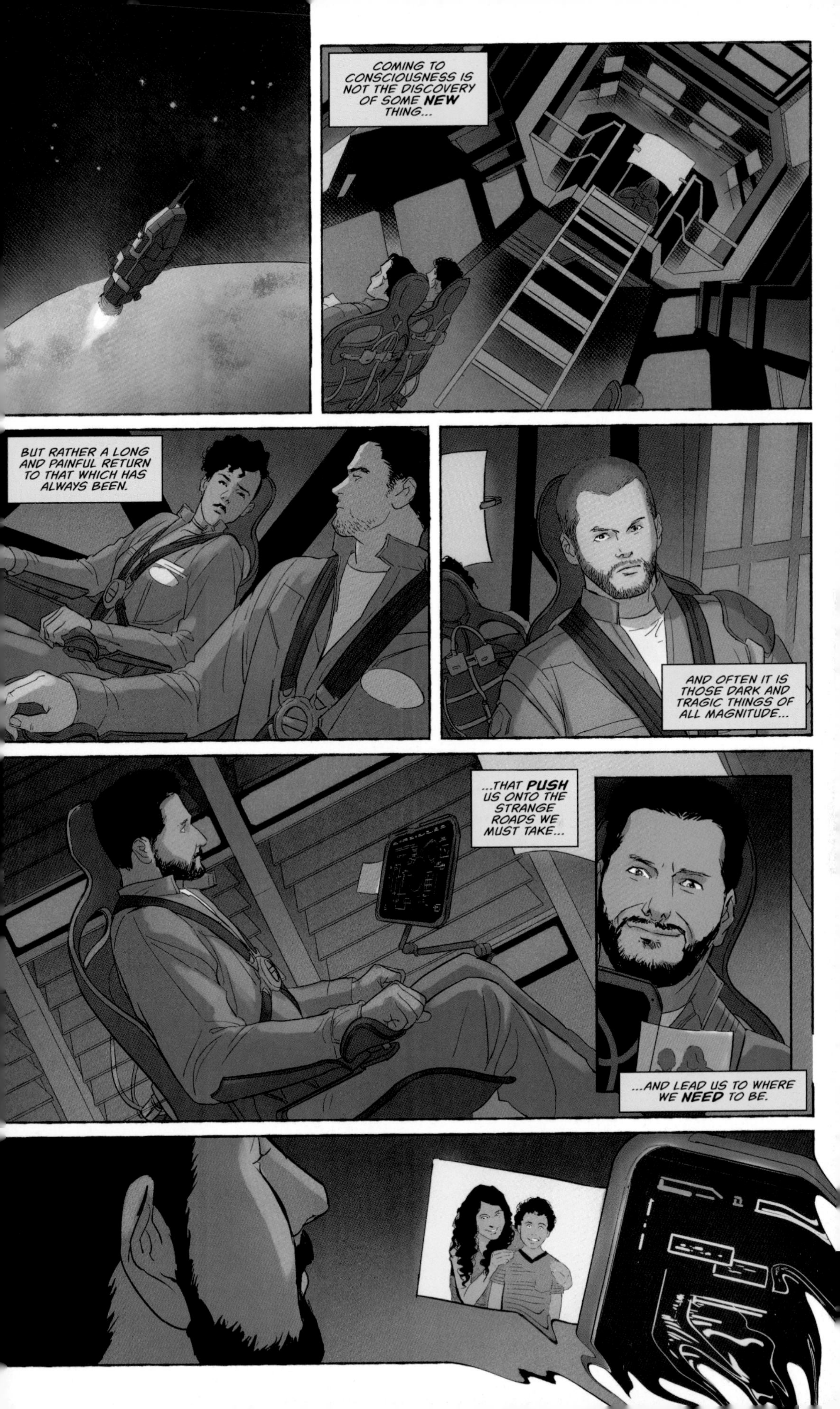
COMING TO CONSCIOUSNESS IS NOT THE DISCOVERY OF SOME **NEW** THING...
BUT RATHER A LONG AND PAINFUL RETURN TO THAT WHICH HAS ALWAYS BEEN.
AND OFTEN IT IS THOSE DARK AND TRAGIC THINGS OF ALL MAGNITUDE...
...THAT **PUSH** US ONTO THE STRANGE ROADS WE MUST TAKE...
...AND LEAD US TO WHERE WE **NEED** TO BE.

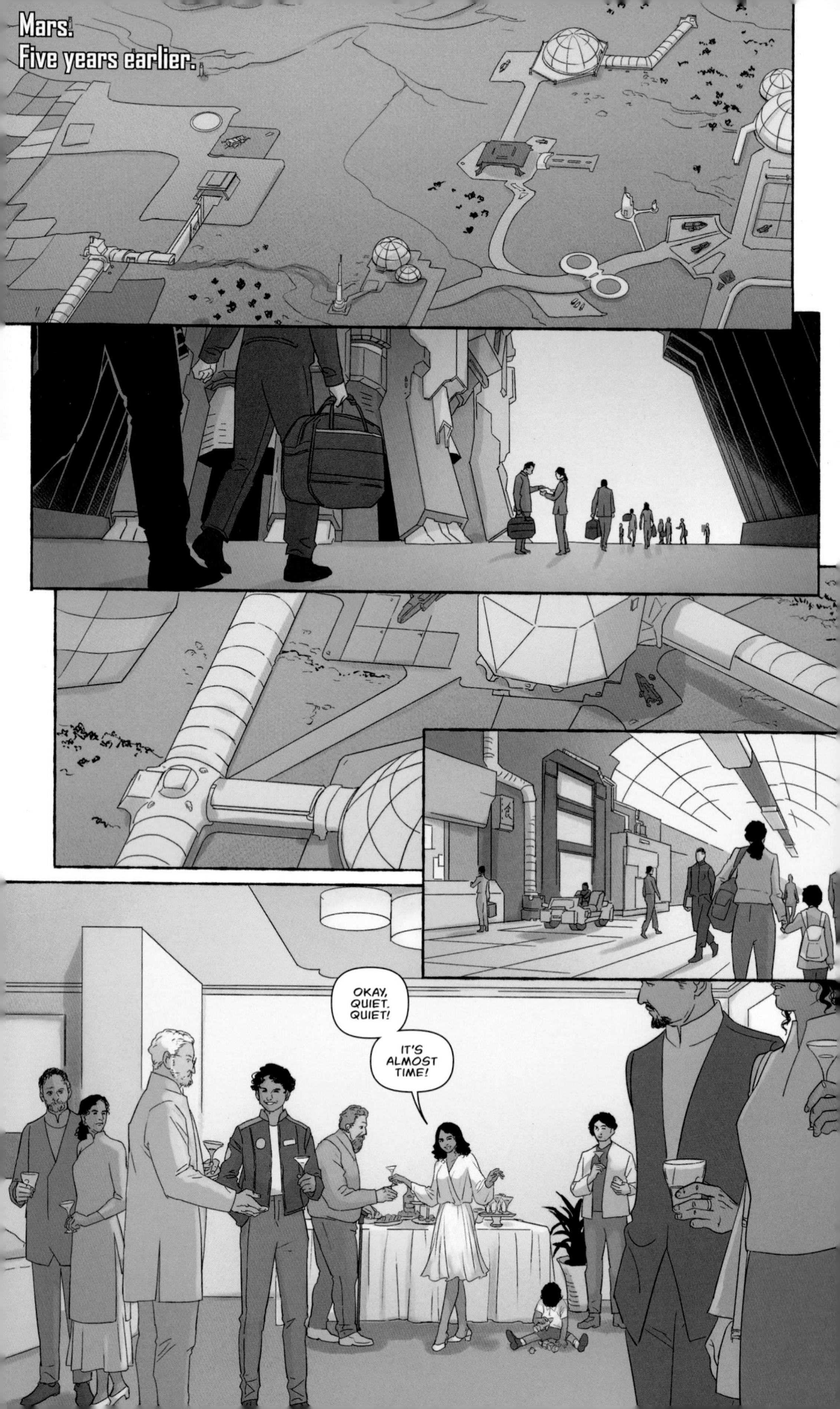
Mars.
Five years earlier.
OKAY, QUIET. QUIET!
IT'S ALMOST TIME!

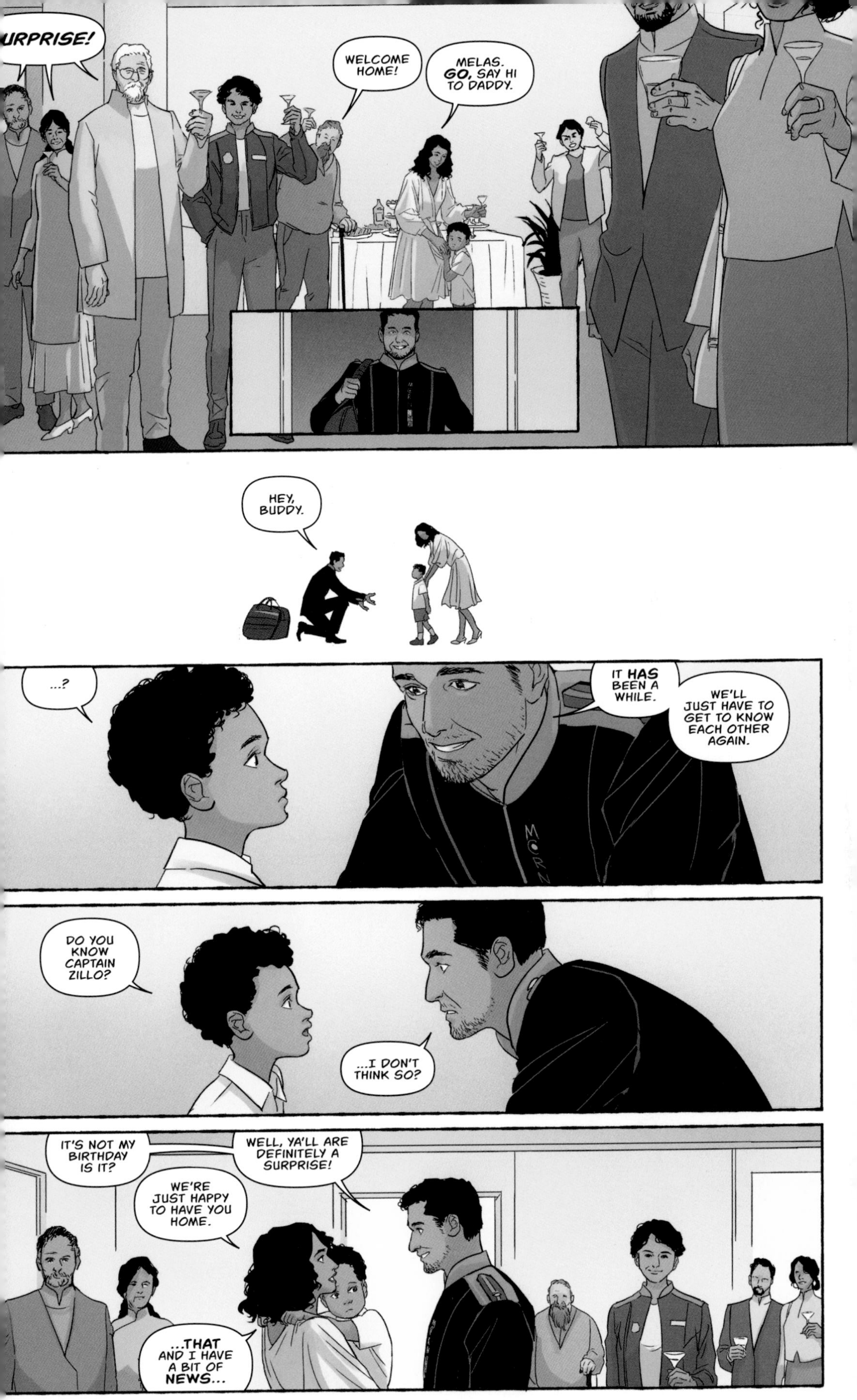

URPRISE!
WELCOME HOME!
MELAS. GO, SAY HI TO DADDY.
HEY, BUDDY.
...?
IT HAS BEEN A WHILE.
WE'LL JUST HAVE TO GET TO KNOW EACH OTHER AGAIN.
DO YOU KNOW CAPTAIN ZILLO?
...I DON'T THINK SO?
IT'S NOT MY BIRTHDAY IS IT?
WELL, YA'LL ARE DEFINITELY A SURPRISE!
WE'RE JUST HAPPY TO HAVE YOU HOME.
...THAT AND I HAVE A BIT OF NEWS...

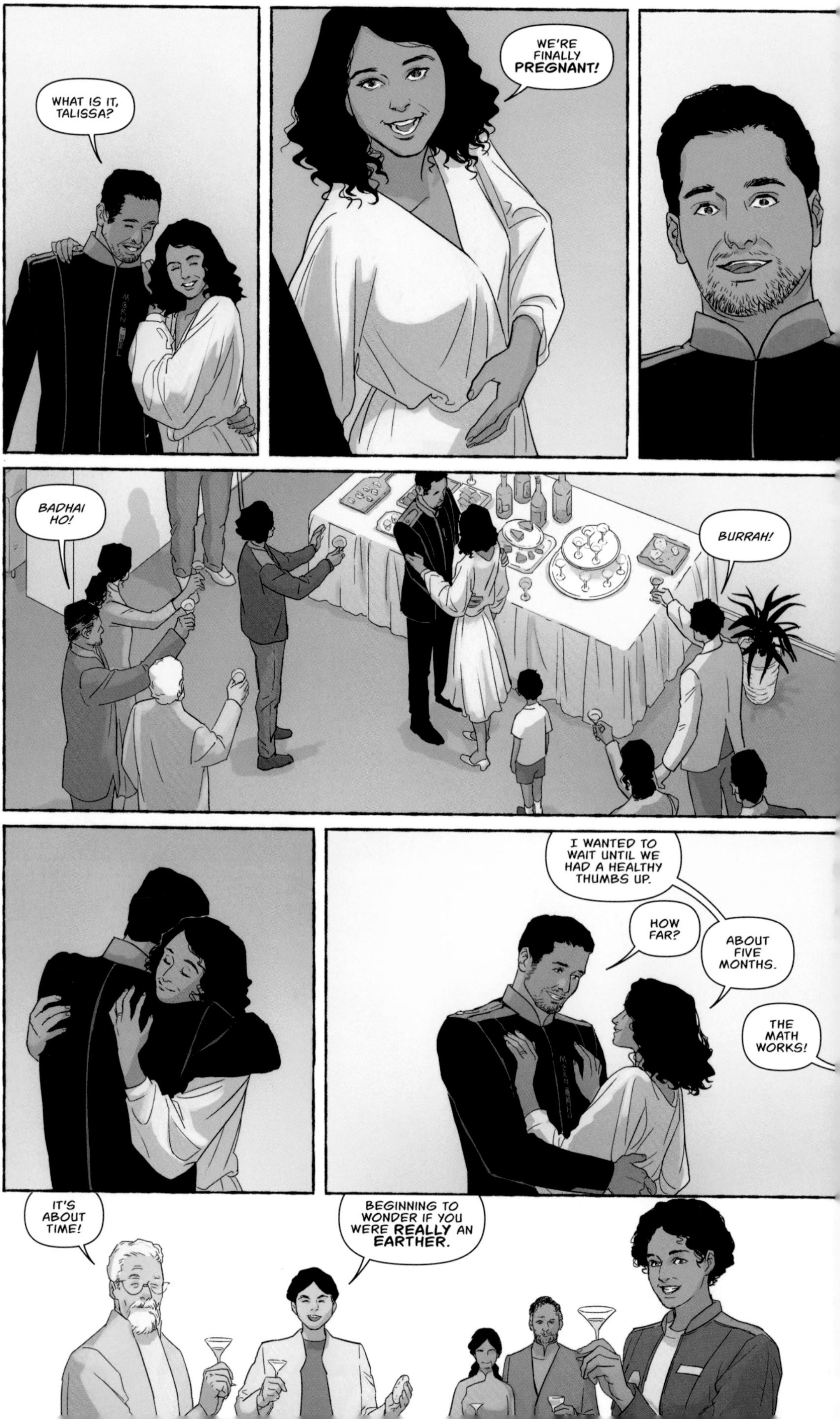
WHAT IS IT, TALISSA?
WE'RE FINALLY PREGNANT!
BADHAI HO!
BURRAH!
I WANTED TO WAIT UNTIL WE HAD A HEALTHY THUMBS UP.
HOW FAR?
ABOUT FIVE MONTHS.
THE MATH WORKS!
IT'S ABOUT TIME!
BEGINNING TO WONDER IF YOU WERE REALLY AN EARTHER.

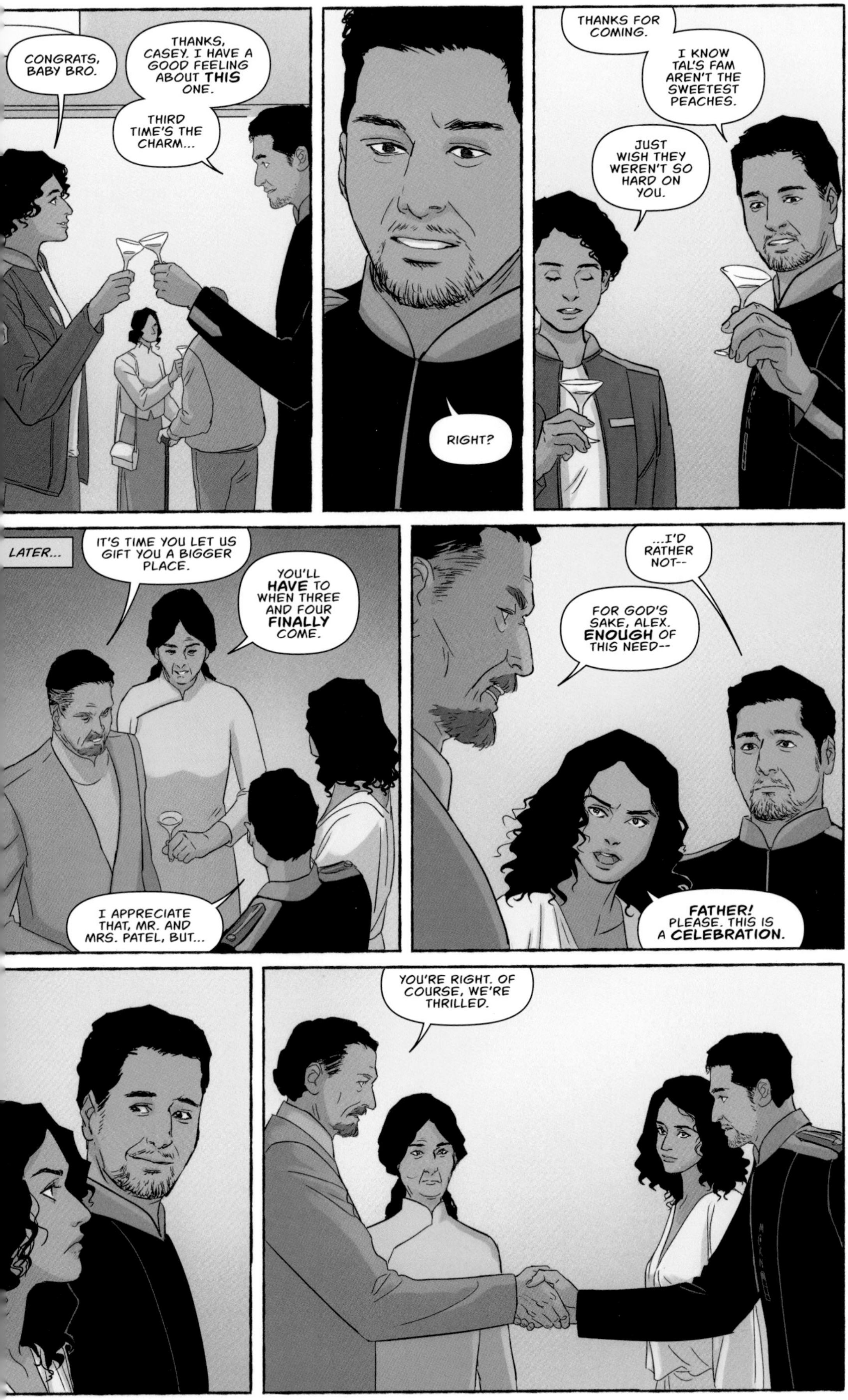
CONGRATS, BABY BRO.
THANKS, CASEY. I HAVE A GOOD FEELING ABOUT THIS ONE.
THIRD TIME'S THE CHARM...
RIGHT?
THANKS FOR COMING.
I KNOW TAL'S FAM AREN'T THE SWEETEST PEACHES.
JUST WISH THEY WEREN'T SO HARD ON YOU.
LATER...
IT'S TIME YOU LET US GIFT YOU A BIGGER PLACE.
YOU'LL HAVE TO WHEN THREE AND FOUR FINALLY COME.
I APPRECIATE THAT, MR. AND MRS. PATEL, BUT...
...I'D RATHER NOT--
FOR GOD'S SAKE, ALEX. ENOUGH OF THIS NEED--
FATHER! PLEASE. THIS IS A CELEBRATION.
YOU'RE RIGHT. OF COURSE, WE'RE THRILLED.

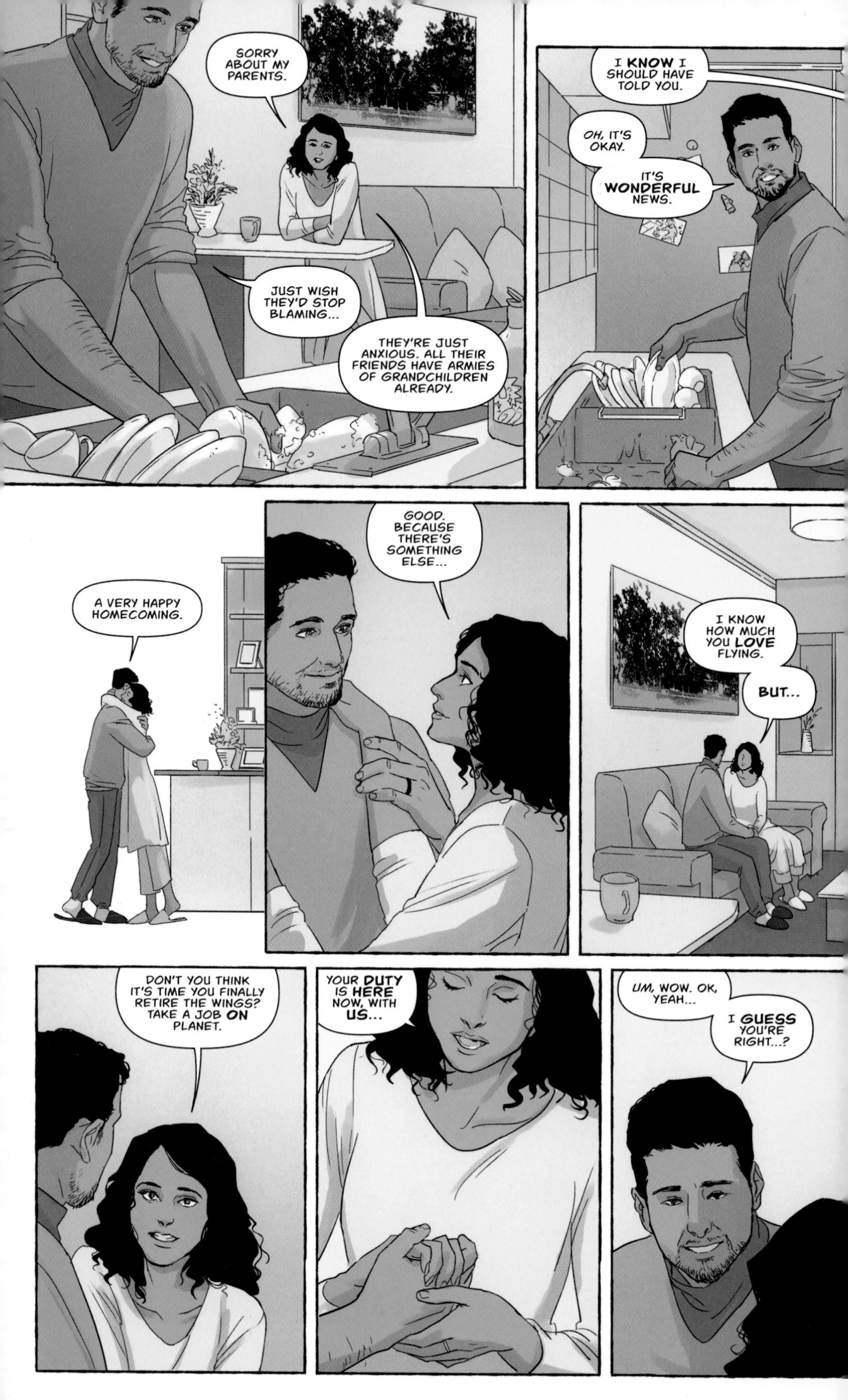

SORRY ABOUT MY PARENTS.
JUST WISH THEY'D STOP BLAMING...
THEY'RE JUST ANXIOUS. ALL THEIR FRIENDS HAVE ARMIES OF GRANDCHILDREN ALREADY.
I KNOW I SHOULD HAVE TOLD YOU.
OH, IT'S OKAY.
IT'S WONDERFUL NEWS.
A VERY HAPPY HOMECOMING.
GOOD. BECAUSE THERE'S SOMETHING ELSE...
I KNOW HOW MUCH YOU LOVE FLYING.
BUT...
DON'T YOU THINK IT'S TIME YOU FINALLY RETIRE THE WINGS? TAKE A JOB ON PLANET.
YOUR DUTY IS HERE NOW, WITH US...
UM, WOW. OK, YEAH...
I GUESS YOU'RE RIGHT...?

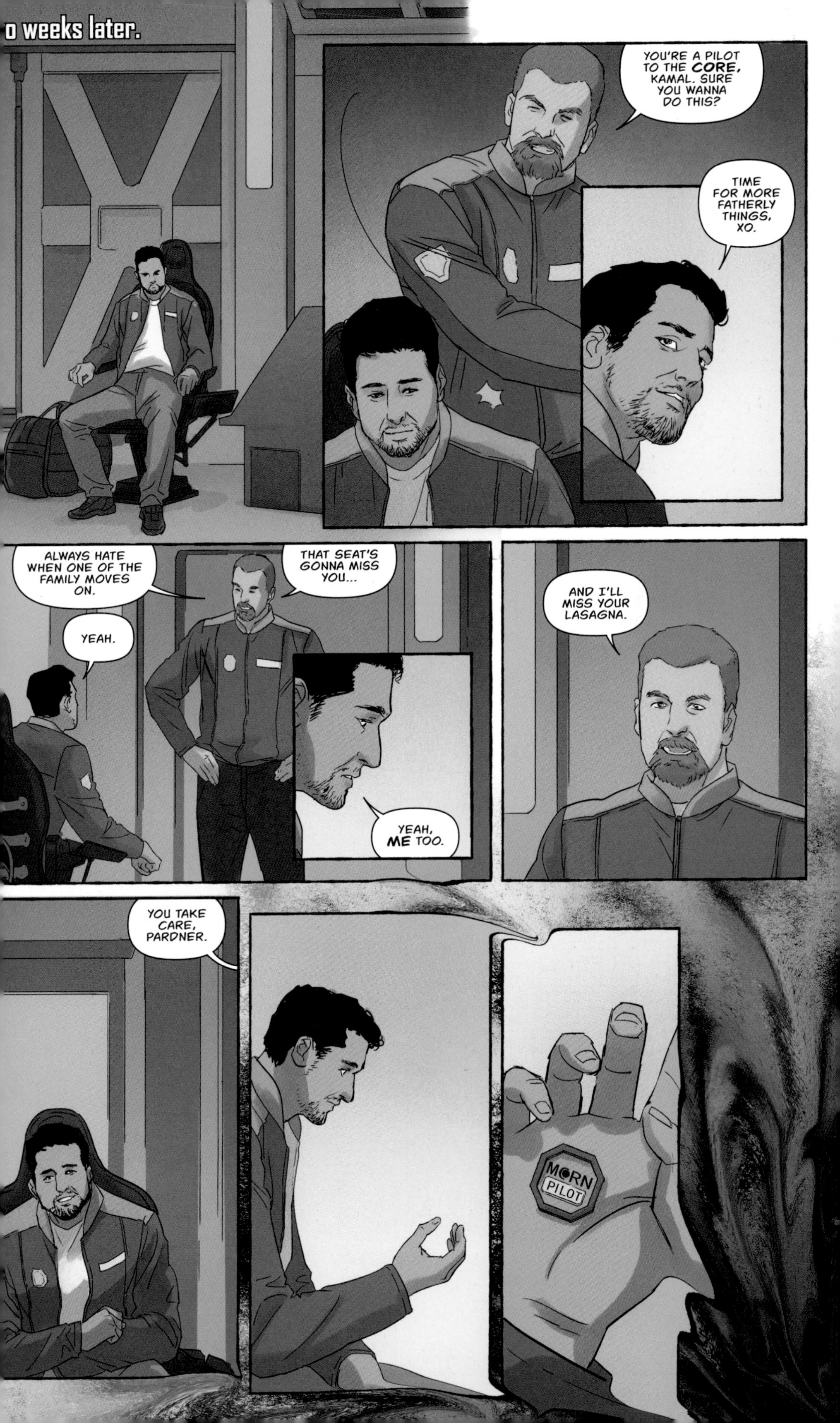
o weeks later.
YOU'RE A PILOT TO THE CORE, KAMAL. SURE YOU WANNA DO THIS?
TIME FOR MORE FATHERLY THINGS, XO.
ALWAYS HATE WHEN ONE OF THE FAMILY MOVES ON.
THAT SEAT'S GONNA MISS YOU...
YEAH.
YEAH, ME TOO.
AND I'LL MISS YOUR LASAGNA.
YOU TAKE CARE, PARDNER.
MORN PILOT

Two weeks later.

PATEL
ERRAFORMING

DUTY.
TOGETHER
AS MARTIANS
WE BUILD

WHEN LIVING FOR OTHERS' EXPECTATIONS IS ALL YOU KNOW...

Three weeks later.

PATEL
RRAFORMIN

DUTY.
TOGETHER
AS MARTIANS
WE BUILD

YUCK!

Five weeks later.

ATE
RAFORMI

TAKE CARE OF ZX3 FILES FOR ME?

HONOR.
TOGETHER
AS MARTI
WE RISE

...TO SEE OUR TRUTH TAKES TIME.

MORN

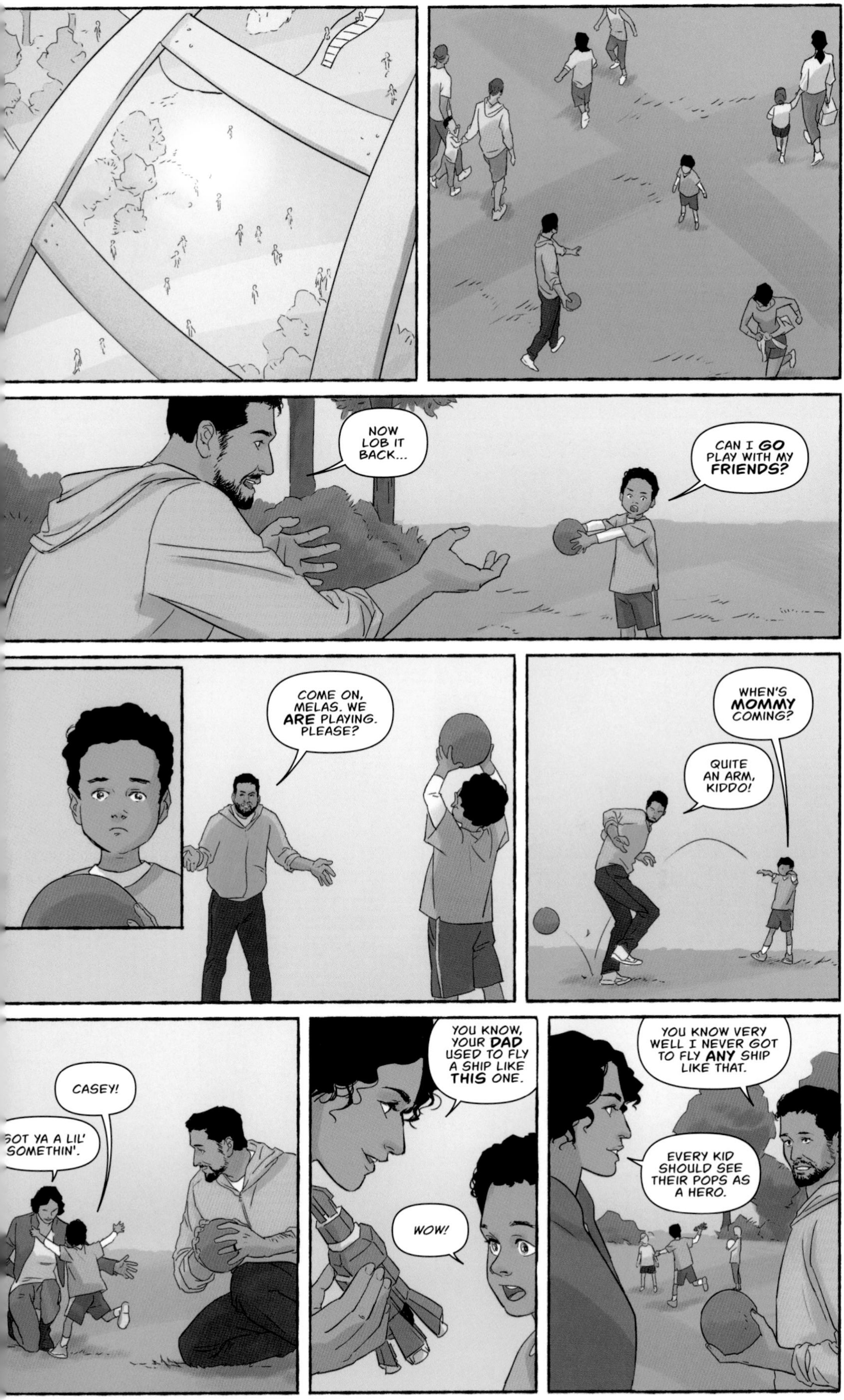
NOW LOB IT BACK...
CAN I GO PLAY WITH MY FRIENDS?
COME ON, MELAS. WE ARE PLAYING. PLEASE?
WHEN'S MOMMY COMING?
QUITE AN ARM, KIDDO!
CASEY!
GOT YA A LIL' SOMETHIN'.
YOU KNOW, YOUR DAD USED TO FLY A SHIP LIKE THIS ONE.
WOW!
YOU KNOW VERY WELL I NEVER GOT TO FLY ANY SHIP LIKE THAT.
EVERY KID SHOULD SEE THEIR POPS AS A HERO.

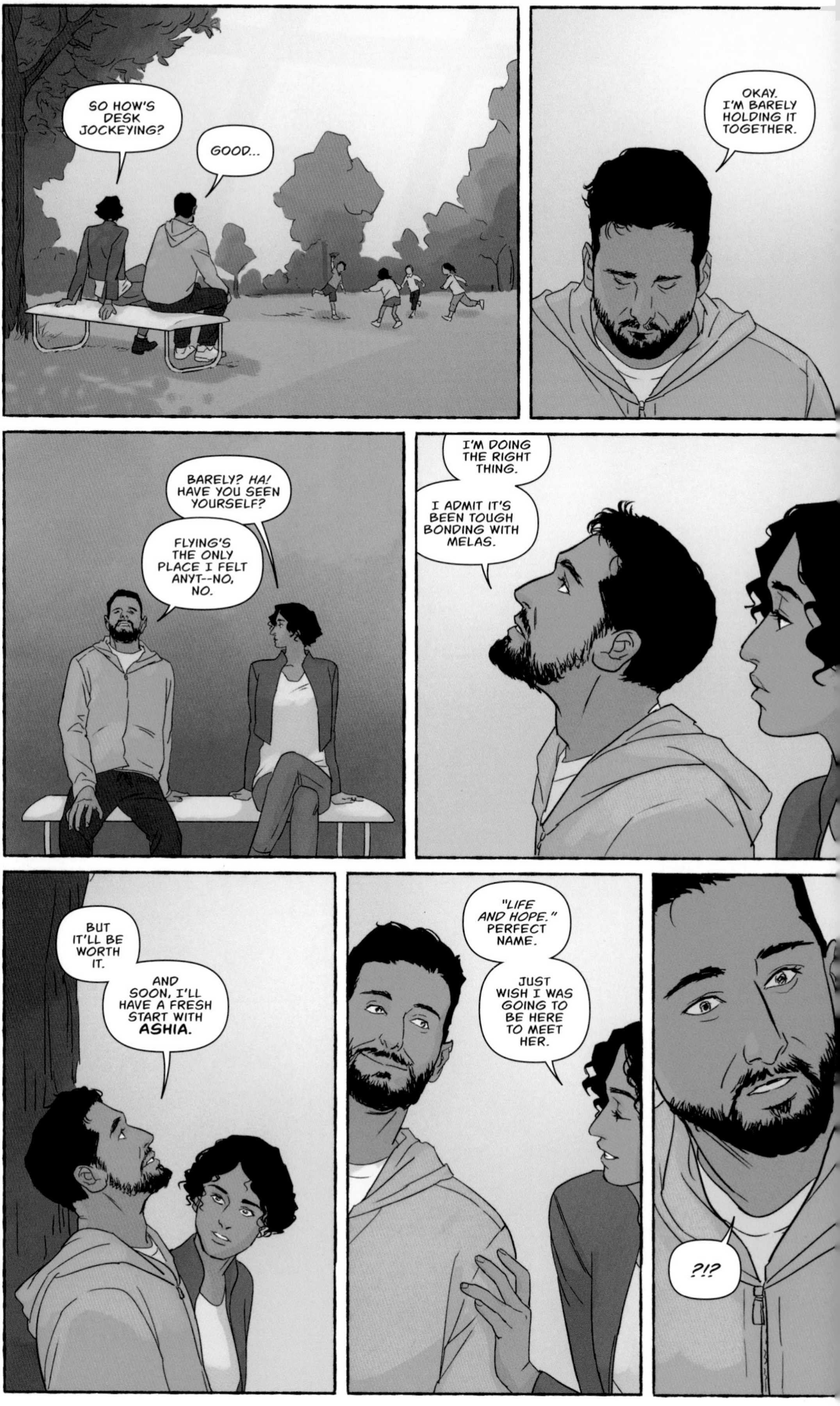
SO HOW'S DESK JOCKEYING?
GOOD...
OKAY. I'M BARELY HOLDING IT TOGETHER.
BARELY? HA! HAVE YOU SEEN YOURSELF?
FLYING'S THE ONLY PLACE I FELT ANYT--NO, NO.
I'M DOING THE RIGHT THING.
I ADMIT IT'S BEEN TOUGH BONDING WITH MELAS.
BUT IT'LL BE WORTH IT.
AND SOON, I'LL HAVE A FRESH START WITH ASHIA.
"LIFE AND HOPE." PERFECT NAME.
JUST WISH I WAS GOING TO BE HERE TO MEET HER.
?!?

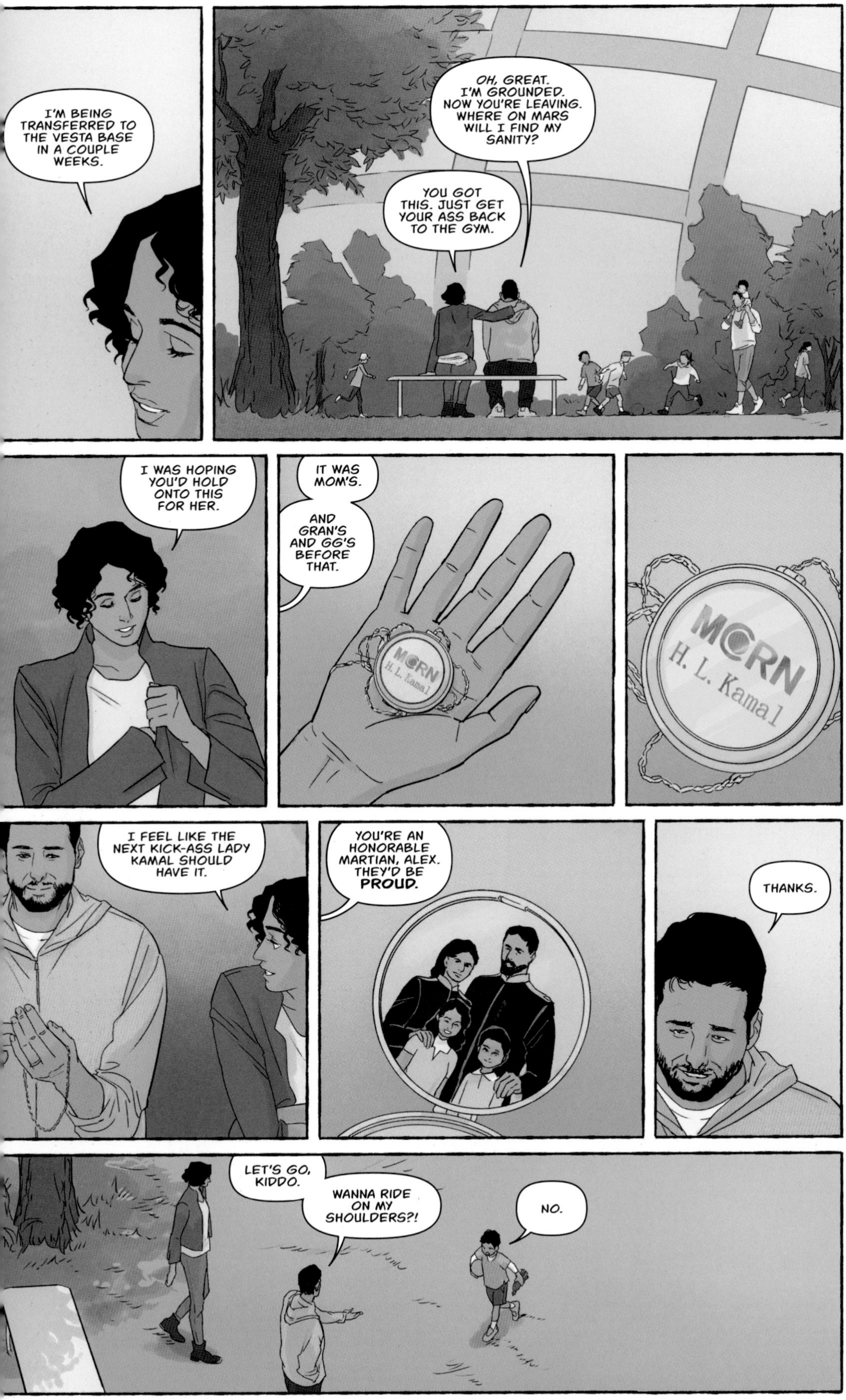
I'M BEING TRANSFERRED TO THE VESTA BASE IN A COUPLE WEEKS.
OH, GREAT. I'M GROUNDED. NOW YOU'RE LEAVING. WHERE ON MARS WILL I FIND MY SANITY?
YOU GOT THIS. JUST GET YOUR ASS BACK TO THE GYM.
I WAS HOPING YOU'D HOLD ONTO THIS FOR HER.
IT WAS MOM'S.
AND GRAN'S AND GG'S BEFORE THAT.
MCRN
H. L. Kamal
MCRN
H. L. Kamal
I FEEL LIKE THE NEXT KICK-ASS LADY KAMAL SHOULD HAVE IT.
YOU'RE AN HONORABLE MARTIAN, ALEX. THEY'D BE **PROUD.**
THANKS.
LET'S GO, KIDDO.
WANNA RIDE ON MY SHOULDERS?!
NO.

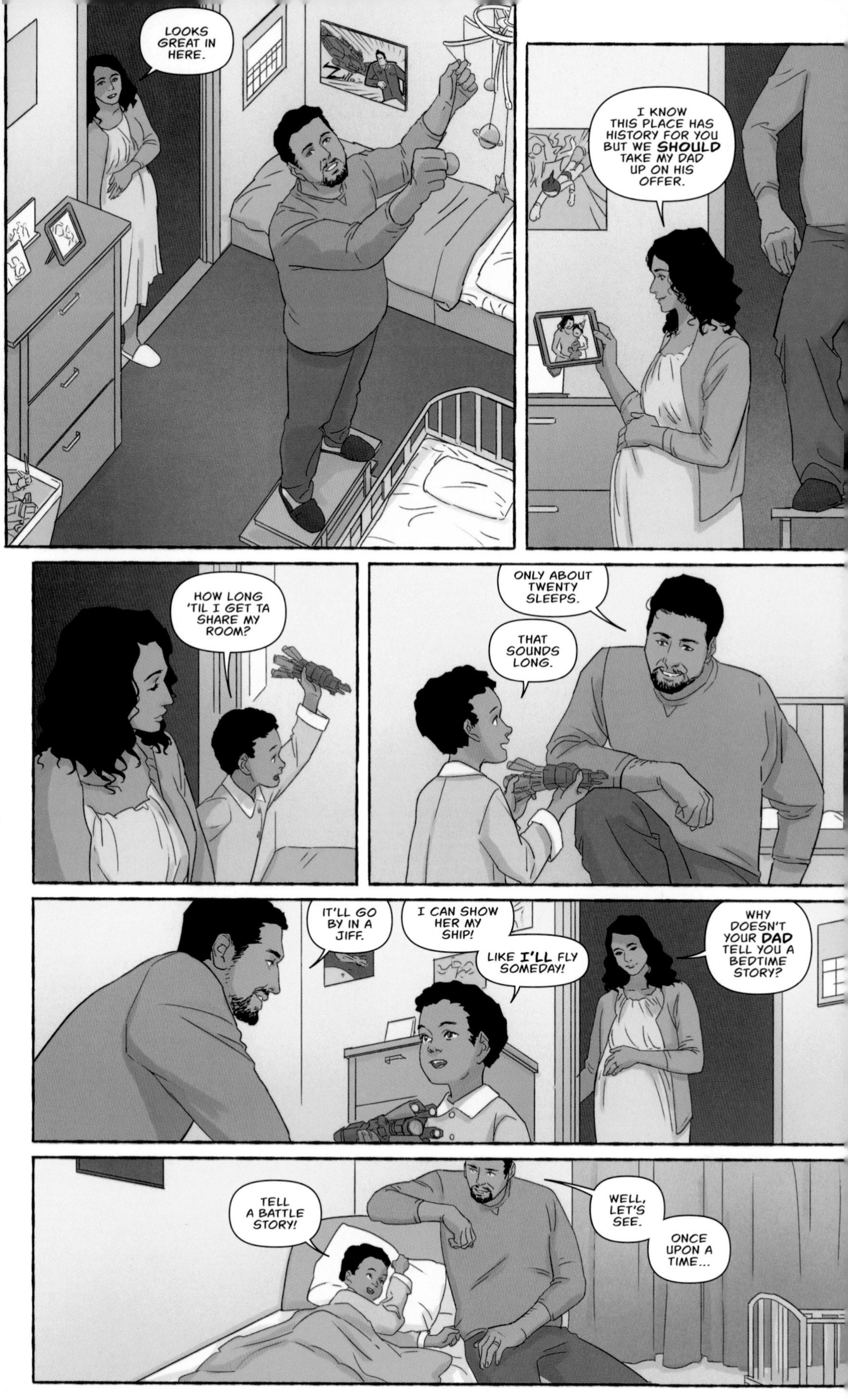
LOOKS GREAT IN HERE.
I KNOW THIS PLACE HAS HISTORY FOR YOU BUT WE SHOULD TAKE MY DAD UP ON HIS OFFER.
HOW LONG 'TIL I GET TA SHARE MY ROOM?
ONLY ABOUT TWENTY SLEEPS.
THAT SOUNDS LONG.
IT'LL GO BY IN A JIFF.
I CAN SHOW HER MY SHIP!
LIKE I'LL FLY SOMEDAY!
WHY DOESN'T YOUR DAD TELL YOU A BEDTIME STORY?
TELL A BATTLE STORY!
WELL, LET'S SEE.
ONCE UPON A TIME...

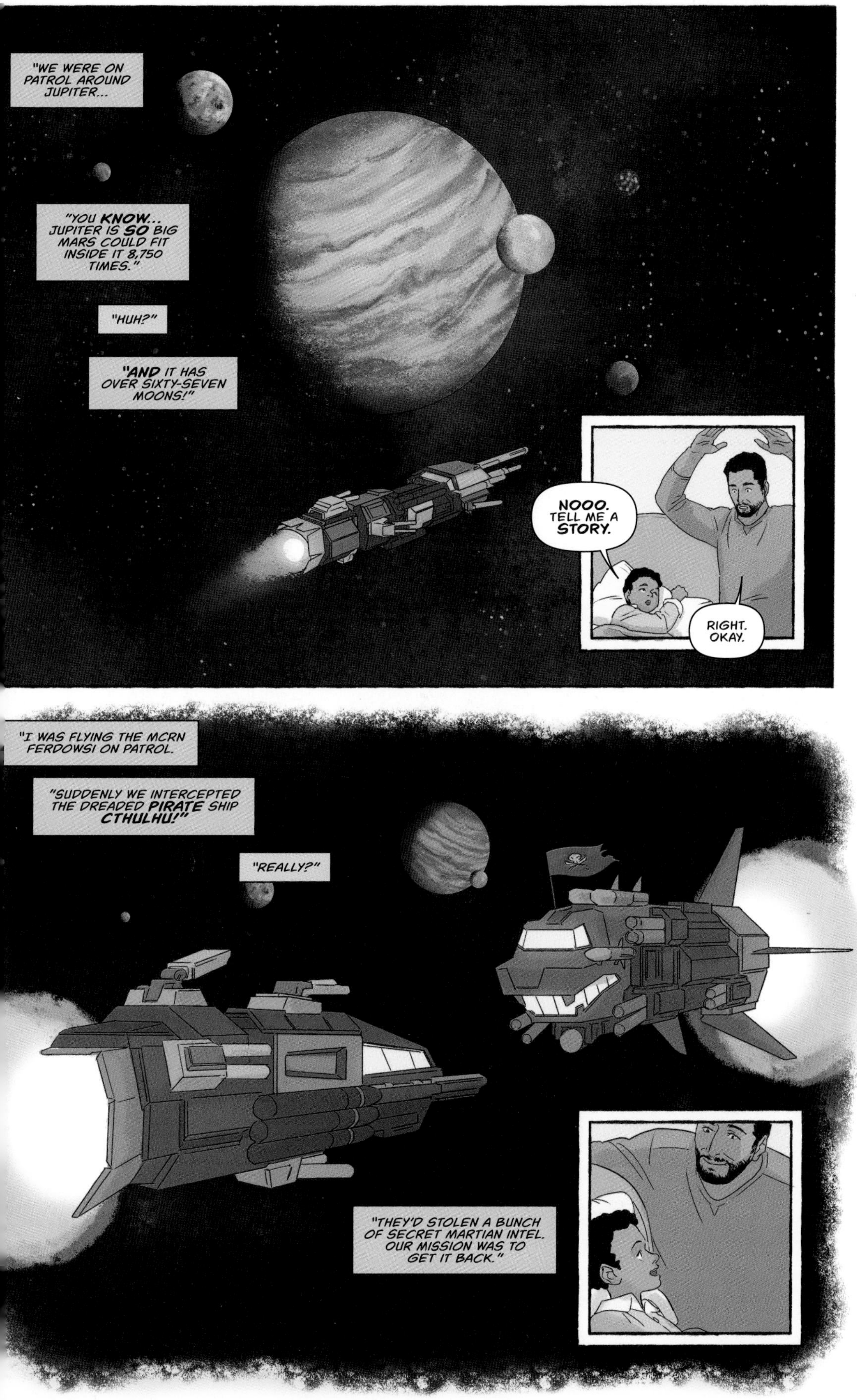
"WE WERE ON PATROL AROUND JUPITER...
"YOU KNOW... JUPITER IS SO BIG MARS COULD FIT INSIDE IT 8,750 TIMES."
"HUH?"
"AND IT HAS OVER SIXTY-SEVEN MOONS!"
NOOO. TELL ME A STORY.
RIGHT. OKAY.
"I WAS FLYING THE MCRN FERDOWSI ON PATROL.
"SUDDENLY WE INTERCEPTED THE DREADED PIRATE SHIP CTHULHU!"
"REALLY?"
"THEY'D STOLEN A BUNCH OF SECRET MARTIAN INTEL. OUR MISSION WAS TO GET IT BACK."

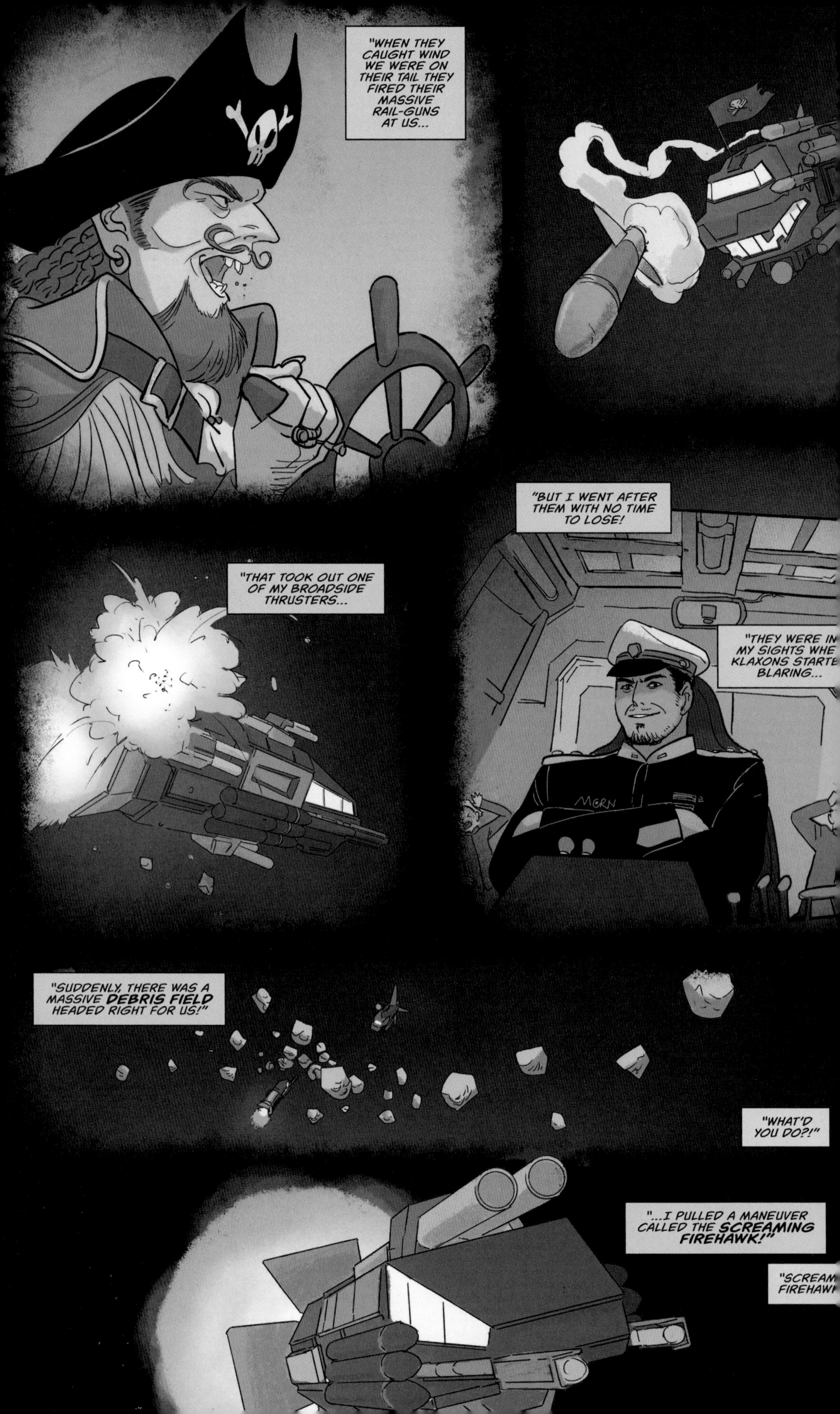
"WHEN THEY CAUGHT WIND WE WERE ON THEIR TAIL THEY FIRED THEIR MASSIVE RAIL-GUNS AT US...
"THAT TOOK OUT ONE OF MY BROADSIDE THRUSTERS...
"BUT I WENT AFTER THEM WITH NO TIME TO LOSE!
MORN
"SUDDENLY, THERE WAS A MASSIVE DEBRIS FIELD HEADED RIGHT FOR US!"
"WHAT'D YOU DO?!"
"...I PULLED A MANEUVER CALLED THE SCREAMING FIREHAWK!"

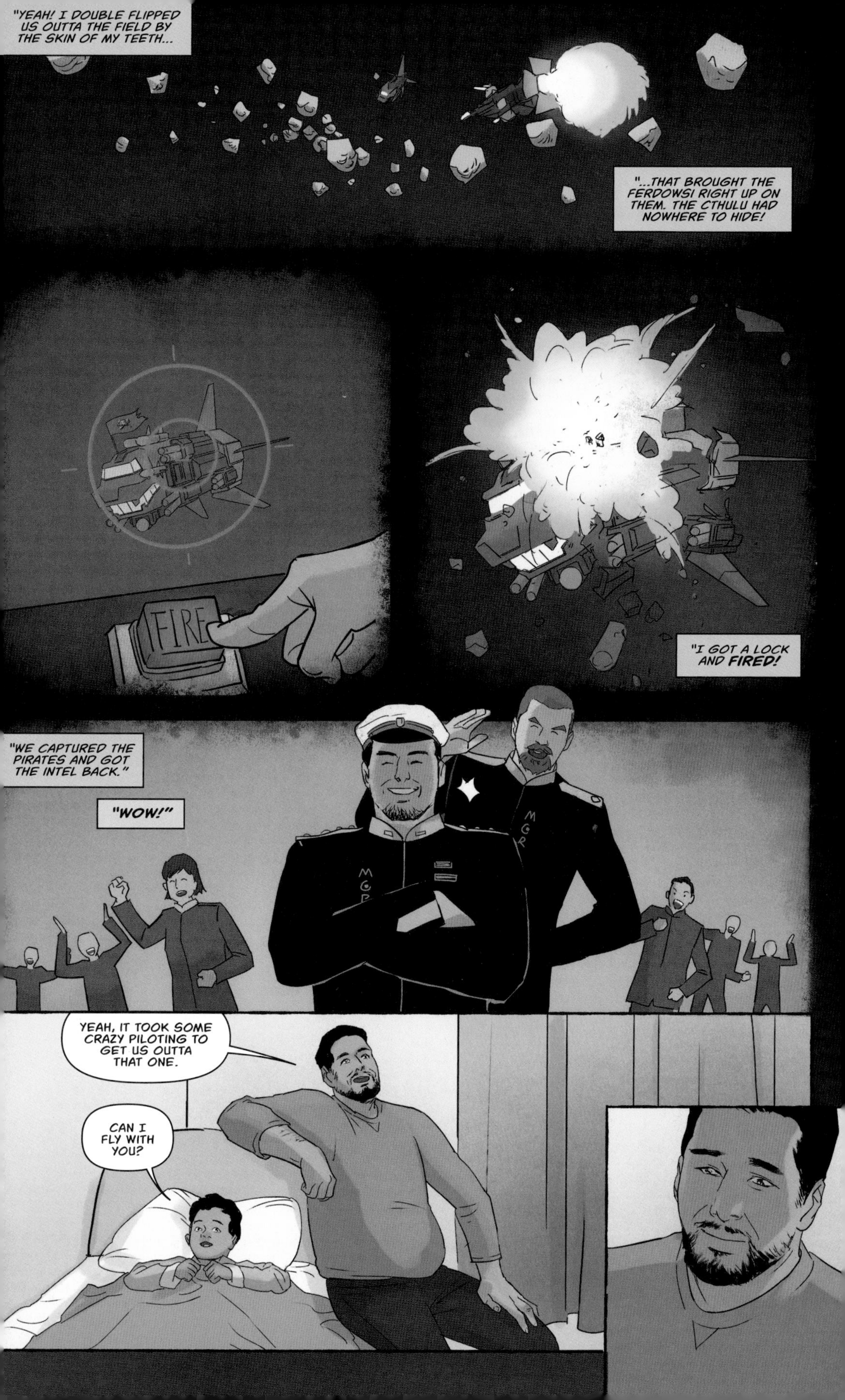
"YEAH! I DOUBLE FLIPPED US OUTTA THE FIELD BY THE SKIN OF MY TEETH...
"...THAT BROUGHT THE FERDOWSI RIGHT UP ON THEM. THE CTHULU HAD NOWHERE TO HIDE!
FIRE
"I GOT A LOCK AND FIRED!
"WE CAPTURED THE PIRATES AND GOT THE INTEL BACK."
"WOW!"
MGR
MGR
YEAH, IT TOOK SOME CRAZY PILOTING TO GET US OUTTA THAT ONE.
CAN I FLY WITH YOU?

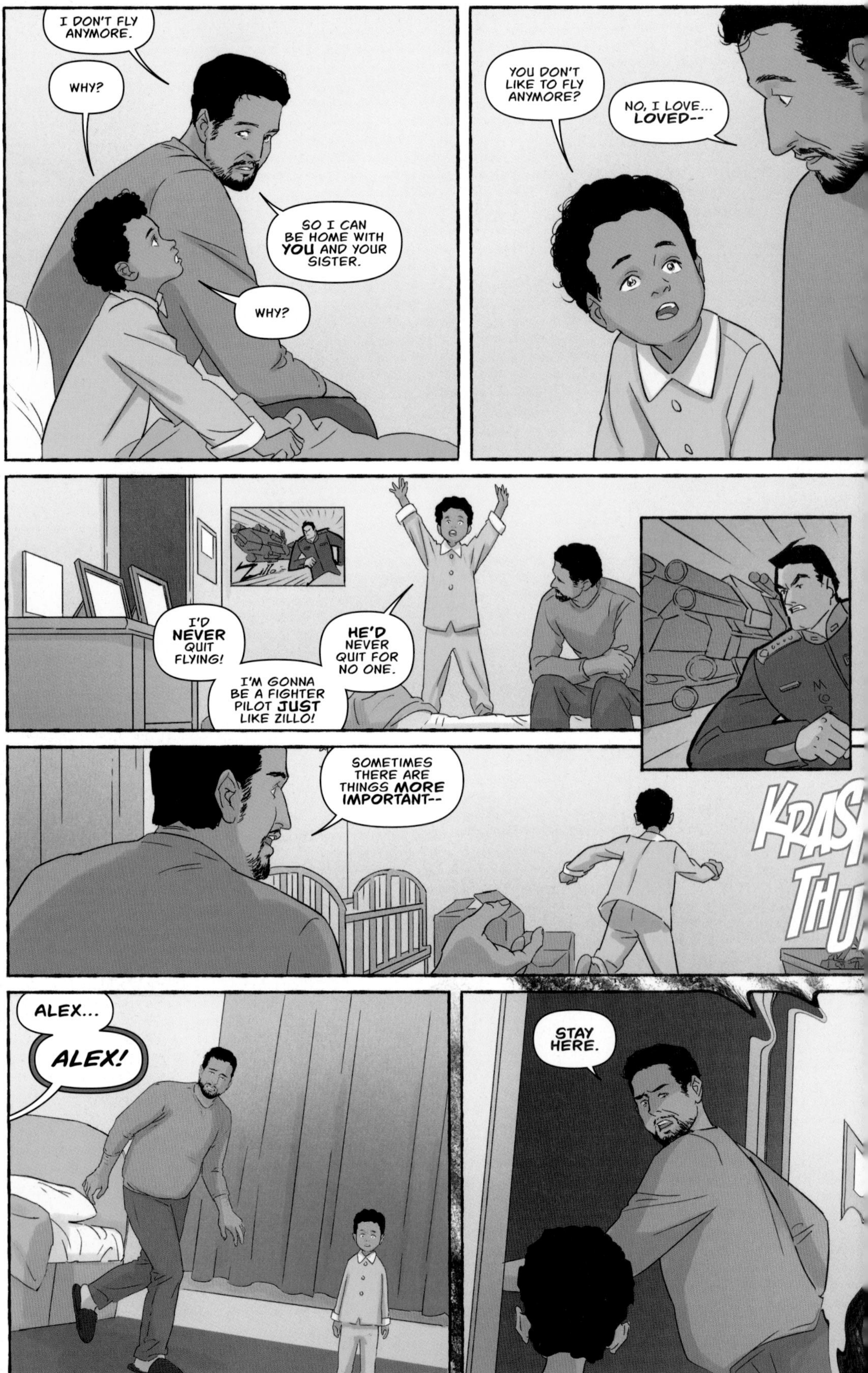
I DON'T FLY ANYMORE.
WHY?
SO I CAN BE HOME WITH **YOU** AND YOUR SISTER.
WHY?
YOU DON'T LIKE TO FLY ANYMORE?
NO, I LOVE... **LOVED--**
I'D **NEVER** QUIT FLYING!
I'M GONNA BE A FIGHTER PILOT **JUST** LIKE ZILLO!
HE'D NEVER QUIT FOR NO ONE.
SOMETIMES THERE ARE THINGS **MORE IMPORTANT--**
ALEX...
ALEX!
STAY HERE.

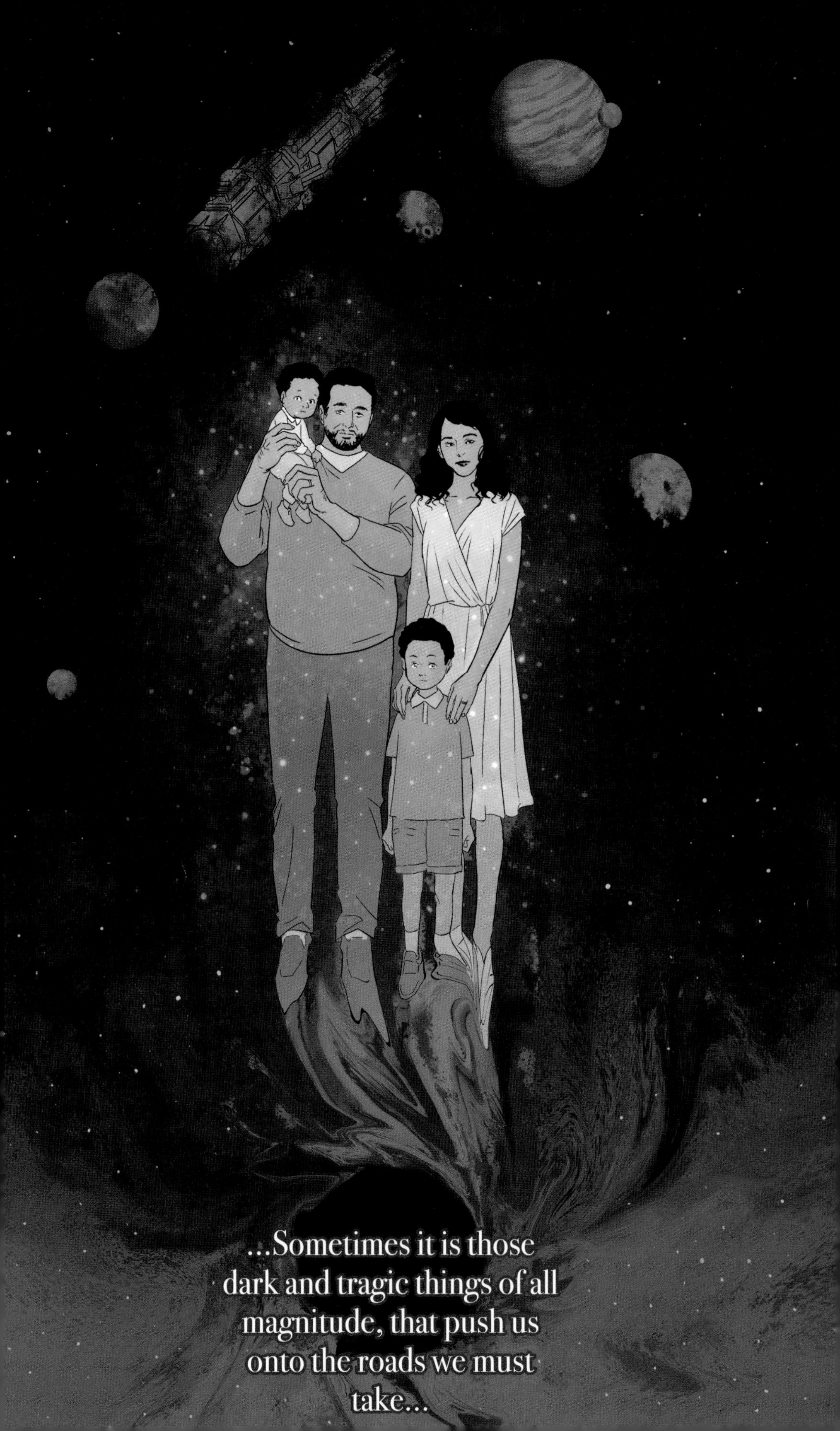
...Sometimes it is those dark and tragic things of all magnitude, that push us onto the roads we must take...

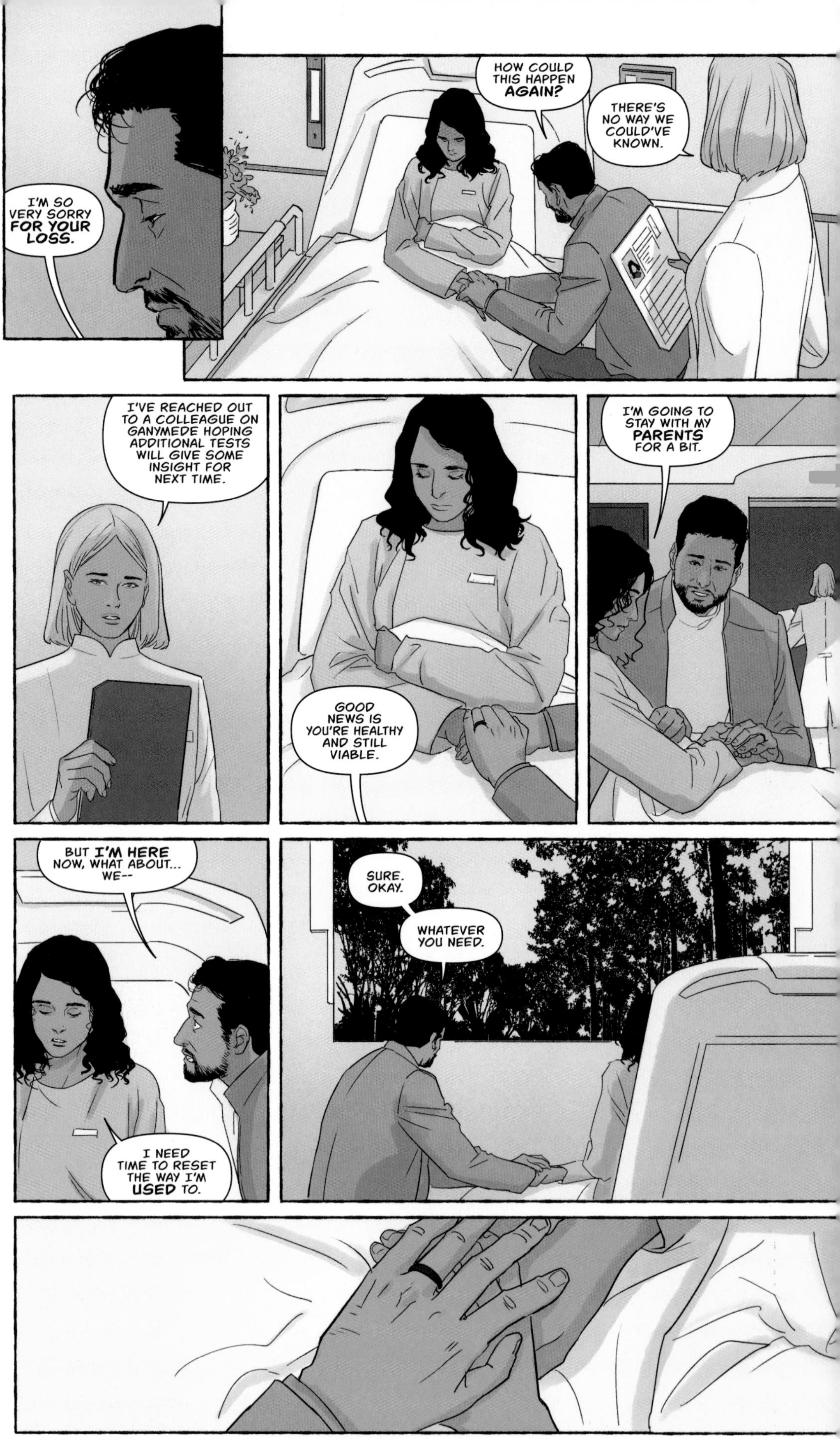
I'M SO VERY SORRY FOR YOUR LOSS.
HOW COULD THIS HAPPEN AGAIN?
THERE'S NO WAY WE COULD'VE KNOWN.
I'VE REACHED OUT TO A COLLEAGUE ON GANYMEDE HOPING ADDITIONAL TESTS WILL GIVE SOME INSIGHT FOR NEXT TIME.
GOOD NEWS IS YOU'RE HEALTHY AND STILL VIABLE.
I'M GOING TO STAY WITH MY PARENTS FOR A BIT.
BUT I'M HERE NOW, WHAT ABOUT... WE--
I NEED TIME TO RESET THE WAY I'M USED TO.
SURE. OKAY.
WHATEVER YOU NEED.

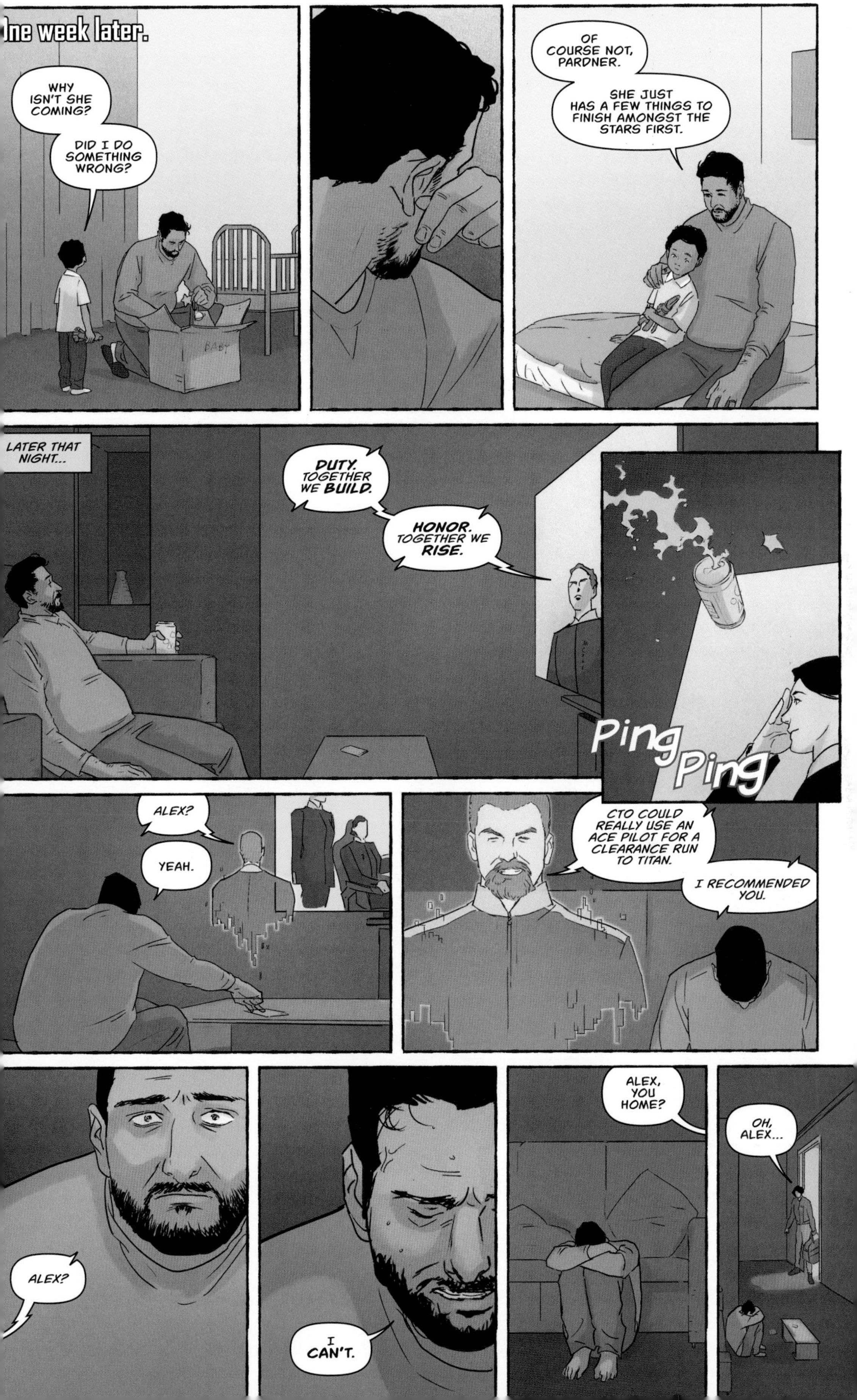
One week later.
WHY ISN'T SHE COMING?
DID I DO SOMETHING WRONG?
BABY
OF COURSE NOT, PARDNER.
SHE JUST HAS A FEW THINGS TO FINISH AMONGST THE STARS FIRST.
LATER THAT NIGHT...
DUTY. TOGETHER WE BUILD.
HONOR. TOGETHER WE RISE.
Ping Ping
ALEX?
YEAH.
CTO COULD REALLY USE AN ACE PILOT FOR A CLEARANCE RUN TO TITAN.
I RECOMMENDED YOU.
ALEX?
I CAN'T.
ALEX, YOU HOME?
OH, ALEX...

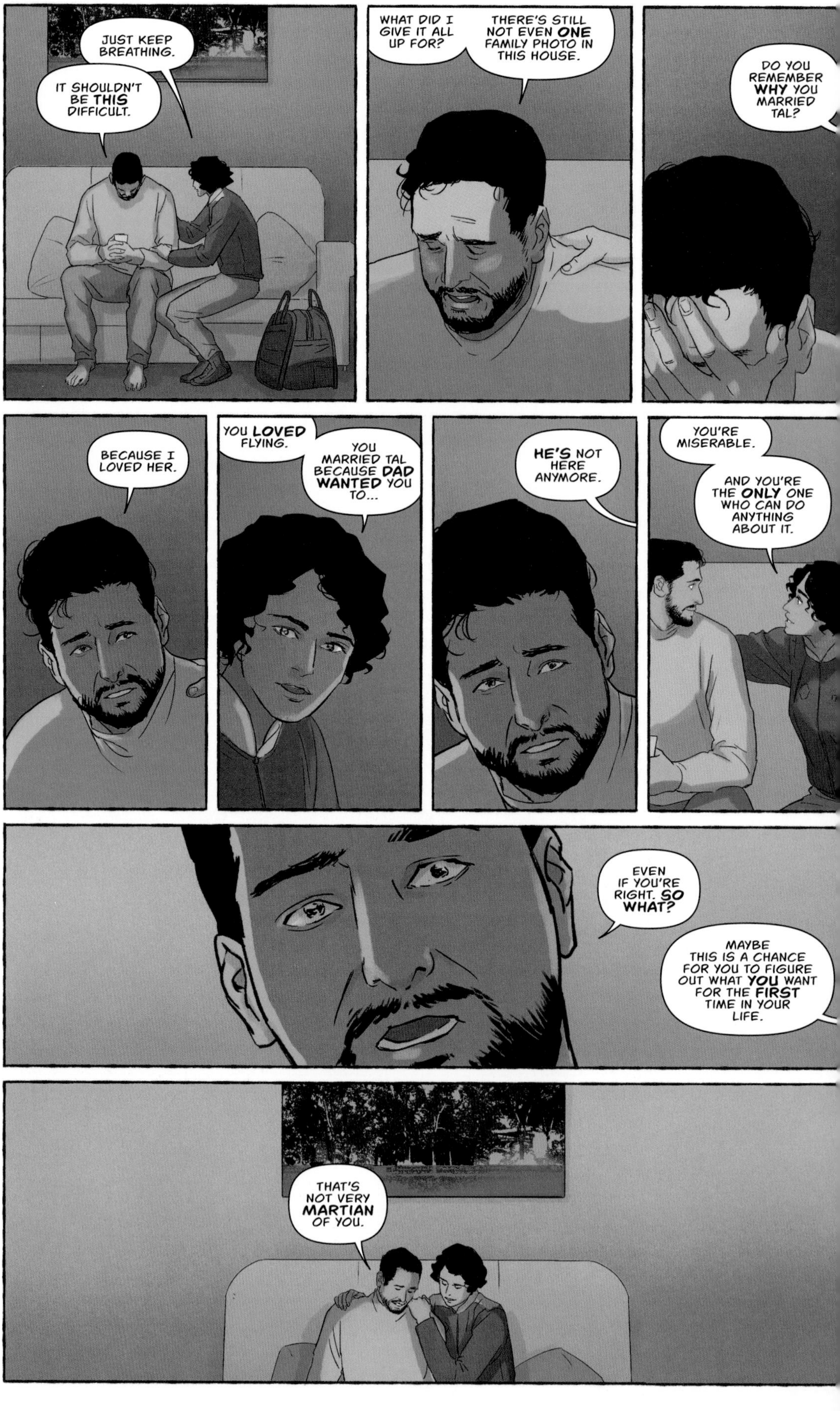
JUST KEEP BREATHING.
IT SHOULDN'T BE THIS DIFFICULT.
WHAT DID I GIVE IT ALL UP FOR?
THERE'S STILL NOT EVEN ONE FAMILY PHOTO IN THIS HOUSE.
DO YOU REMEMBER WHY YOU MARRIED TAL?
BECAUSE I LOVED HER.
YOU LOVED FLYING.
YOU MARRIED TAL BECAUSE DAD WANTED YOU TO...
HE'S NOT HERE ANYMORE.
YOU'RE MISERABLE.
AND YOU'RE THE ONLY ONE WHO CAN DO ANYTHING ABOUT IT.
EVEN IF YOU'RE RIGHT. SO WHAT?
MAYBE THIS IS A CHANCE FOR YOU TO FIGURE OUT WHAT YOU WANT FOR THE FIRST TIME IN YOUR LIFE.
THAT'S NOT VERY MARTIAN OF YOU.

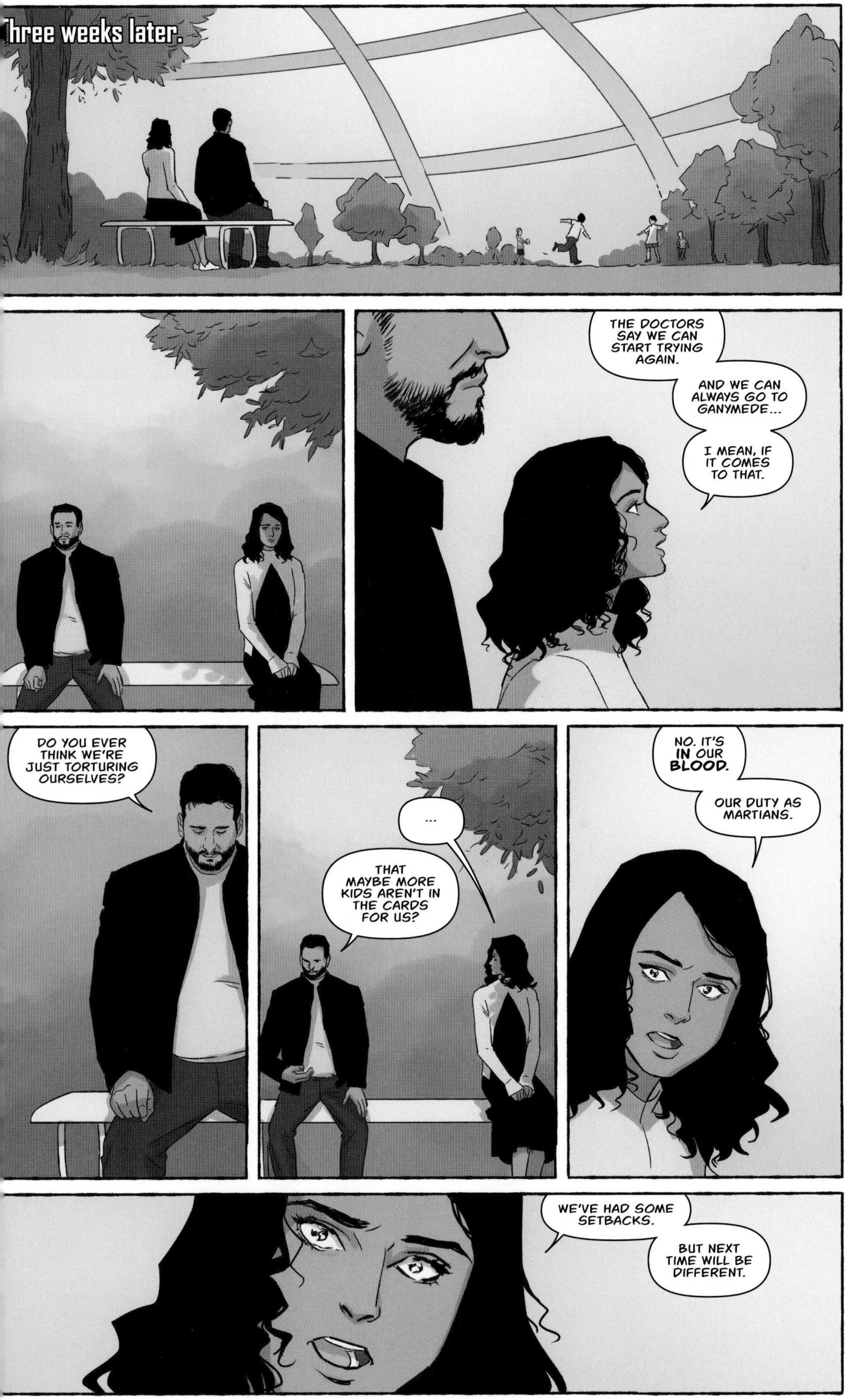
Three weeks later.
THE DOCTORS SAY WE CAN START TRYING AGAIN.
AND WE CAN ALWAYS GO TO GANYMEDE...
I MEAN, IF IT COMES TO THAT.
DO YOU EVER THINK WE'RE JUST TORTURING OURSELVES?
...
THAT MAYBE MORE KIDS AREN'T IN THE CARDS FOR US?
NO. IT'S IN OUR BLOOD.
OUR DUTY AS MARTIANS.
WE'VE HAD SOME SETBACKS.
BUT NEXT TIME WILL BE DIFFERENT.

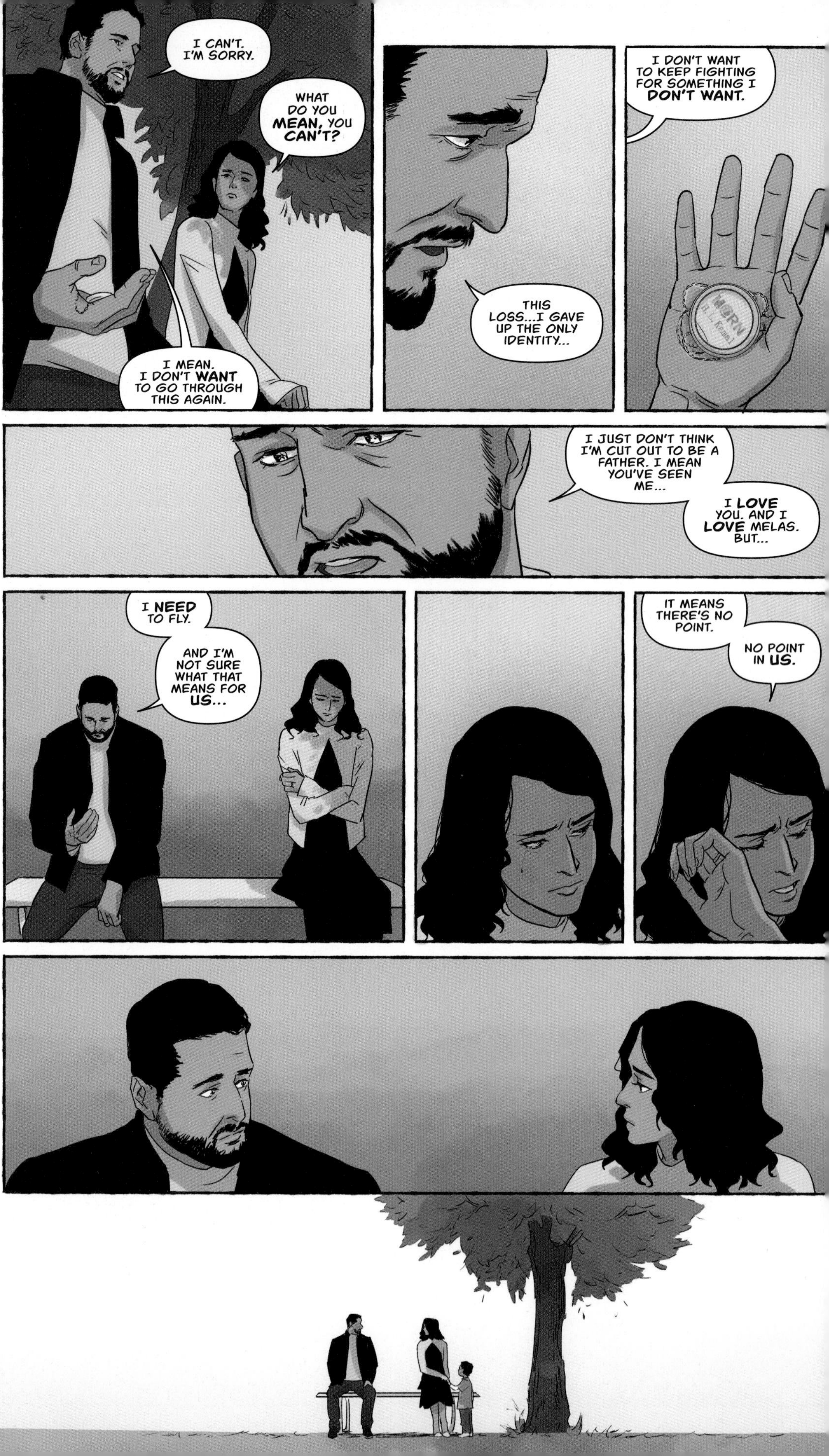

I CAN'T. I'M SORRY.
WHAT DO YOU **MEAN,** YOU **CAN'T?**
I MEAN. I DON'T **WANT** TO GO THROUGH THIS AGAIN.
THIS LOSS...I GAVE UP THE ONLY IDENTITY...
I DON'T WANT TO KEEP FIGHTING FOR SOMETHING I **DON'T WANT.**
I JUST DON'T THINK I'M CUT OUT TO BE A FATHER. I MEAN YOU'VE SEEN ME...
I **LOVE** YOU. AND I **LOVE** MELAS. BUT...
I **NEED** TO FLY.
AND I'M NOT SURE WHAT THAT MEANS FOR **US...**
IT MEANS THERE'S NO POINT.
NO POINT IN **US.**

CHAPTER_004

AMOS BURTON

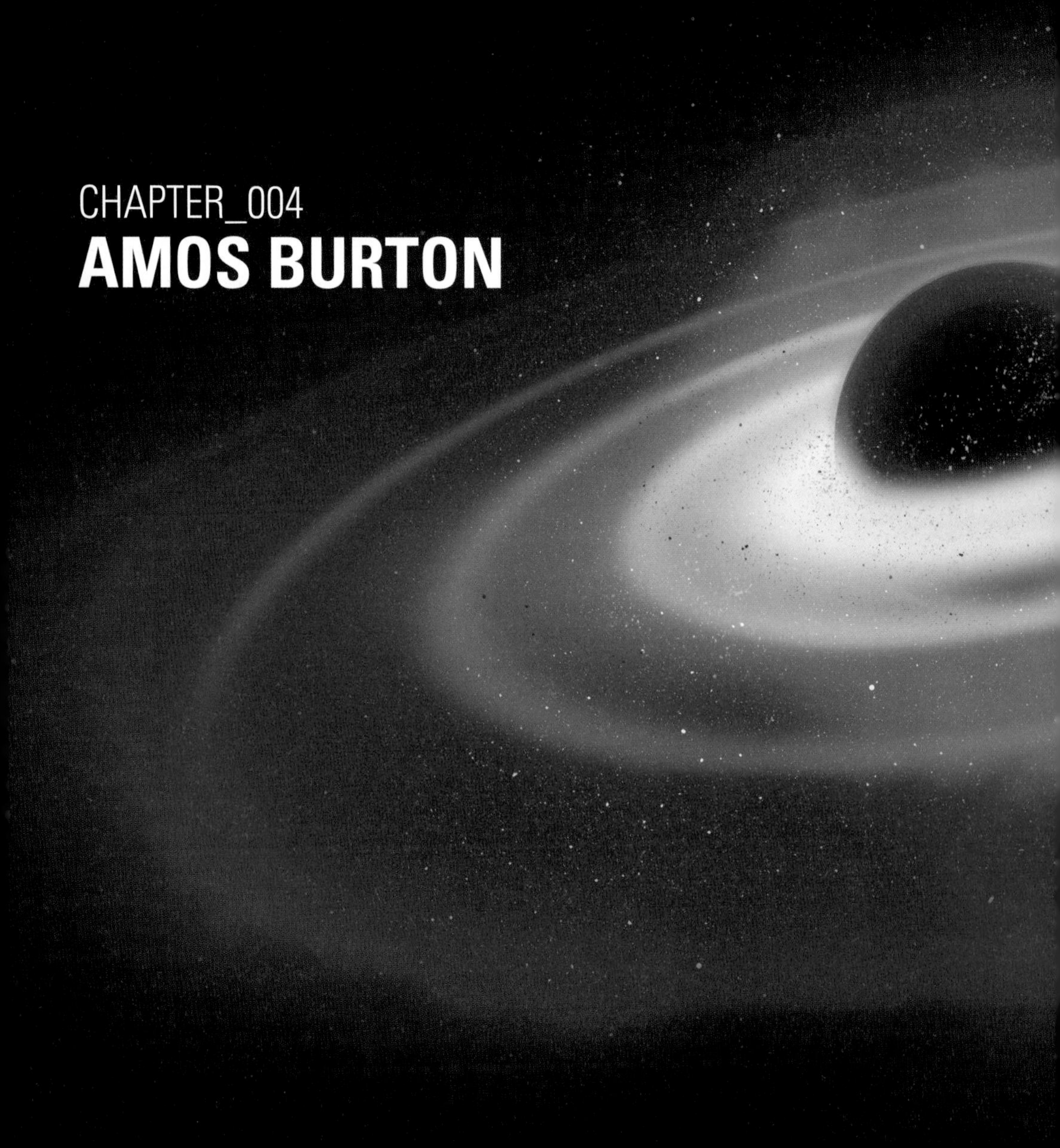

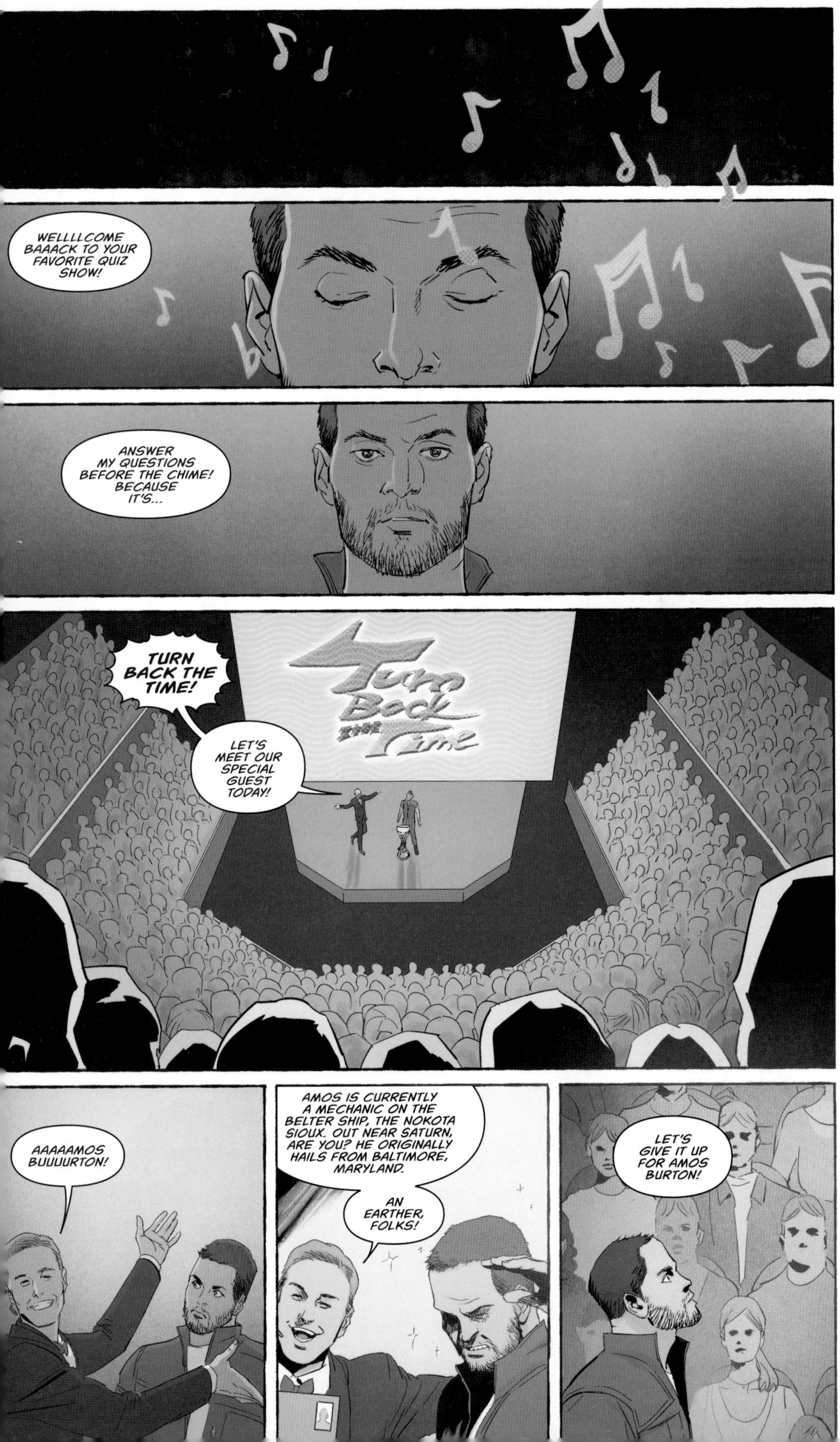
WELLLLCOME BAAACK TO YOUR FAVORITE QUIZ SHOW!
ANSWER MY QUESTIONS BEFORE THE CHIME! BECAUSE IT'S...
TURN BACK THE TIME!
Turn Back the Time
LET'S MEET OUR SPECIAL GUEST TODAY!
AAAAAMOS BUUUURTON!
AMOS IS CURRENTLY A MECHANIC ON THE BELTER SHIP, THE NOKOTA SIOUX. OUT NEAR SATURN, ARE YOU? HE ORIGINALLY HAILS FROM BALTIMORE, MARYLAND.
AN EARTHER, FOLKS!
LET'S GIVE IT UP FOR AMOS BURTON!

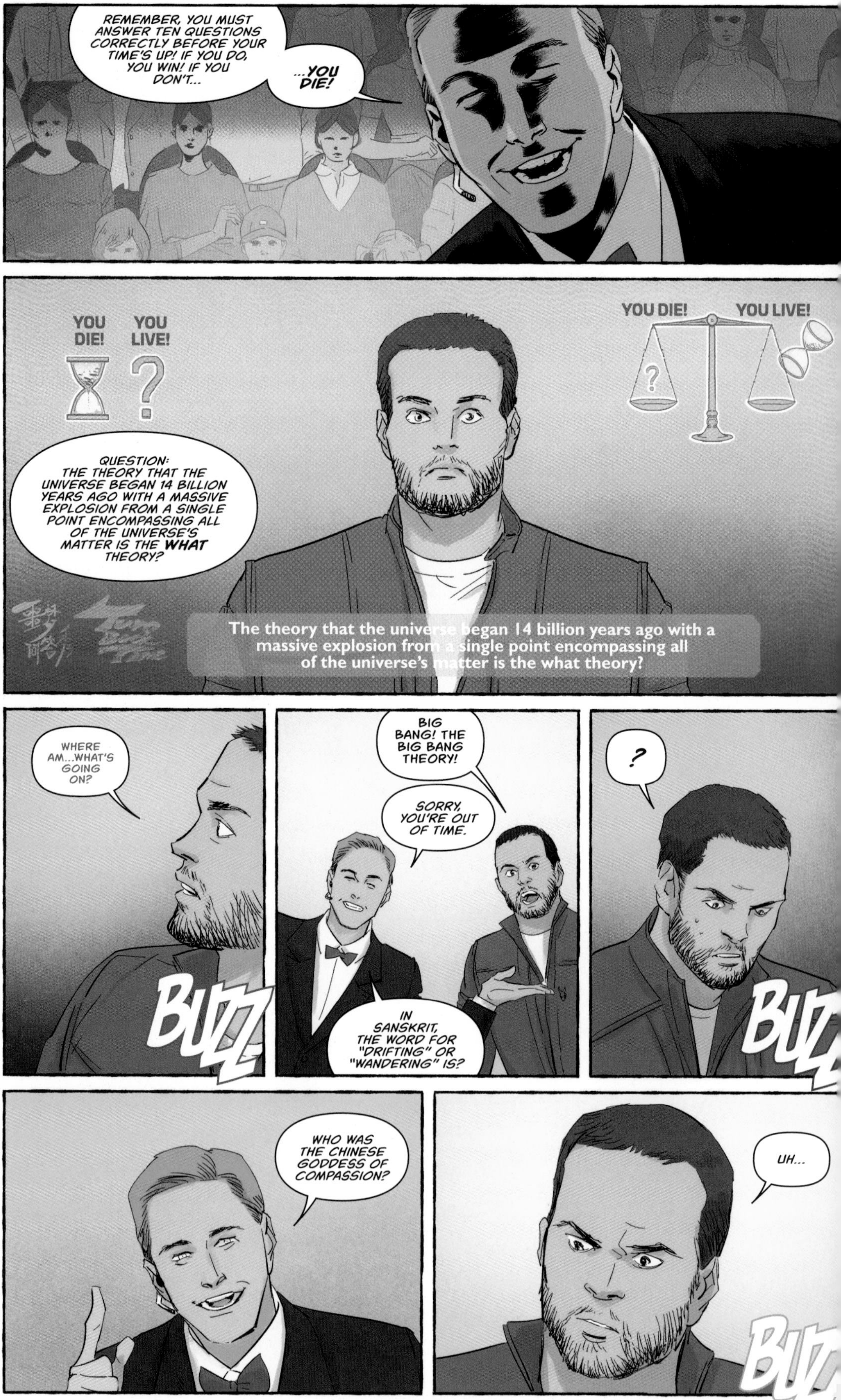
REMEMBER, YOU MUST ANSWER TEN QUESTIONS CORRECTLY BEFORE YOUR TIME'S UP! IF YOU DO, YOU WIN! IF YOU DON'T...
...YOU DIE!
YOU DIE!
YOU LIVE!
?
YOU DIE!
YOU LIVE!
?
QUESTION: THE THEORY THAT THE UNIVERSE BEGAN 14 BILLION YEARS AGO WITH A MASSIVE EXPLOSION FROM A SINGLE POINT ENCOMPASSING ALL OF THE UNIVERSE'S MATTER IS THE WHAT THEORY?
The theory that the universe began 14 billion years ago with a massive explosion from a single point encompassing all of the universe's matter is the what theory?
WHERE AM...WHAT'S GOING ON?
BUZZ
BIG BANG! THE BIG BANG THEORY!
SORRY, YOU'RE OUT OF TIME.
IN SANSKRIT, THE WORD FOR "DRIFTING" OR "WANDERING" IS?
?
BUZZ
WHO WAS THE CHINESE GODDESS OF COMPASSION?
UH...
BUZZ

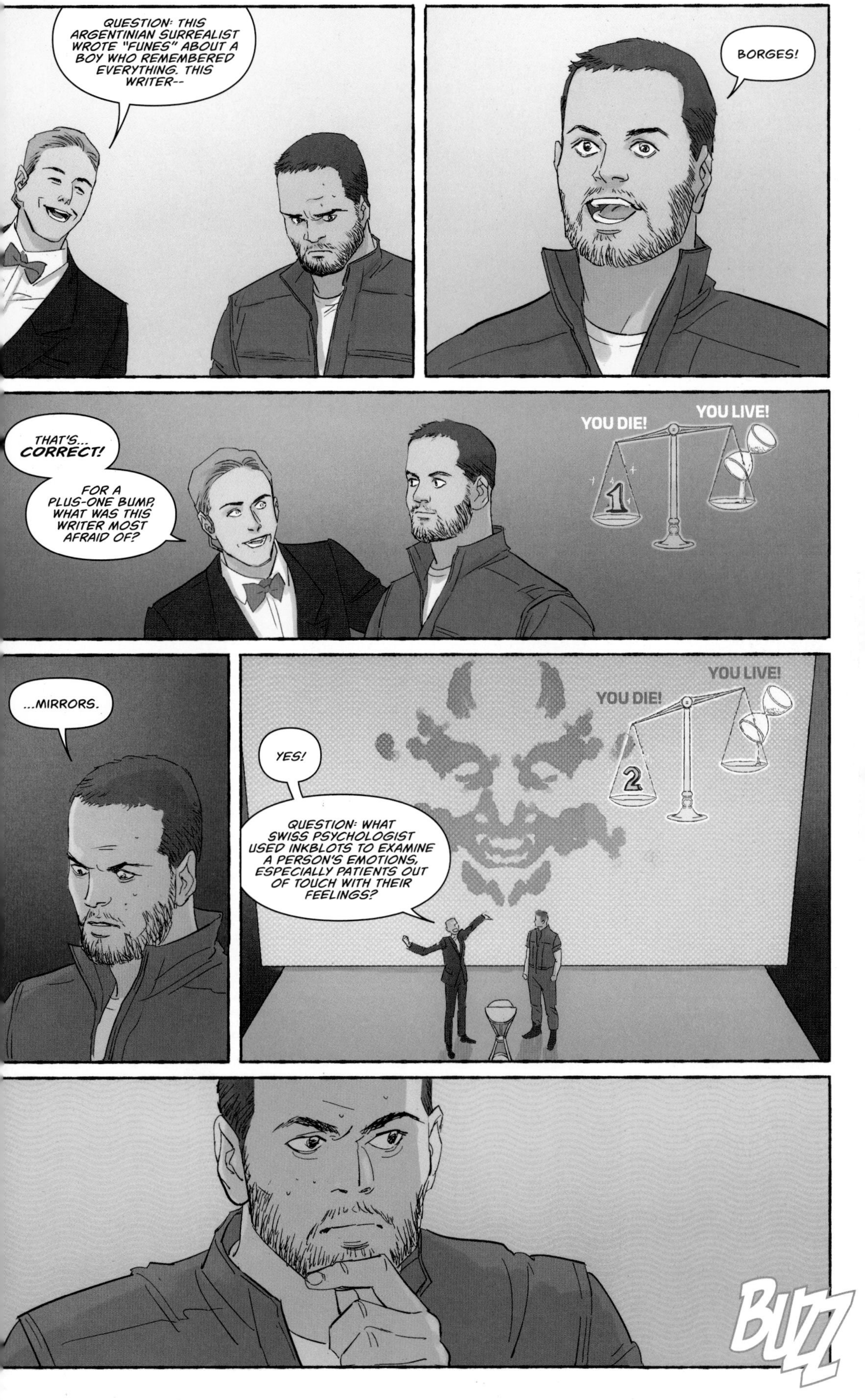
QUESTION: THIS ARGENTINIAN SURREALIST WROTE "FUNES" ABOUT A BOY WHO REMEMBERED EVERYTHING. THIS WRITER--
BORGES!
THAT'S... CORRECT!
FOR A PLUS-ONE BUMP, WHAT WAS THIS WRITER MOST AFRAID OF?
YOU DIE!
YOU LIVE!
1
...MIRRORS.
YOU LIVE!
YOU DIE!
2
YES!
QUESTION: WHAT SWISS PSYCHOLOGIST USED INKBLOTS TO EXAMINE A PERSON'S EMOTIONS, ESPECIALLY PATIENTS OUT OF TOUCH WITH THEIR FEELINGS?
BUZZ

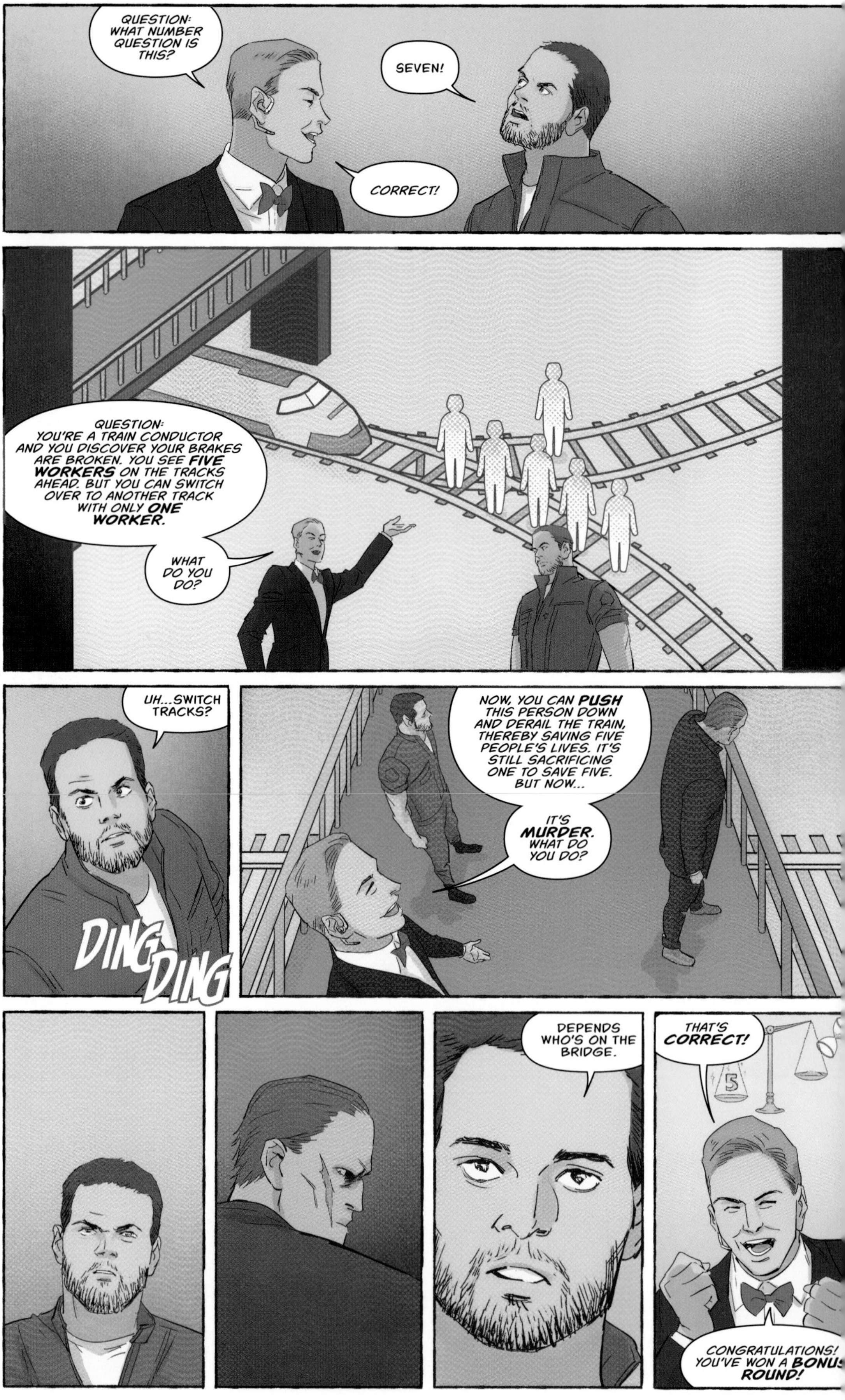
QUESTION: WHAT NUMBER QUESTION IS THIS?
SEVEN!
CORRECT!
QUESTION: YOU'RE A TRAIN CONDUCTOR AND YOU DISCOVER YOUR BRAKES ARE BROKEN. YOU SEE **FIVE WORKERS** ON THE TRACKS AHEAD. BUT YOU CAN SWITCH OVER TO ANOTHER TRACK WITH ONLY **ONE WORKER.**
WHAT DO YOU DO?
UH...SWITCH TRACKS?
DING DING
NOW, YOU CAN **PUSH** THIS PERSON DOWN AND DERAIL THE TRAIN, THEREBY SAVING FIVE PEOPLE'S LIVES. IT'S STILL SACRIFICING ONE TO SAVE FIVE. BUT NOW...
IT'S **MURDER.** WHAT DO YOU DO?
DEPENDS WHO'S ON THE BRIDGE.
THAT'S **CORRECT!**
5
CONGRATULATIONS! YOU'VE WON A **BONUS ROUND!**

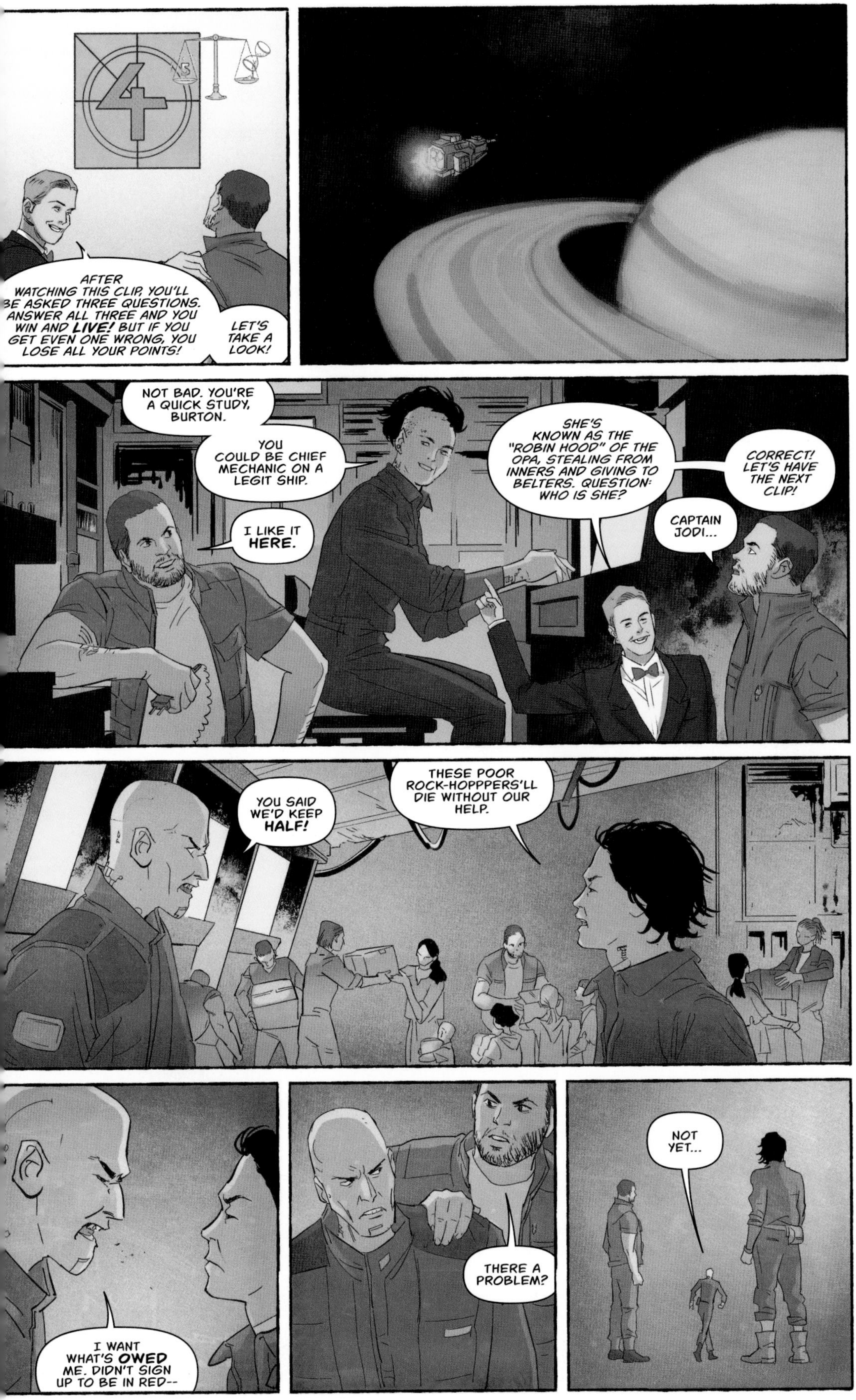
AFTER WATCHING THIS CLIP, YOU'LL BE ASKED THREE QUESTIONS. ANSWER ALL THREE AND YOU WIN AND LIVE! BUT IF YOU GET EVEN ONE WRONG, YOU LOSE ALL YOUR POINTS!
LET'S TAKE A LOOK!
NOT BAD. YOU'RE A QUICK STUDY, BURTON.
YOU COULD BE CHIEF MECHANIC ON A LEGIT SHIP.
I LIKE IT HERE.
SHE'S KNOWN AS THE "ROBIN HOOD" OF THE OPA, STEALING FROM INNERS AND GIVING TO BELTERS. QUESTION: WHO IS SHE?
CAPTAIN JODI...
CORRECT! LET'S HAVE THE NEXT CLIP!
YOU SAID WE'D KEEP HALF!
THESE POOR ROCK-HOPPPERS'LL DIE WITHOUT OUR HELP.
I WANT WHAT'S OWED ME. DIDN'T SIGN UP TO BE IN RED--
THERE A PROBLEM?
NOT YET...

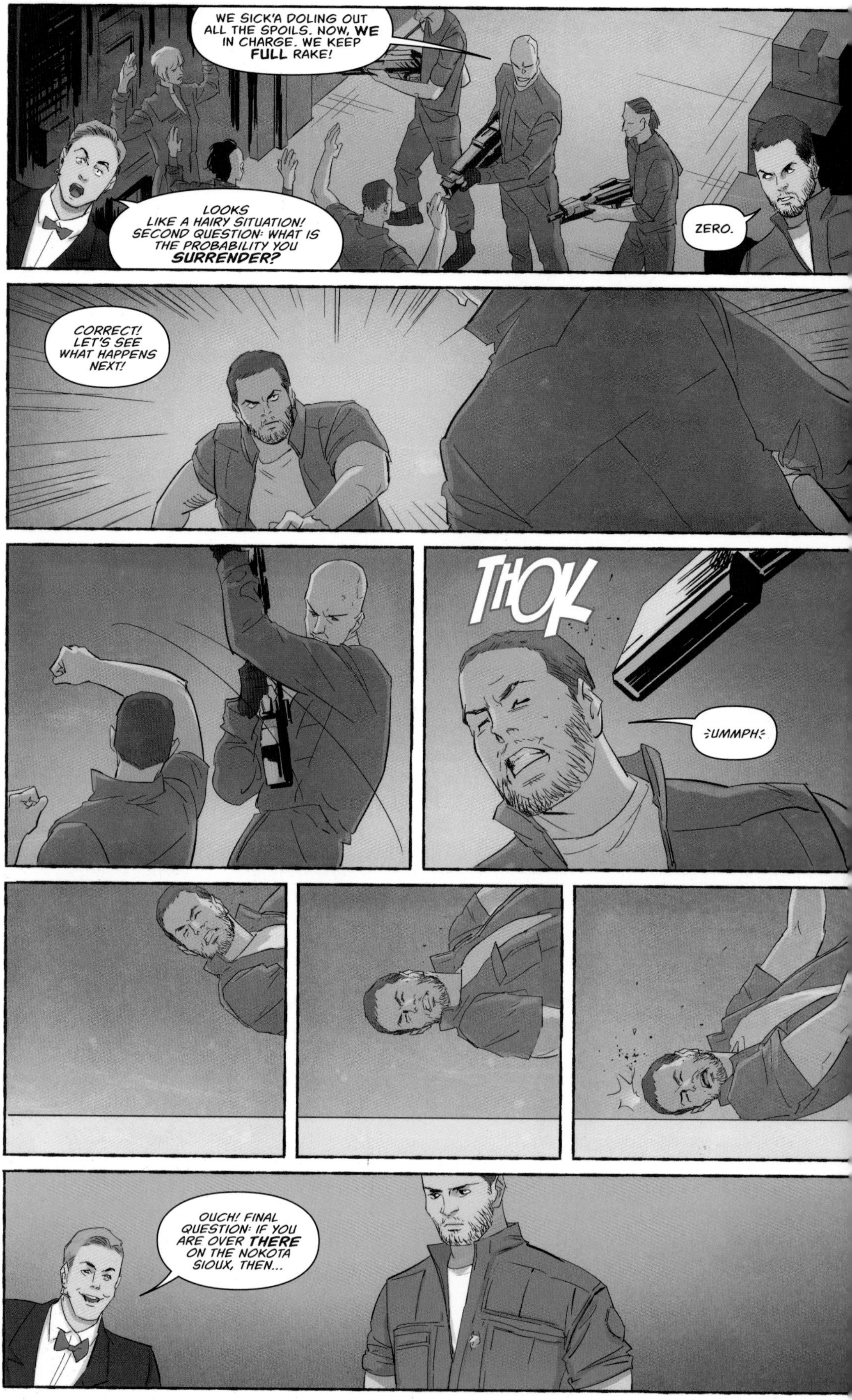
WE SICK'A DOLING OUT ALL THE SPOILS. NOW, WE IN CHARGE. WE KEEP FULL RAKE!
LOOKS LIKE A HAIRY SITUATION! SECOND QUESTION: WHAT IS THE PROBABILITY YOU SURRENDER?
ZERO.
CORRECT! LET'S SEE WHAT HAPPENS NEXT!
THOK
UMMPH
OUCH! FINAL QUESTION: IF YOU ARE OVER THERE ON THE NOKOTA SIOUX, THEN...

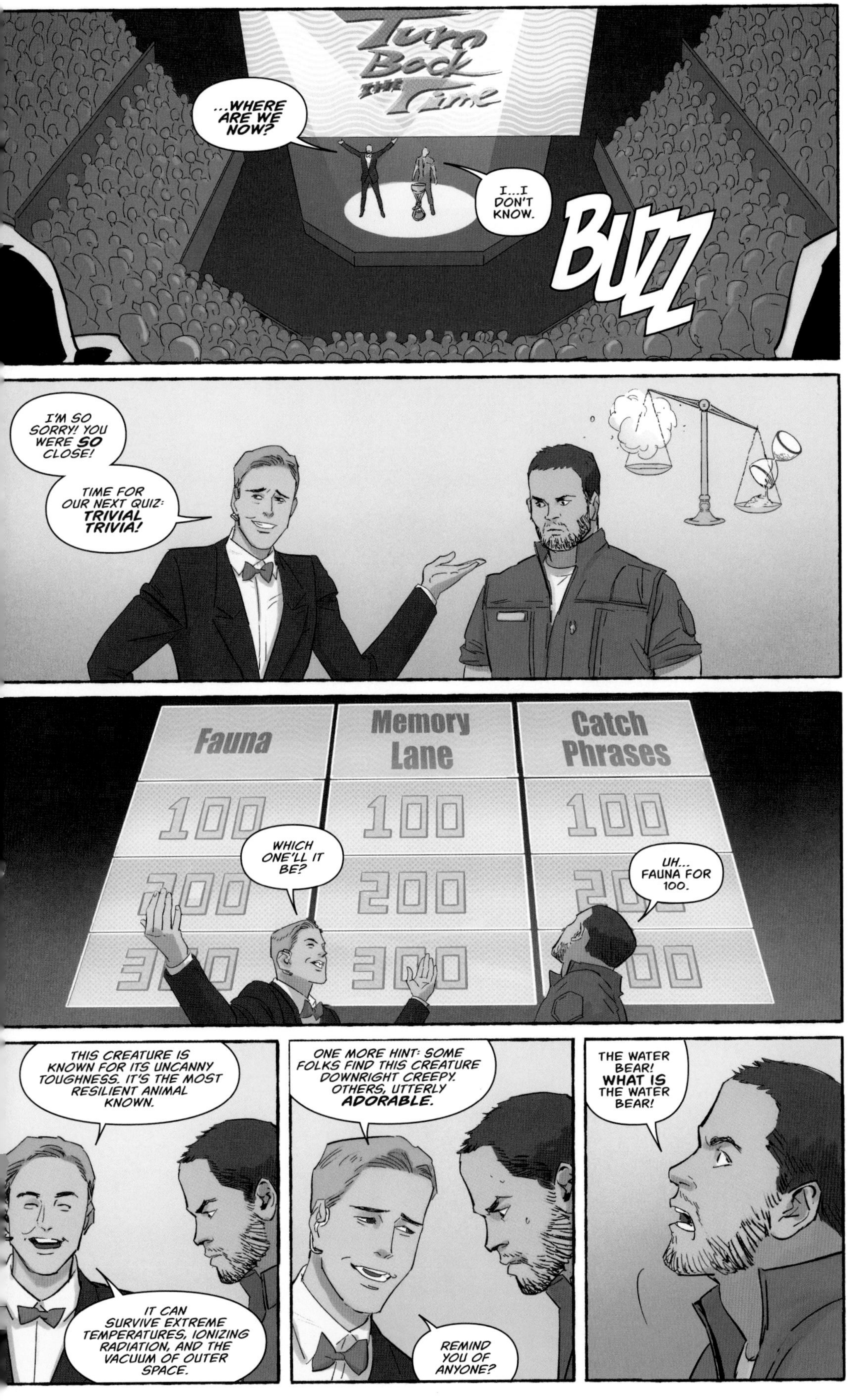
Turn Back the Time
...WHERE ARE WE NOW?
I...I DON'T KNOW.
BUZZ
I'M SO SORRY! YOU WERE SO CLOSE!
TIME FOR OUR NEXT QUIZ: TRIVIAL TRIVIA!
Fauna
Memory Lane
Catch Phrases
WHICH ONE'LL IT BE?
UH... FAUNA FOR 100.
THIS CREATURE IS KNOWN FOR ITS UNCANNY TOUGHNESS. IT'S THE MOST RESILIENT ANIMAL KNOWN.
IT CAN SURVIVE EXTREME TEMPERATURES, IONIZING RADIATION, AND THE VACUUM OF OUTER SPACE.
ONE MORE HINT: SOME FOLKS FIND THIS CREATURE DOWNRIGHT CREEPY. OTHERS, UTTERLY ADORABLE.
REMIND YOU OF ANYONE?
THE WATER BEAR! WHAT IS THE WATER BEAR!

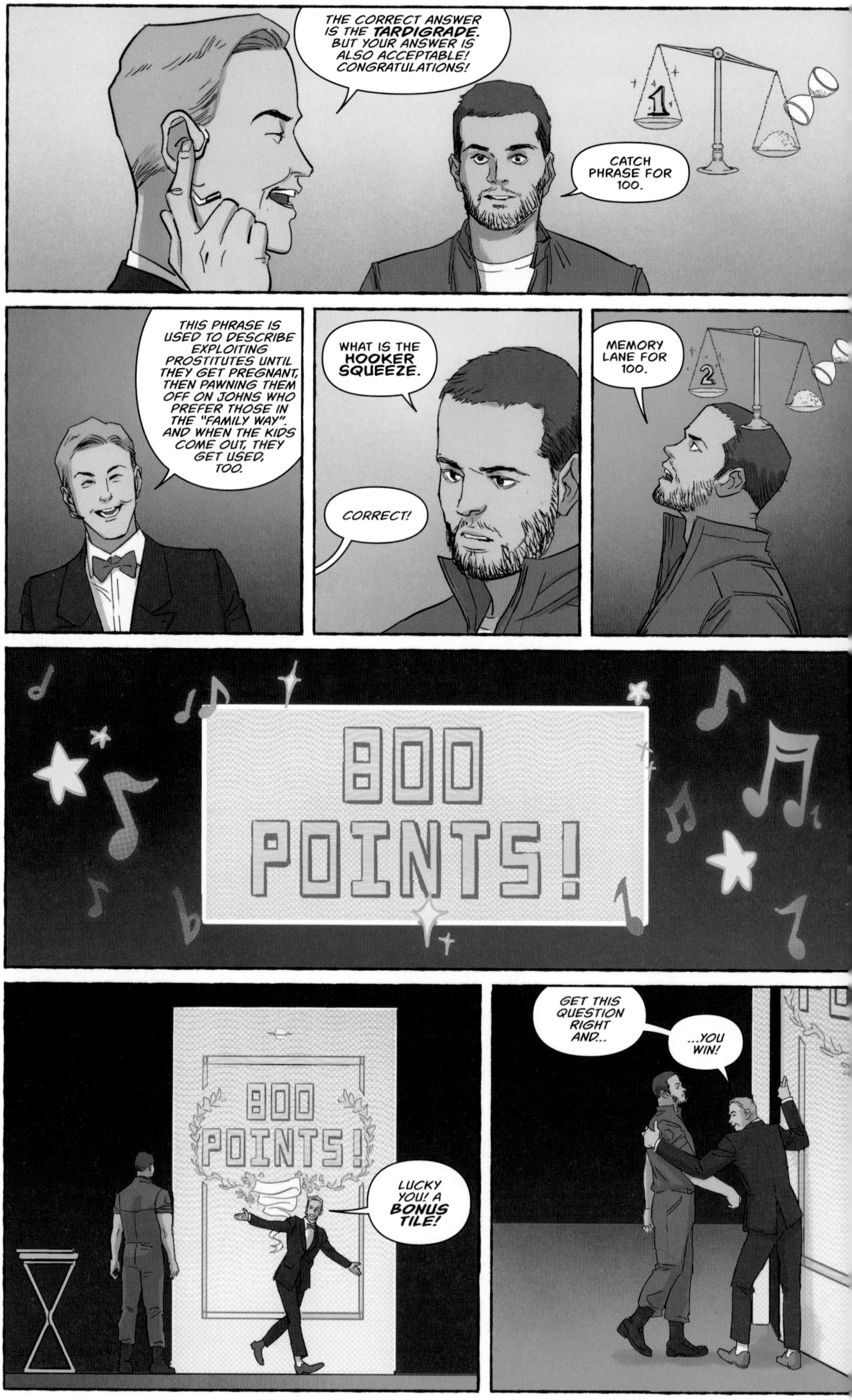
THE CORRECT ANSWER IS THE TARDIGRADE. BUT YOUR ANSWER IS ALSO ACCEPTABLE! CONGRATULATIONS!
1
CATCH PHRASE FOR 100.
THIS PHRASE IS USED TO DESCRIBE EXPLOITING PROSTITUTES UNTIL THEY GET PREGNANT, THEN PAWNING THEM OFF ON JOHNS WHO PREFER THOSE IN THE "FAMILY WAY". AND WHEN THE KIDS COME OUT, THEY GET USED, TOO.
WHAT IS THE HOOKER SQUEEZE.
CORRECT!
MEMORY LANE FOR 100.
2
800 POINTS!
800 POINTS!
LUCKY YOU! A BONUS TILE!
GET THIS QUESTION RIGHT AND...
...YOU WIN!

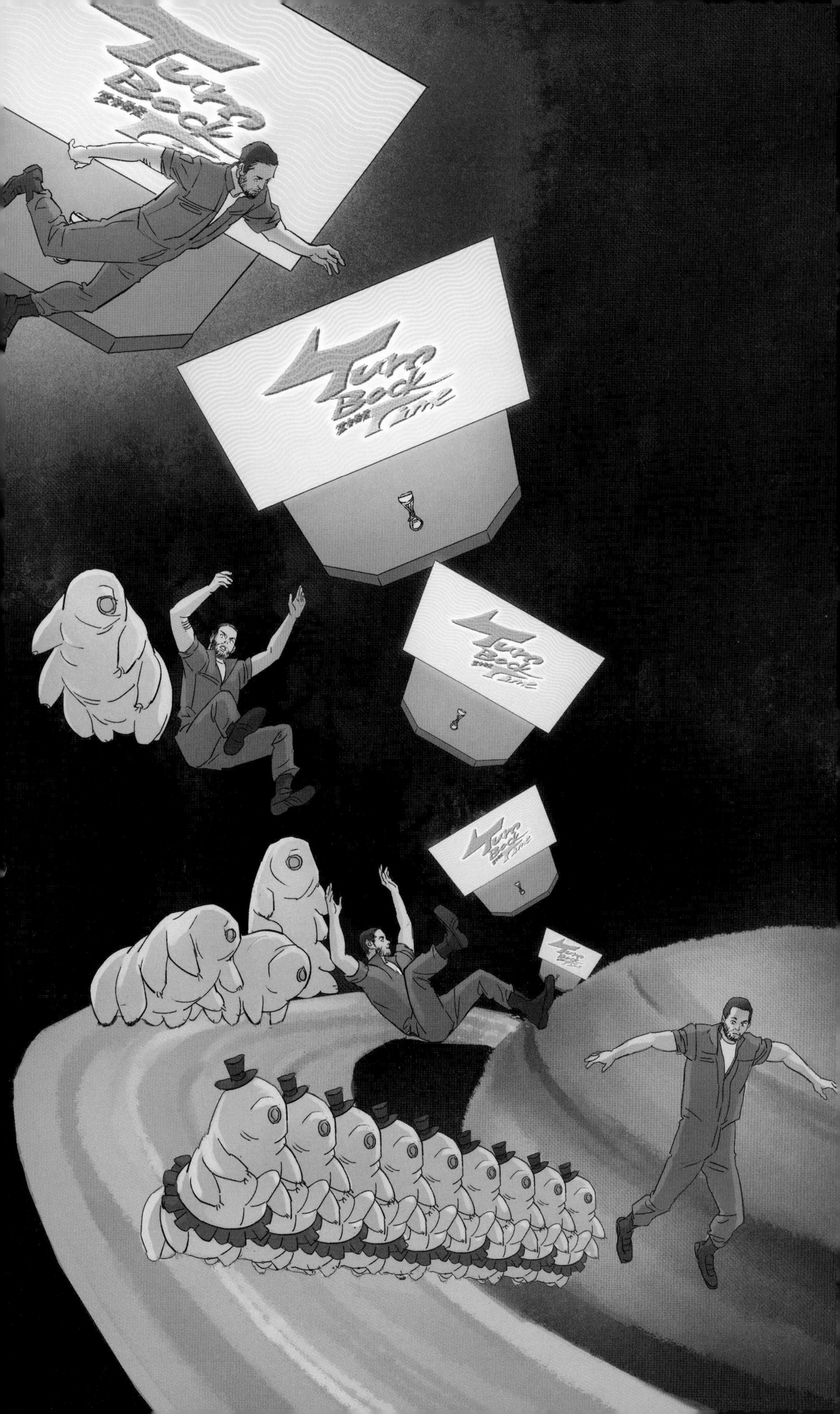
Turn Back Time

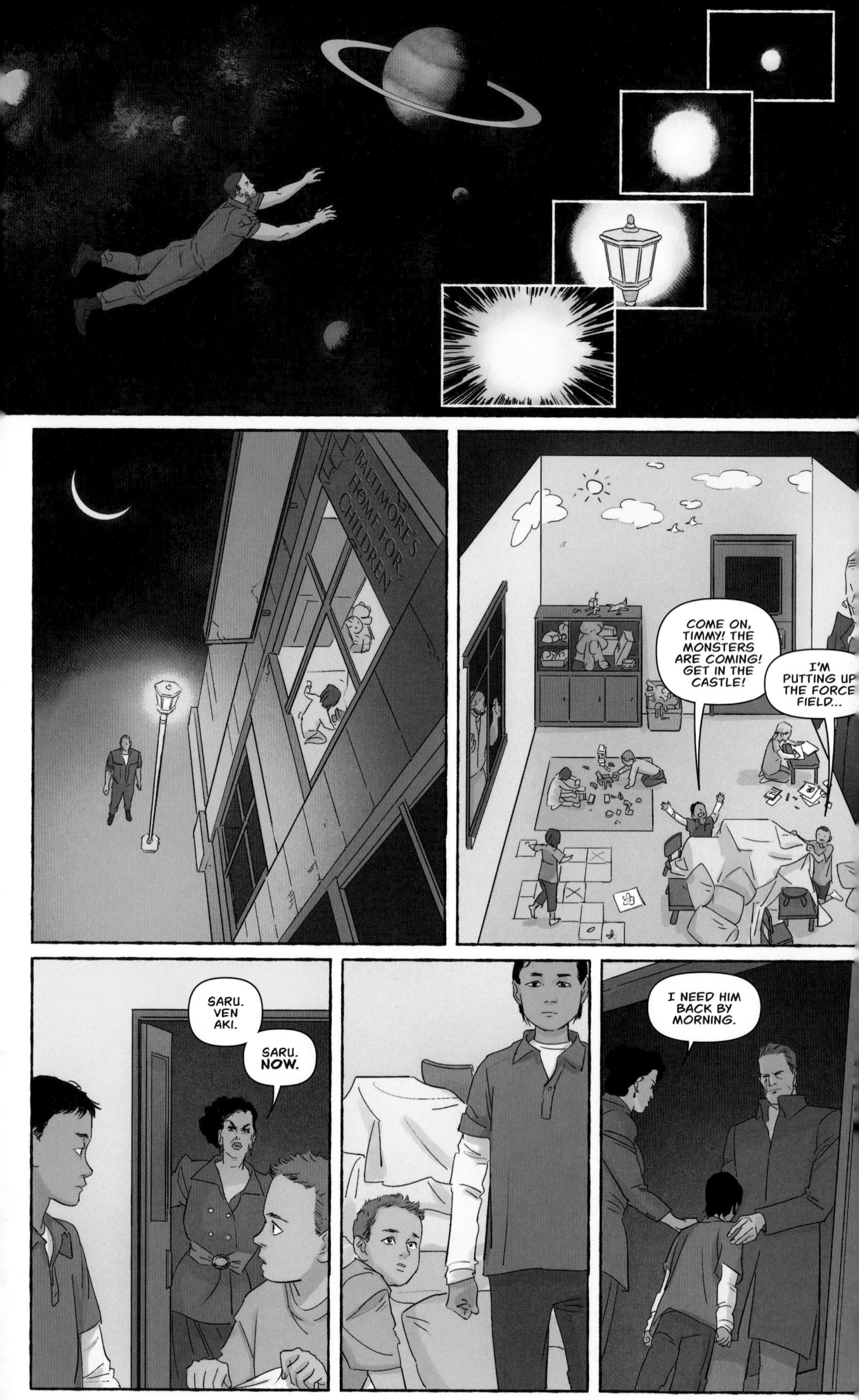
BALTIMORE'S HOME FOR CHILDREN
COME ON, TIMMY! THE MONSTERS ARE COMING! GET IN THE CASTLE!
I'M PUTTING UP THE FORCE FIELD...
SARU. VEN AKI.
SARU. NOW.
I NEED HIM BACK BY MORNING.

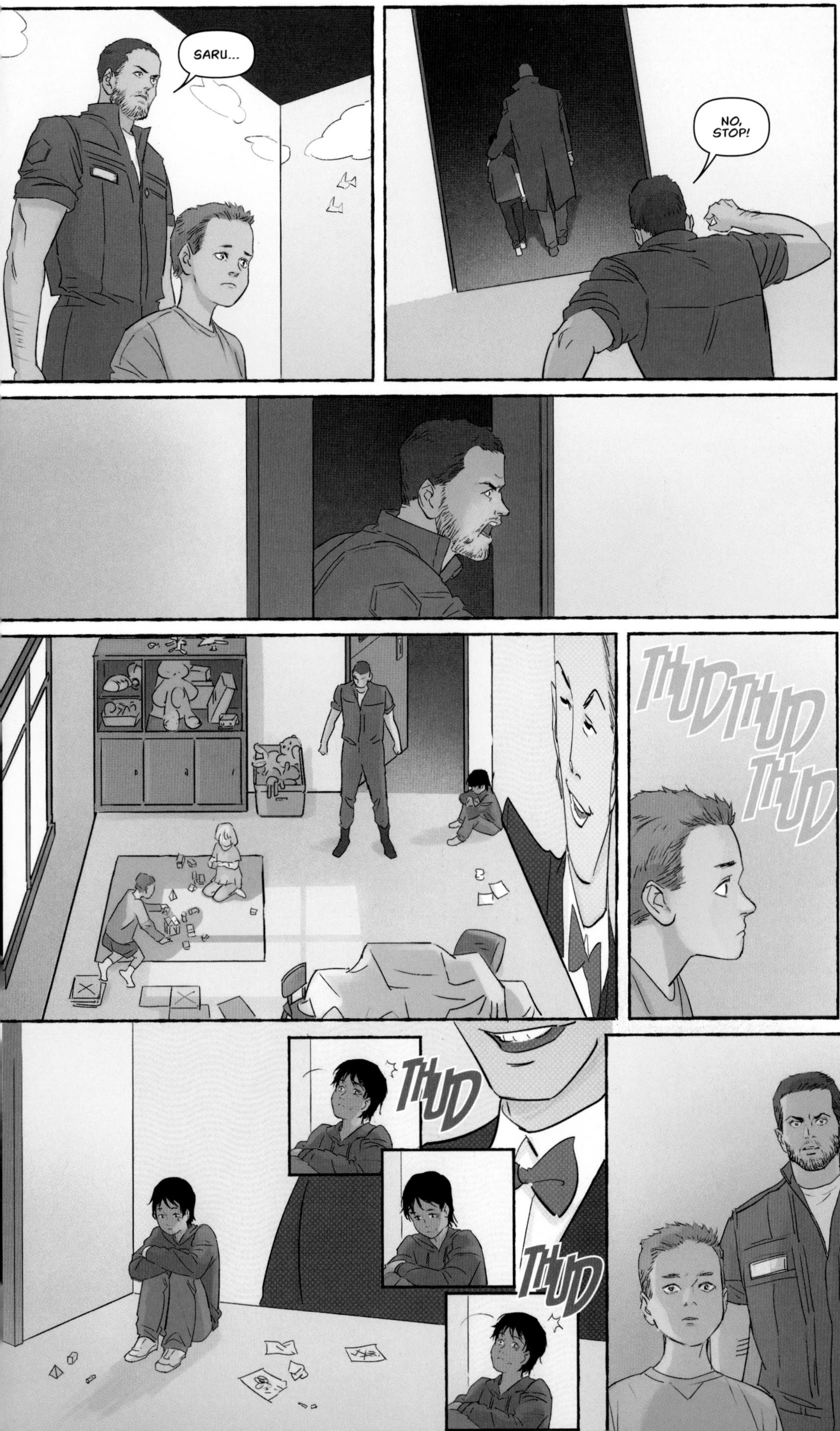

SARU...
NO, STOP!
THUD THUD THUD
THUD
THUD

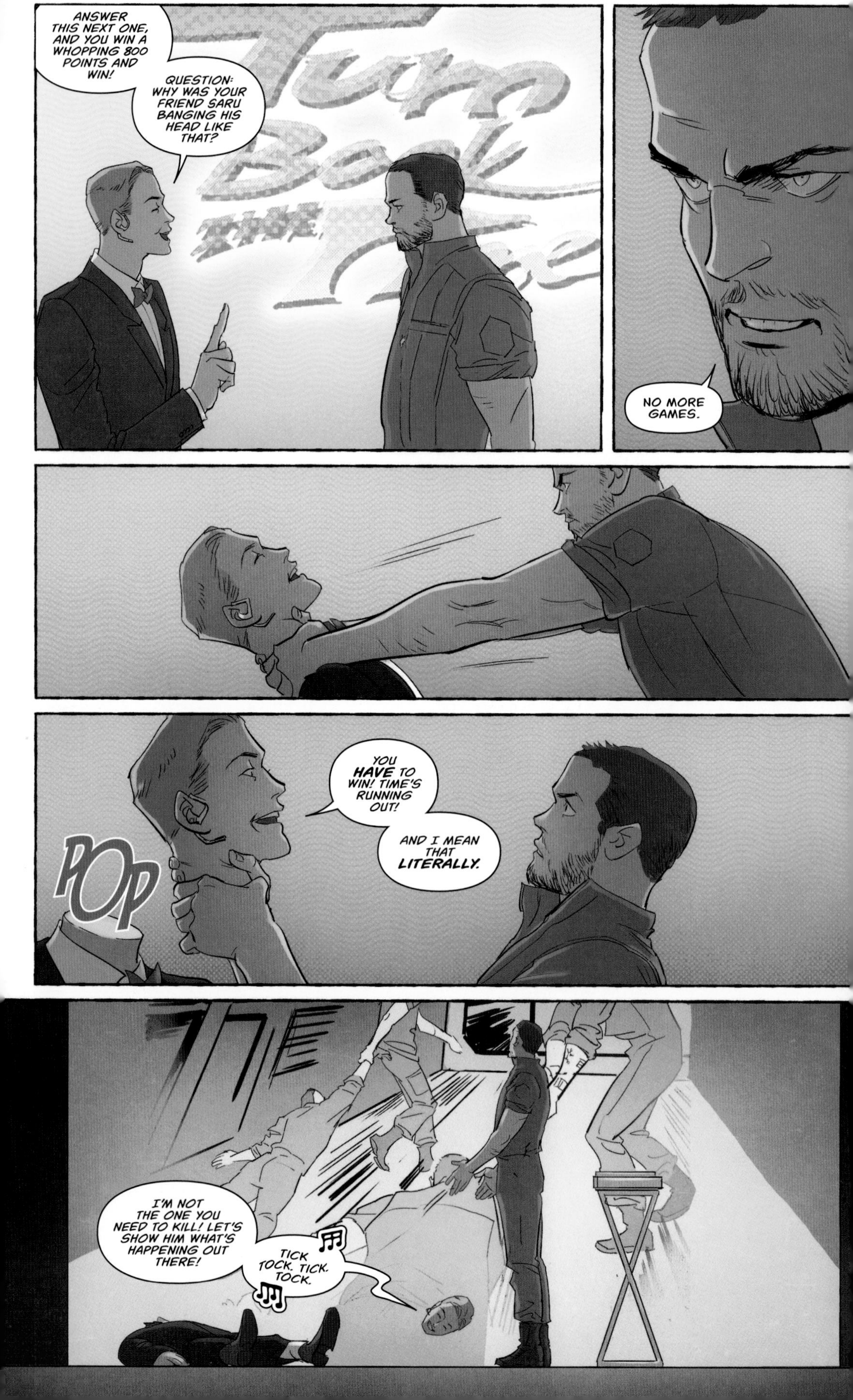
ANSWER THIS NEXT ONE, AND YOU WIN A WHOPPING 800 POINTS AND WIN!
QUESTION: WHY WAS YOUR FRIEND SARU BANGING HIS HEAD LIKE THAT?
NO MORE GAMES.
YOU HAVE TO WIN! TIME'S RUNNING OUT!
AND I MEAN THAT LITERALLY.
POP
I'M NOT THE ONE YOU NEED TO KILL! LET'S SHOW HIM WHAT'S HAPPENING OUT THERE!
TICK TOCK. TICK. TOCK.

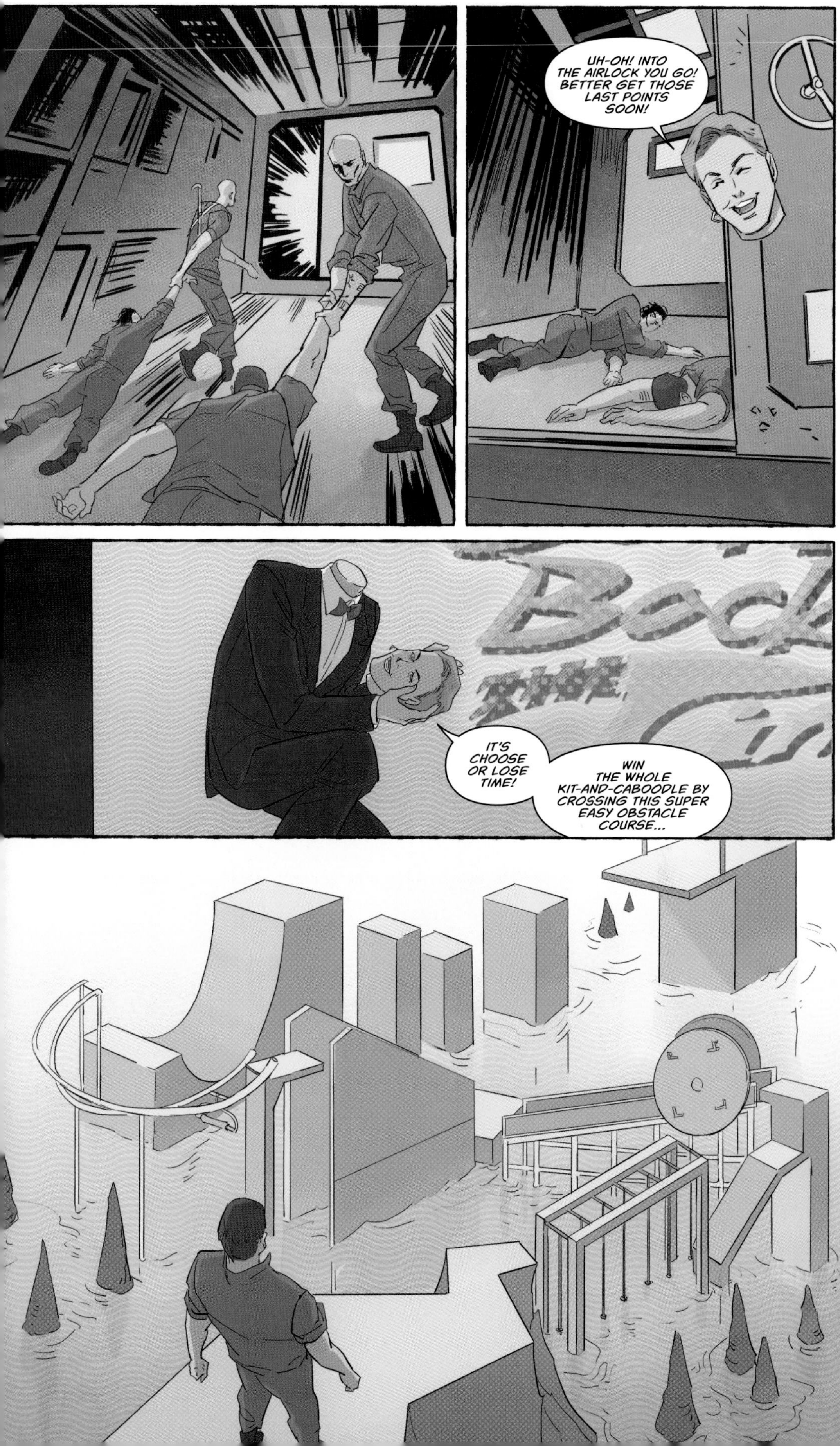
UH-OH! INTO THE AIRLOCK YOU GO! BETTER GET THOSE LAST POINTS SOON!
IT'S CHOOSE OR LOSE TIME!
WIN THE WHOLE KIT-AND-CABOODLE BY CROSSING THIS SUPER EASY OBSTACLE COURSE...

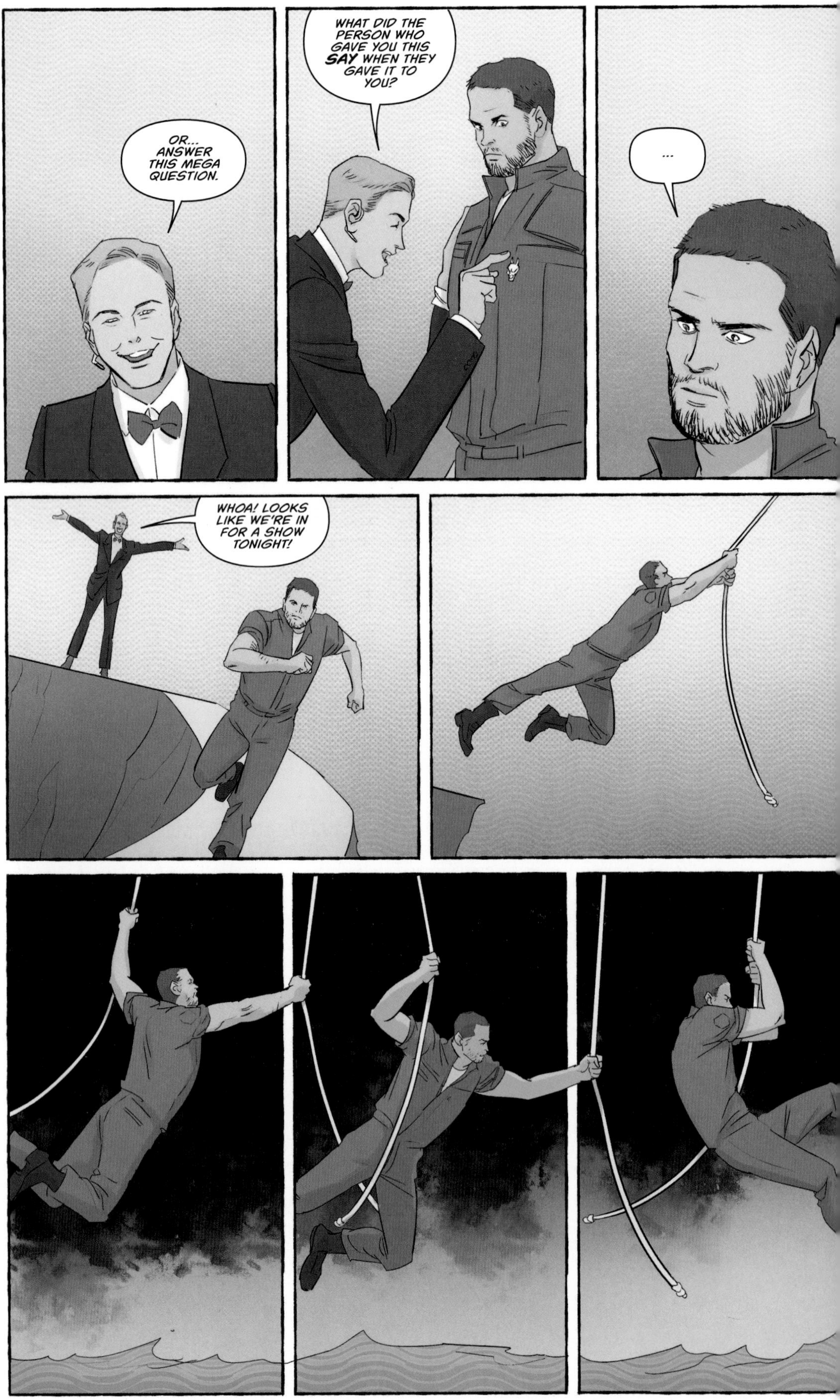
OR... ANSWER THIS MEGA QUESTION.
WHAT DID THE PERSON WHO GAVE YOU THIS SAY WHEN THEY GAVE IT TO YOU?
...
WHOA! LOOKS LIKE WE'RE IN FOR A SHOW TONIGHT!

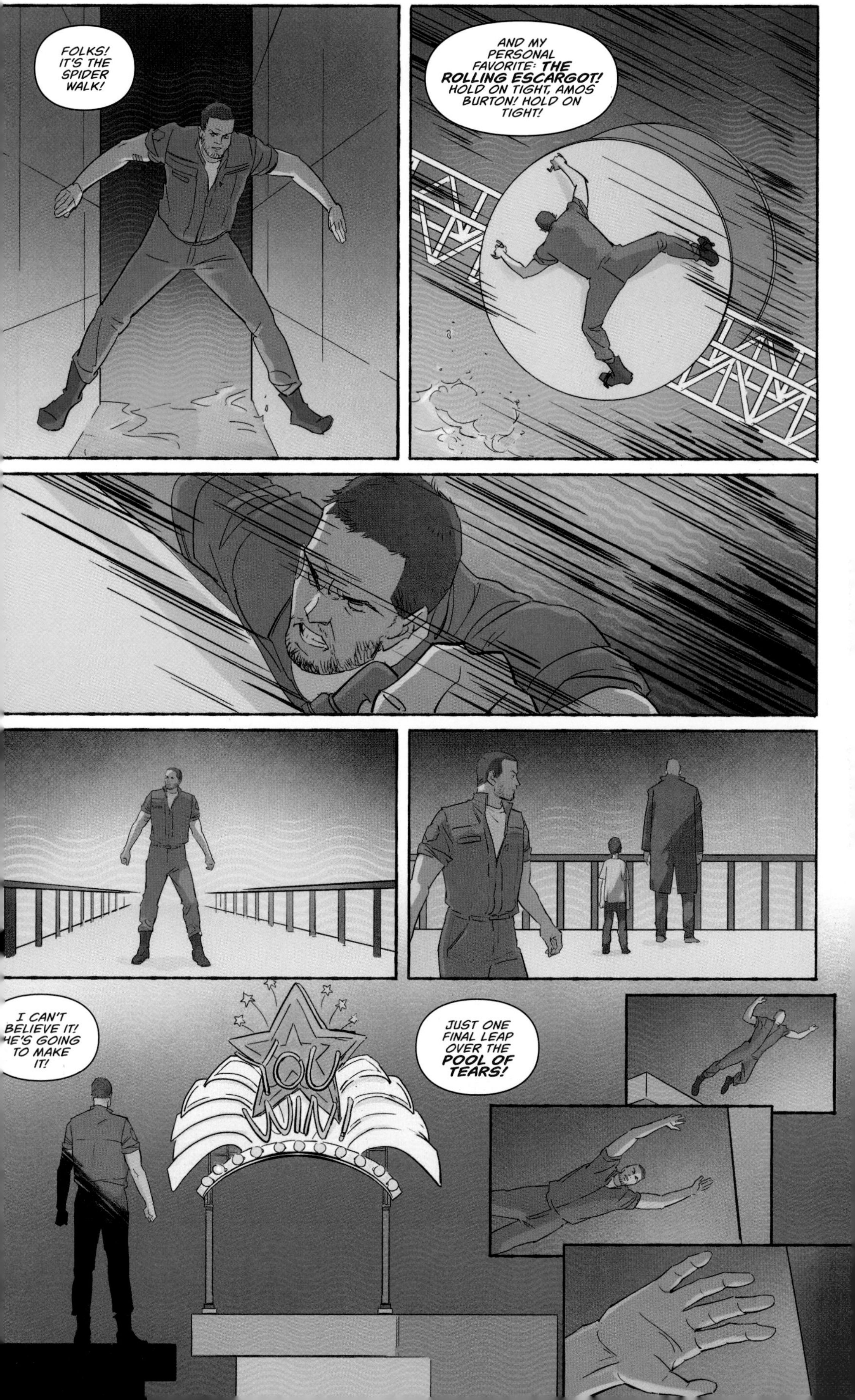
FOLKS! IT'S THE SPIDER WALK!
AND MY PERSONAL FAVORITE: **THE ROLLING ESCARGOT!** HOLD ON TIGHT, AMOS BURTON! HOLD ON TIGHT!
I CAN'T BELIEVE IT! HE'S GOING TO MAKE IT!
YOU WIN!
JUST ONE FINAL LEAP OVER THE **POOL OF TEARS!**

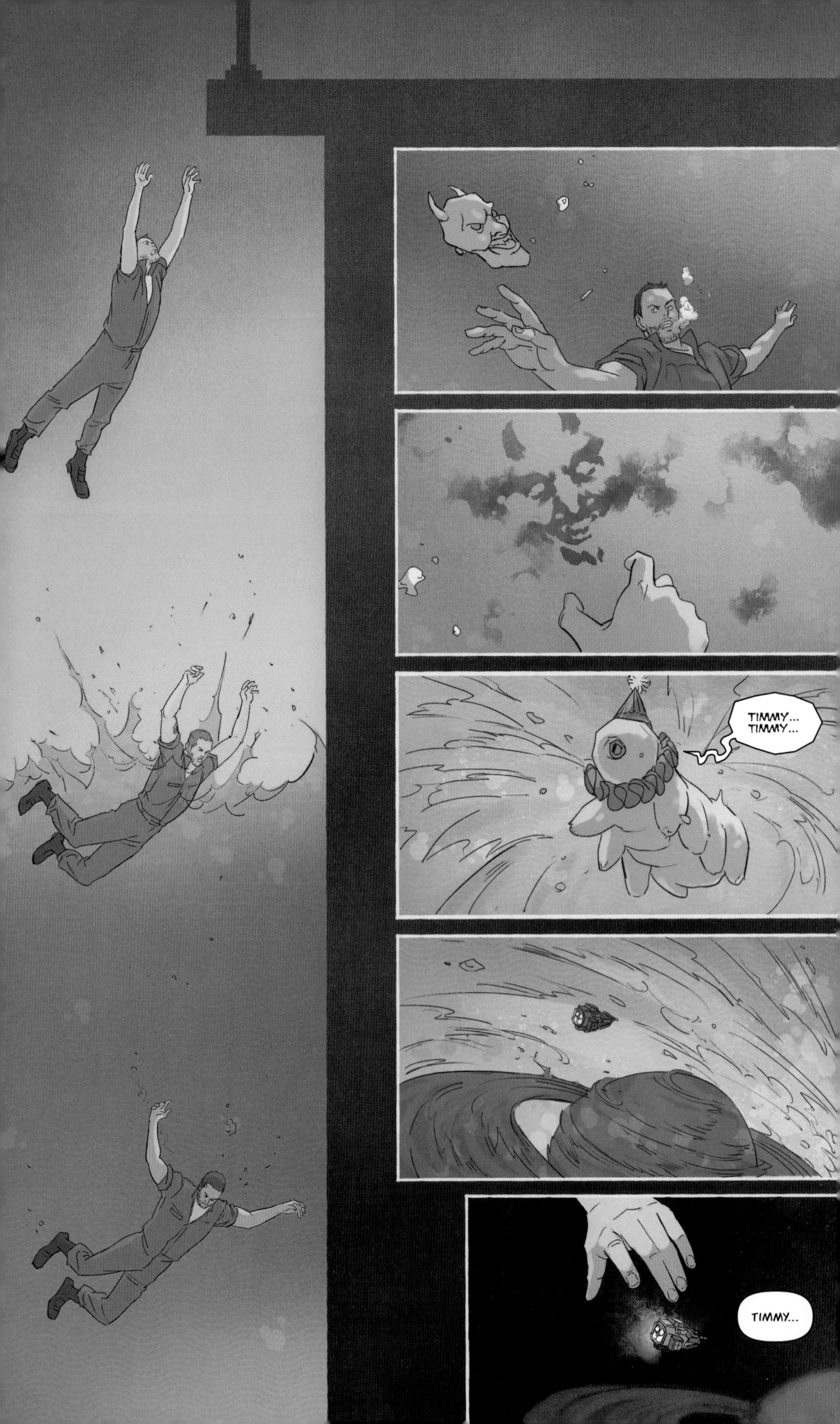
TIMMY...
TIMMY...
TIMMY...

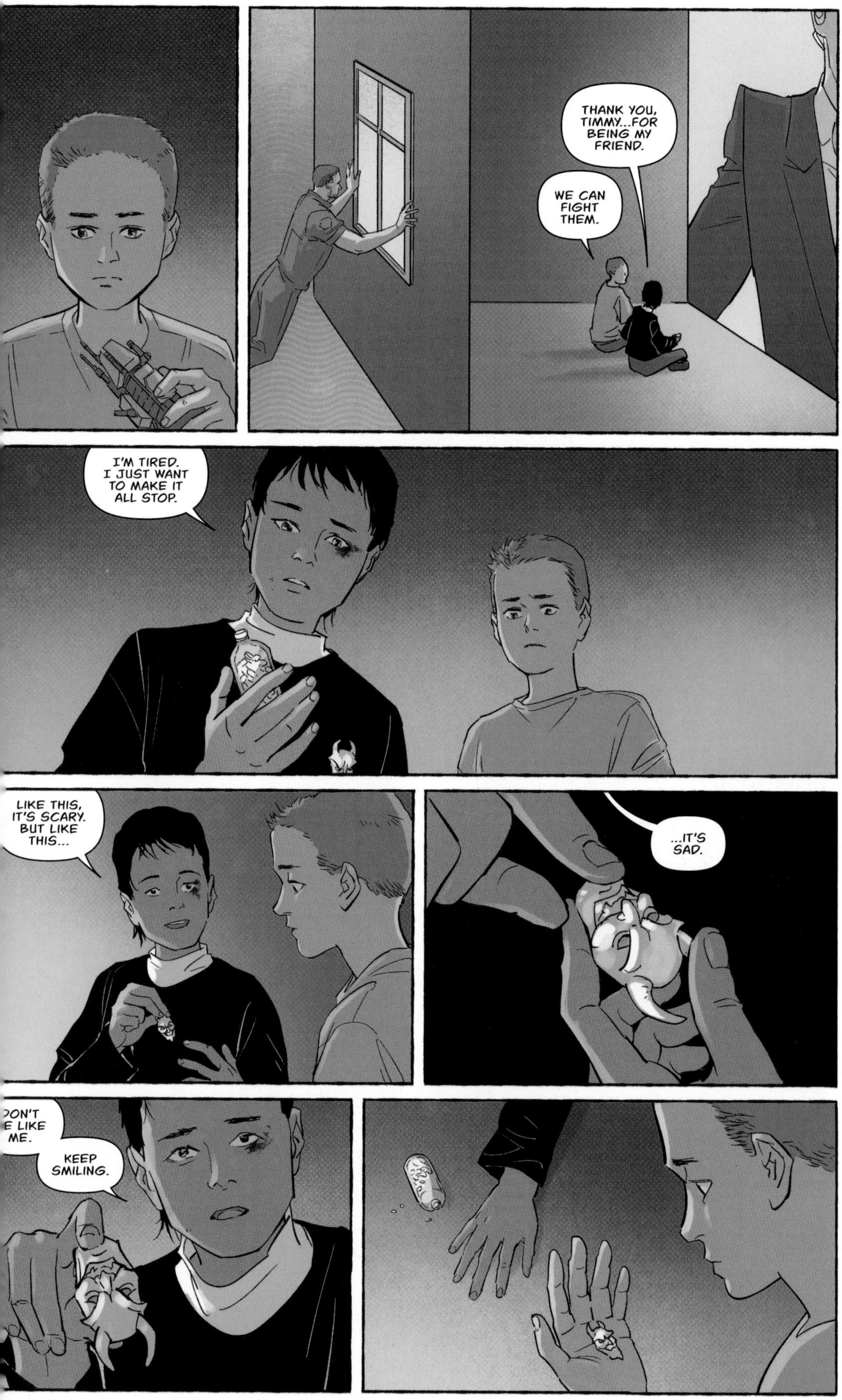
THANK YOU, TIMMY...FOR BEING MY FRIEND.
WE CAN FIGHT THEM.
I'M TIRED. I JUST WANT TO MAKE IT ALL STOP.
LIKE THIS, IT'S SCARY. BUT LIKE THIS...
...IT'S SAD.
E LIKE ME.
KEEP SMILING.

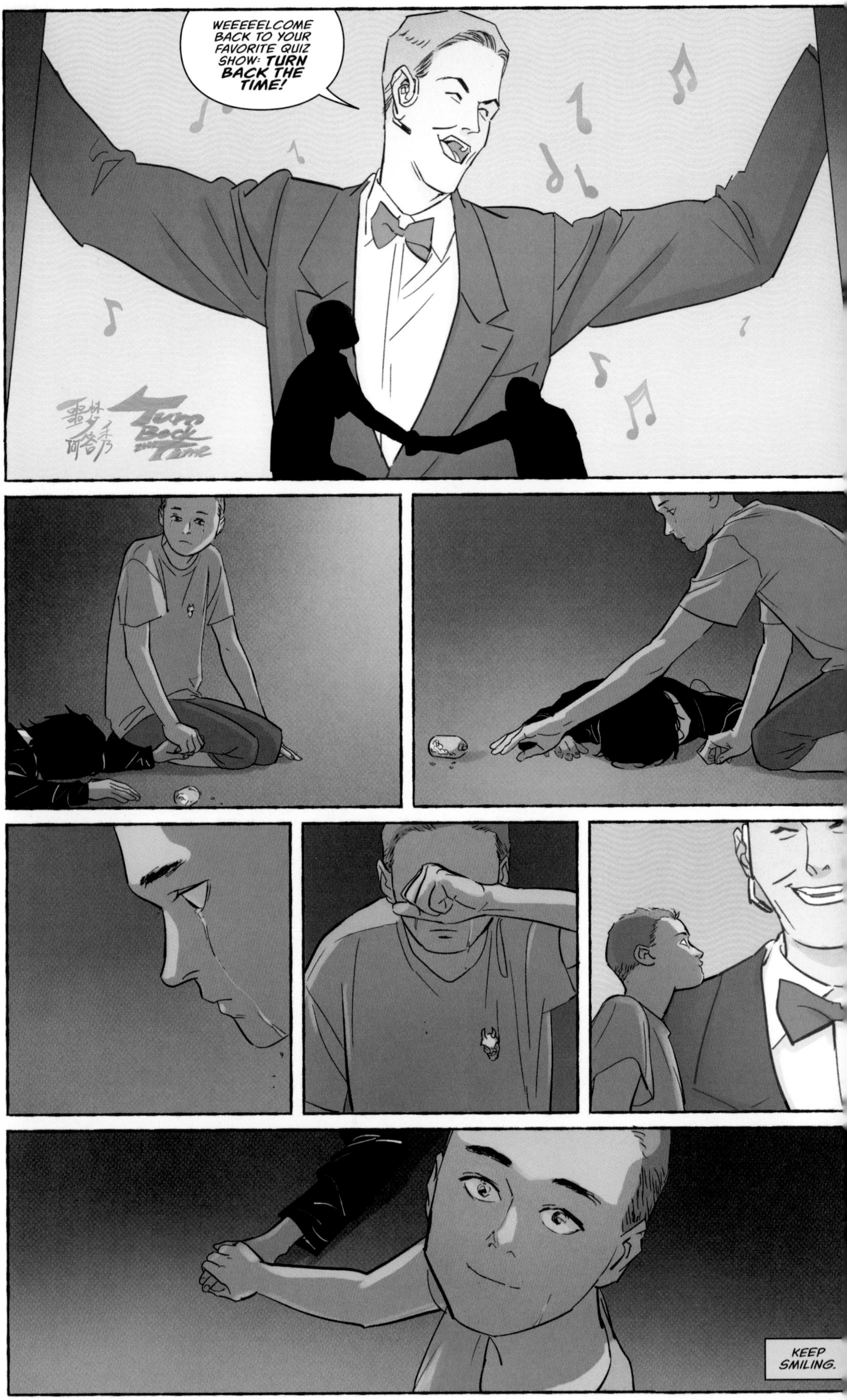
WEEEEELCOME BACK TO YOUR FAVORITE QUIZ SHOW: TURN BACK THE TIME!
KEEP SMILING.

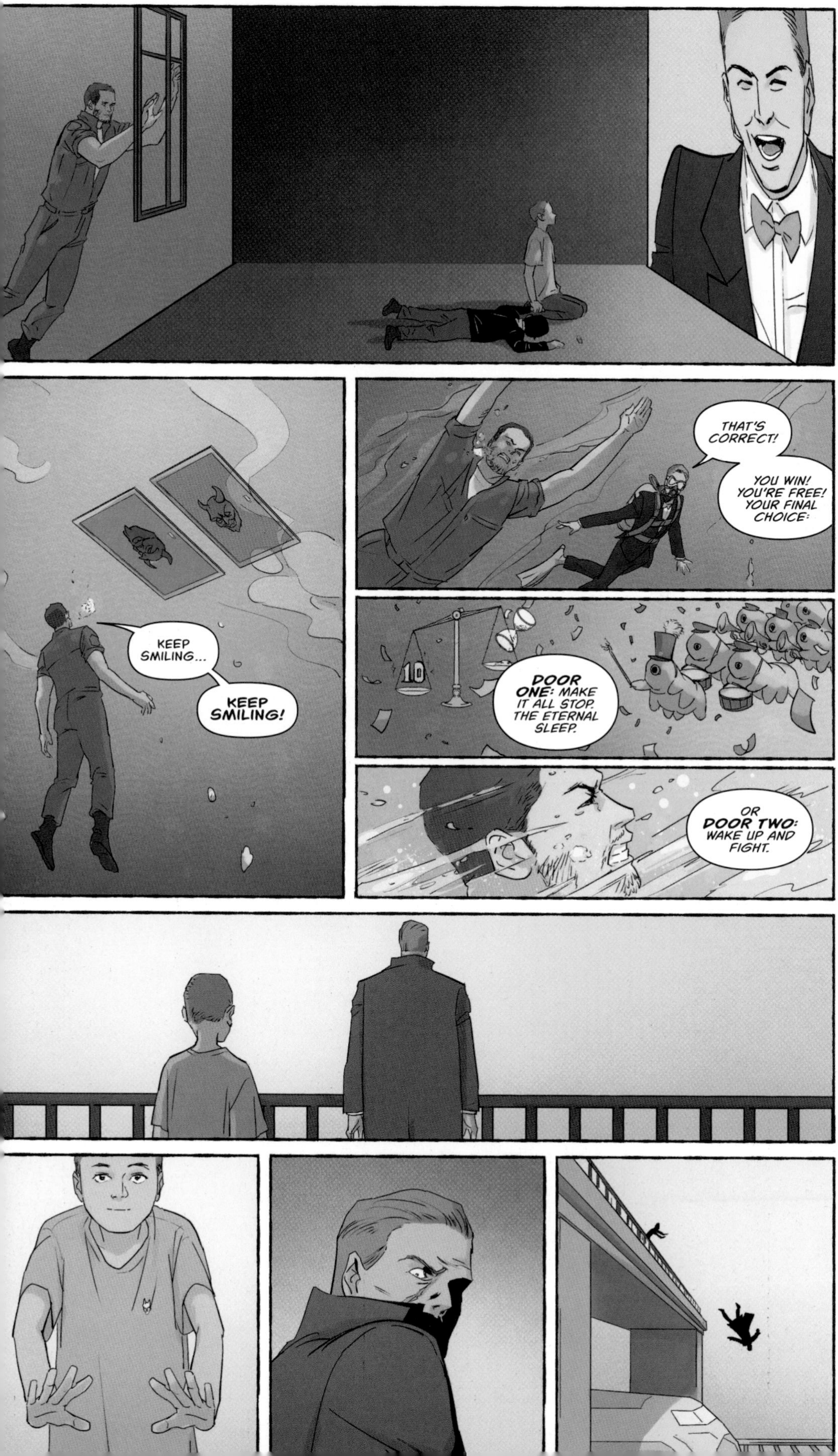
KEEP SMILING...
KEEP SMILING!
THAT'S CORRECT!
YOU WIN! YOU'RE FREE! YOUR FINAL CHOICE:
10
DOOR ONE: MAKE IT ALL STOP. THE ETERNAL SLEEP.
OR DOOR TWO: WAKE UP AND FIGHT.

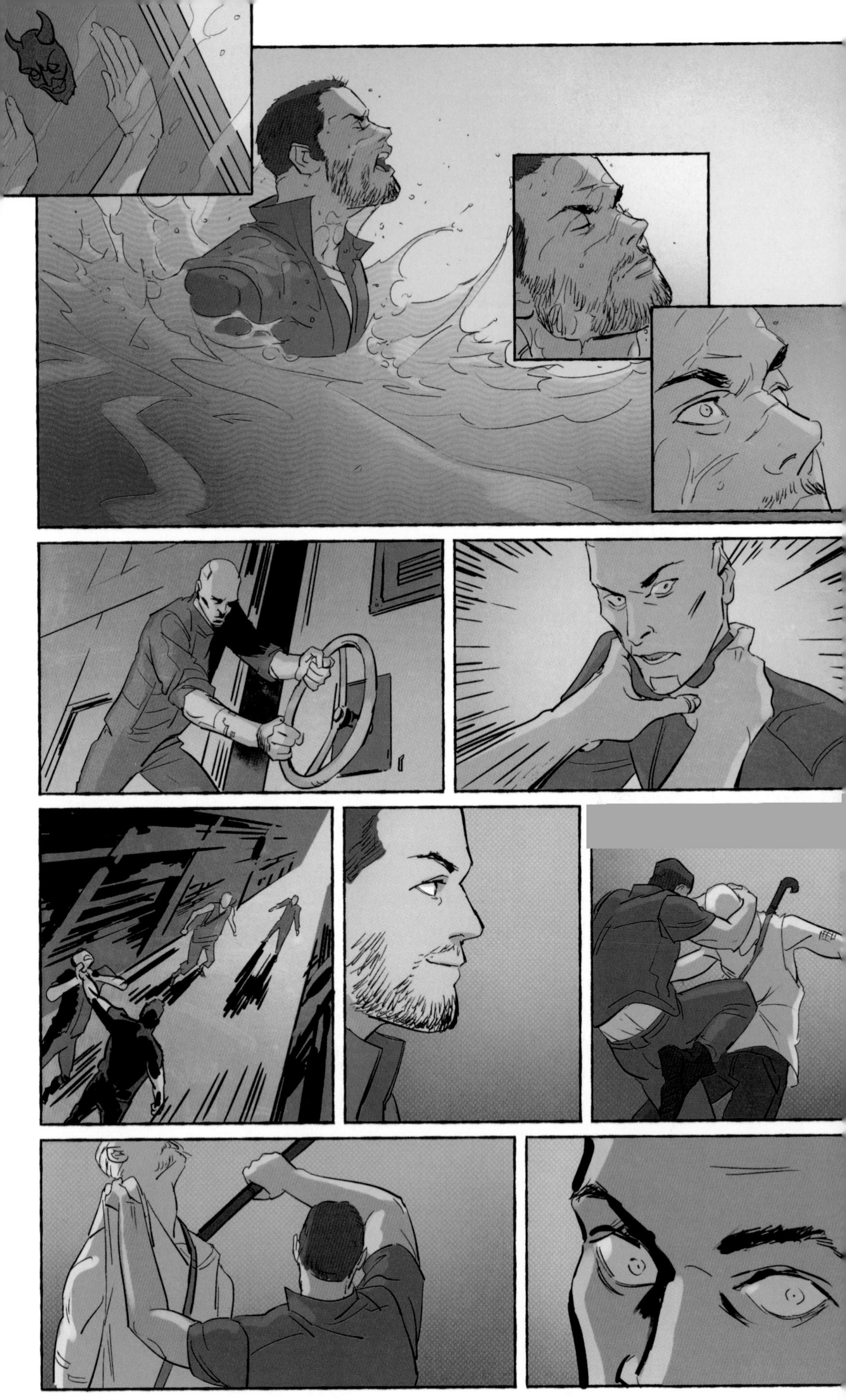

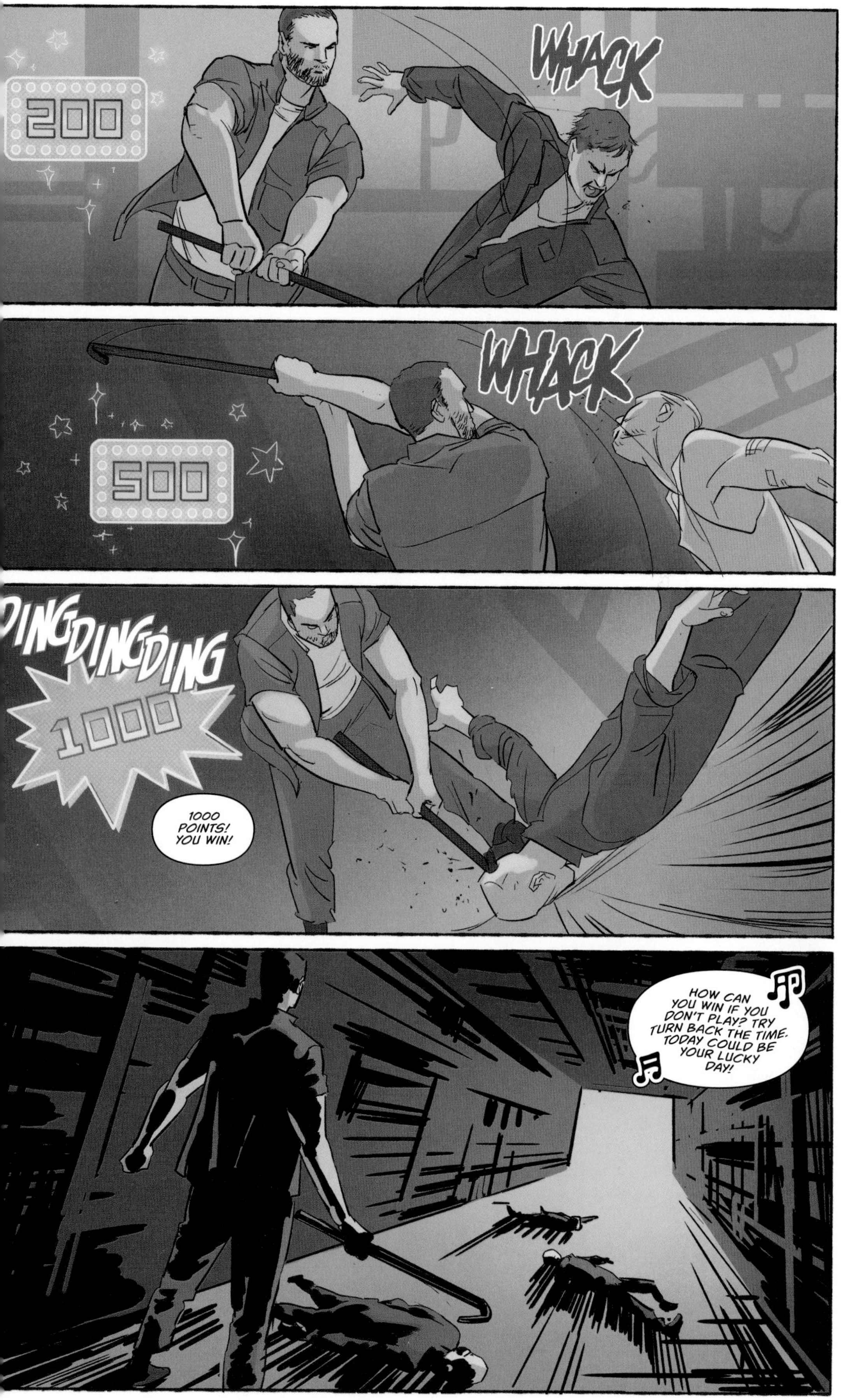
200
WHACK
500
WHACK
DING DING DING
1000
1000 POINTS! YOU WIN!
HOW CAN YOU WIN IF YOU DON'T PLAY? TRY TURN BACK THE TIME. TODAY COULD BE YOUR LUCKY DAY!

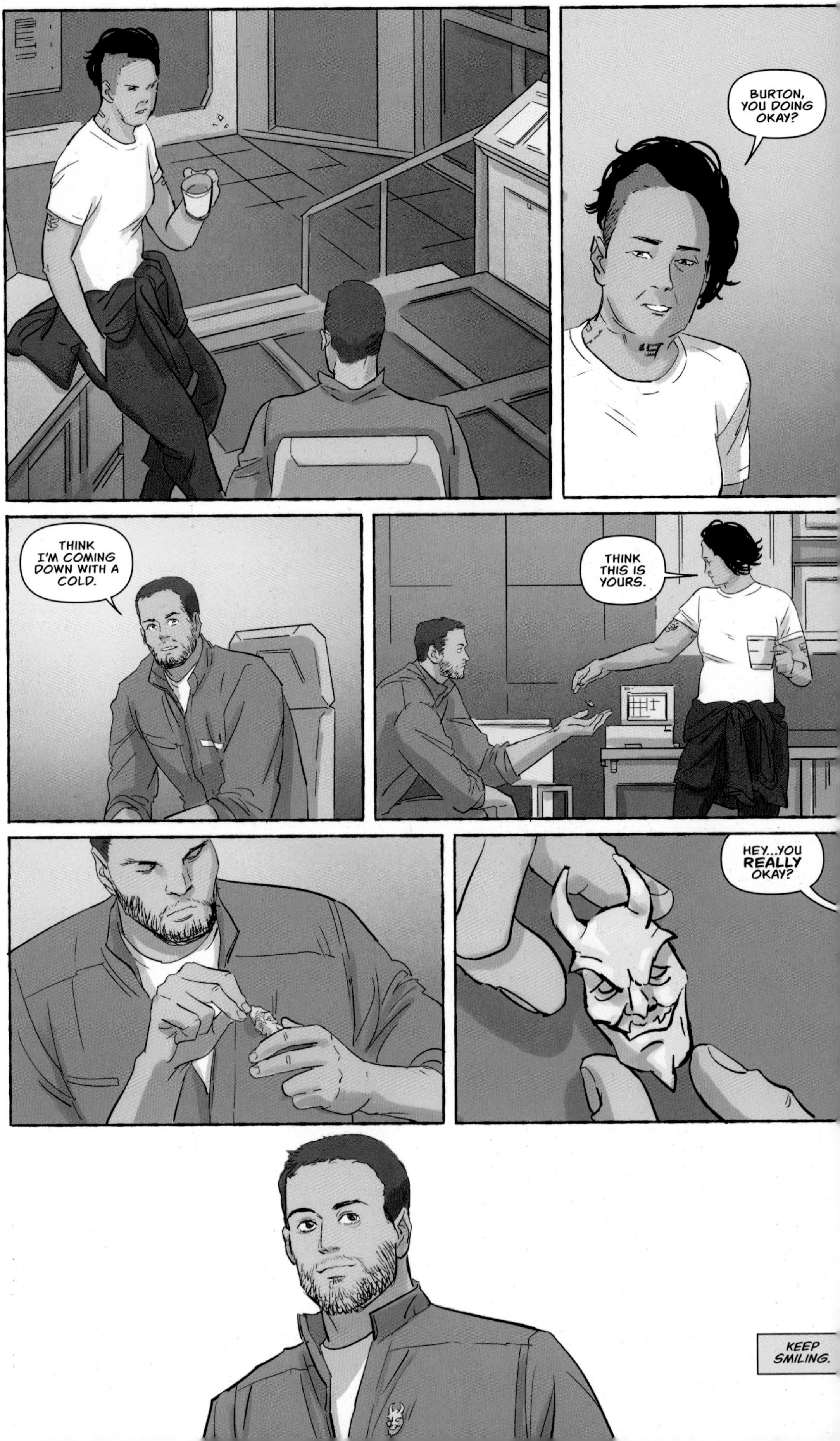
BURTON, YOU DOING OKAY?
THINK I'M COMING DOWN WITH A COLD.
THINK THIS IS YOURS.
HEY...YOU **REALLY** OKAY?
KEEP SMILING.

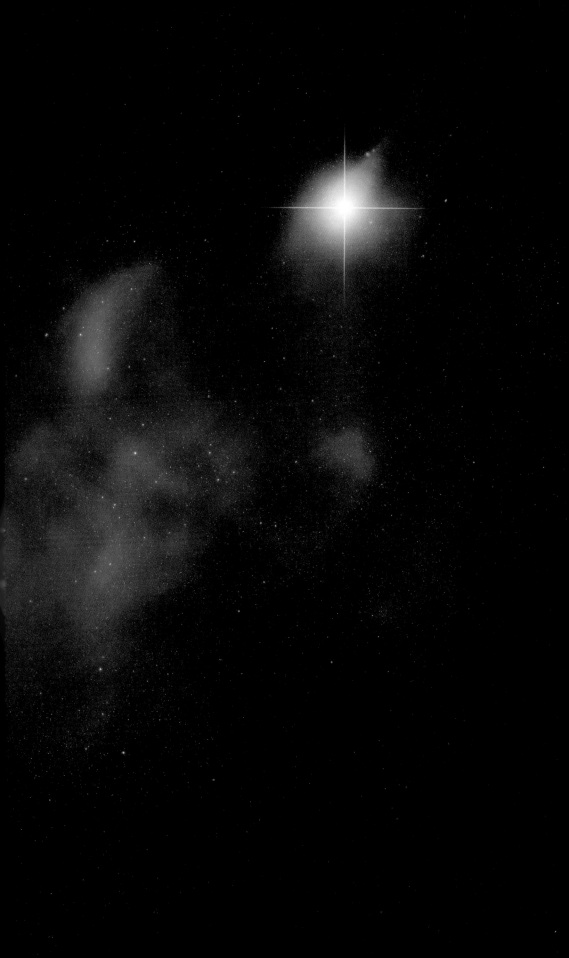

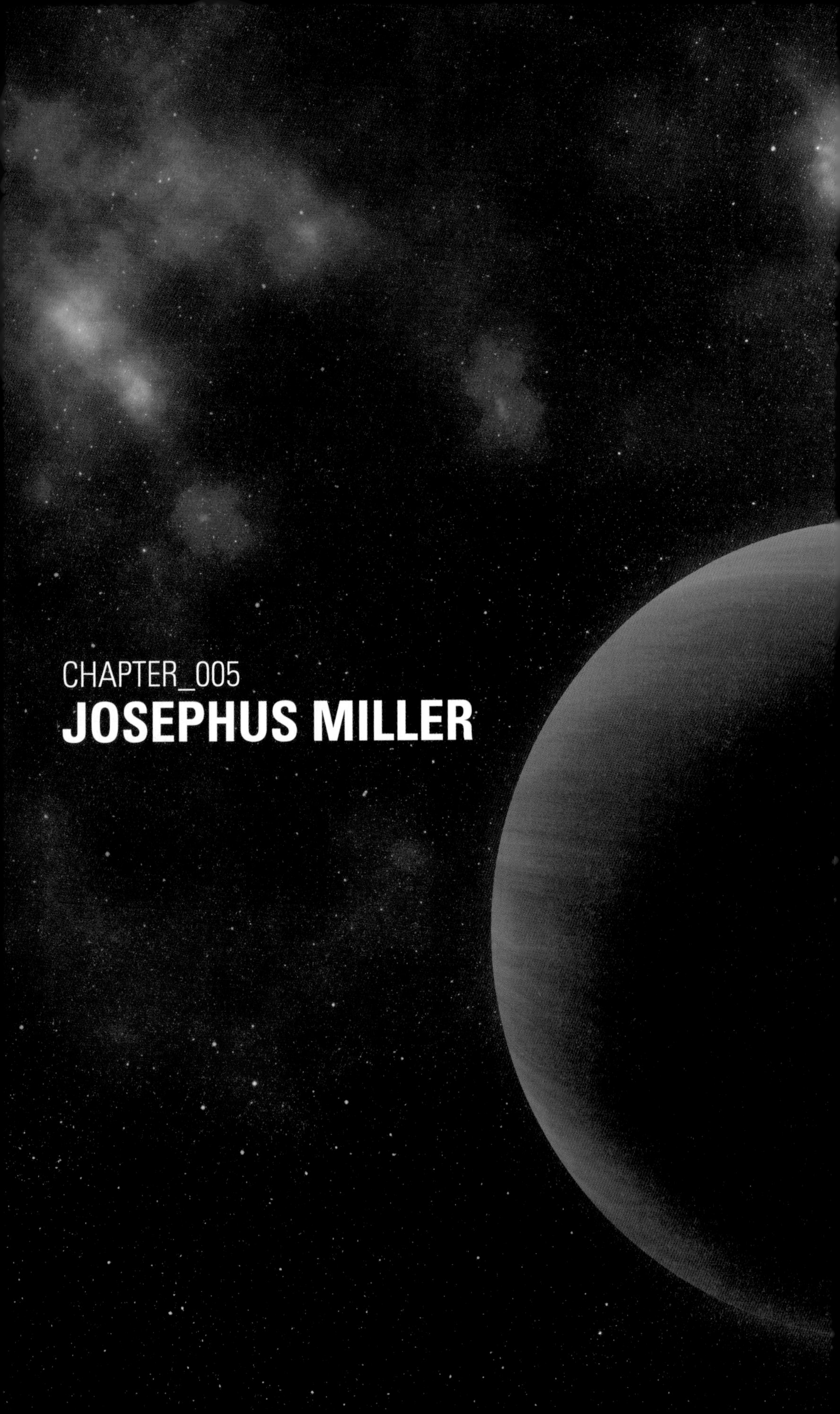

CHAPTER_005

JOSEPHUS MILLER

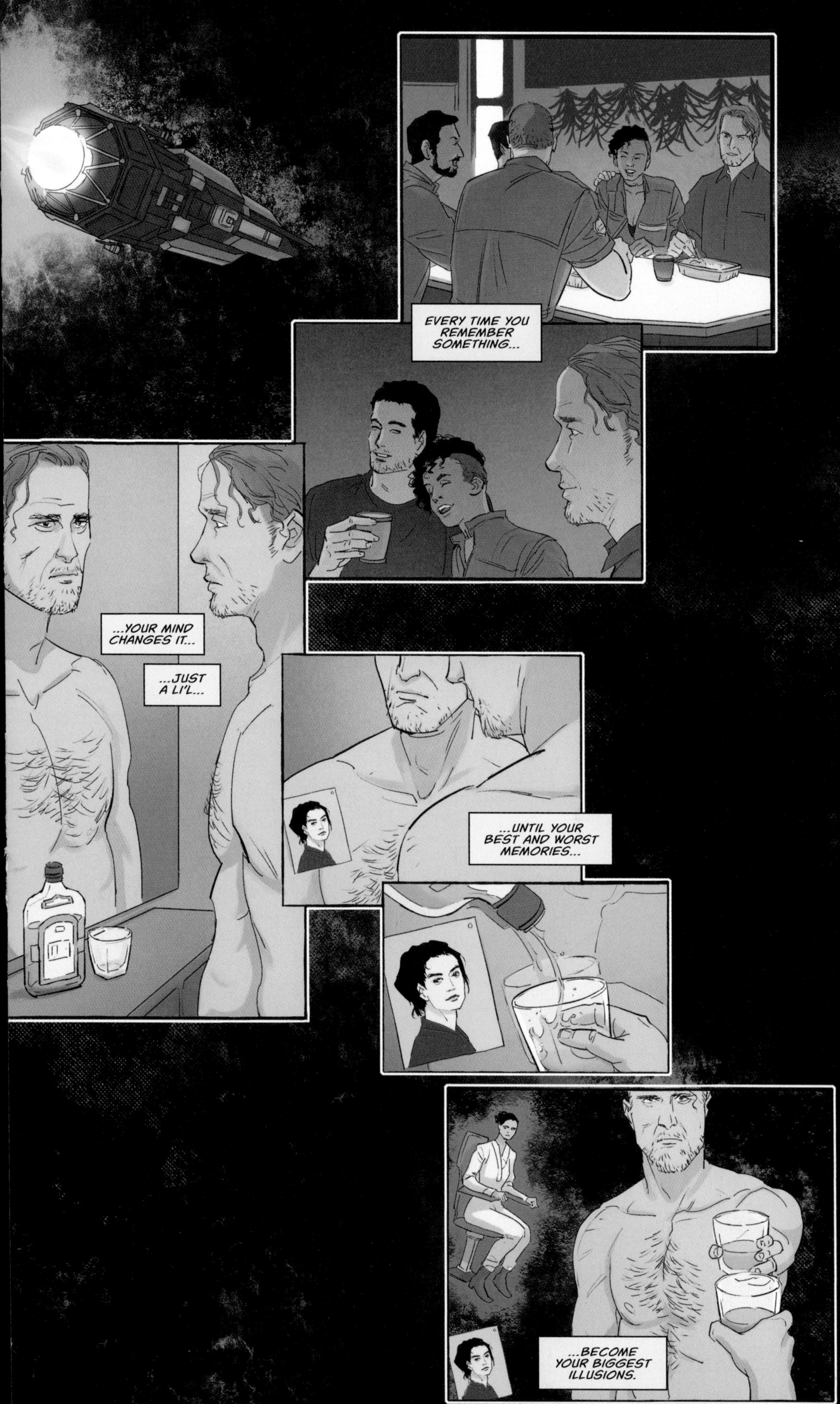
EVERY TIME YOU REMEMBER SOMETHING...
...YOUR MIND CHANGES IT...
...JUST A LI'L...
...UNTIL YOUR BEST AND WORST MEMORIES...
...BECOME YOUR BIGGEST ILLUSIONS.

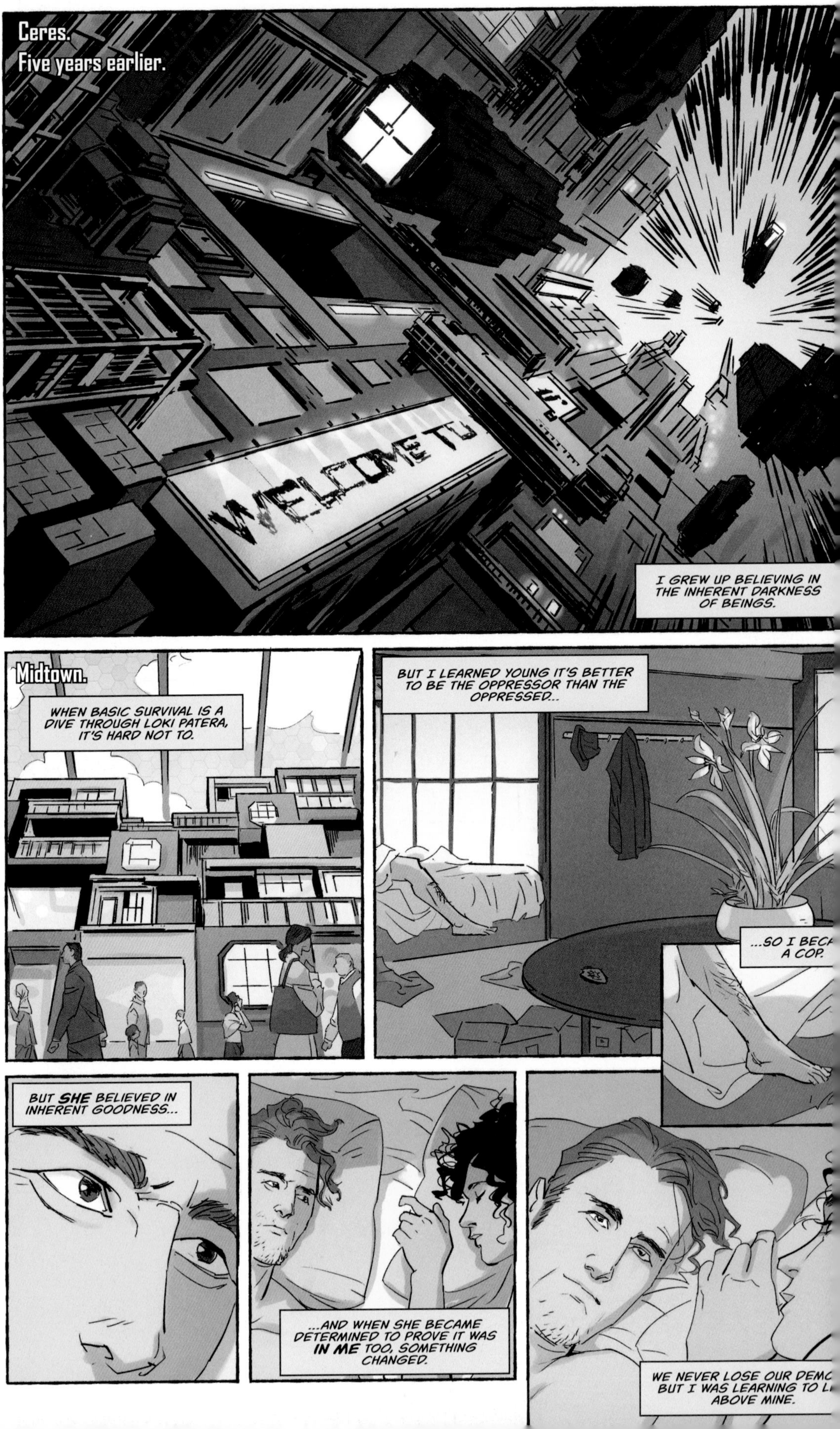

Ceres.
Five years earlier.
WELCOME TO
I GREW UP BELIEVING IN THE INHERENT DARKNESS OF BEINGS.
Midtown.
WHEN BASIC SURVIVAL IS A DIVE THROUGH LOKI PATERA, IT'S HARD NOT TO.
BUT I LEARNED YOUNG IT'S BETTER TO BE THE OPPRESSOR THAN THE OPPRESSED...
...SO I BECA
A COP.
BUT SHE BELIEVED IN INHERENT GOODNESS...
...AND WHEN SHE BECAME DETERMINED TO PROVE IT WAS IN ME TOO, SOMETHING CHANGED.
WE NEVER LOSE OUR DEMO
BUT I WAS LEARNING TO L
ABOVE MINE.

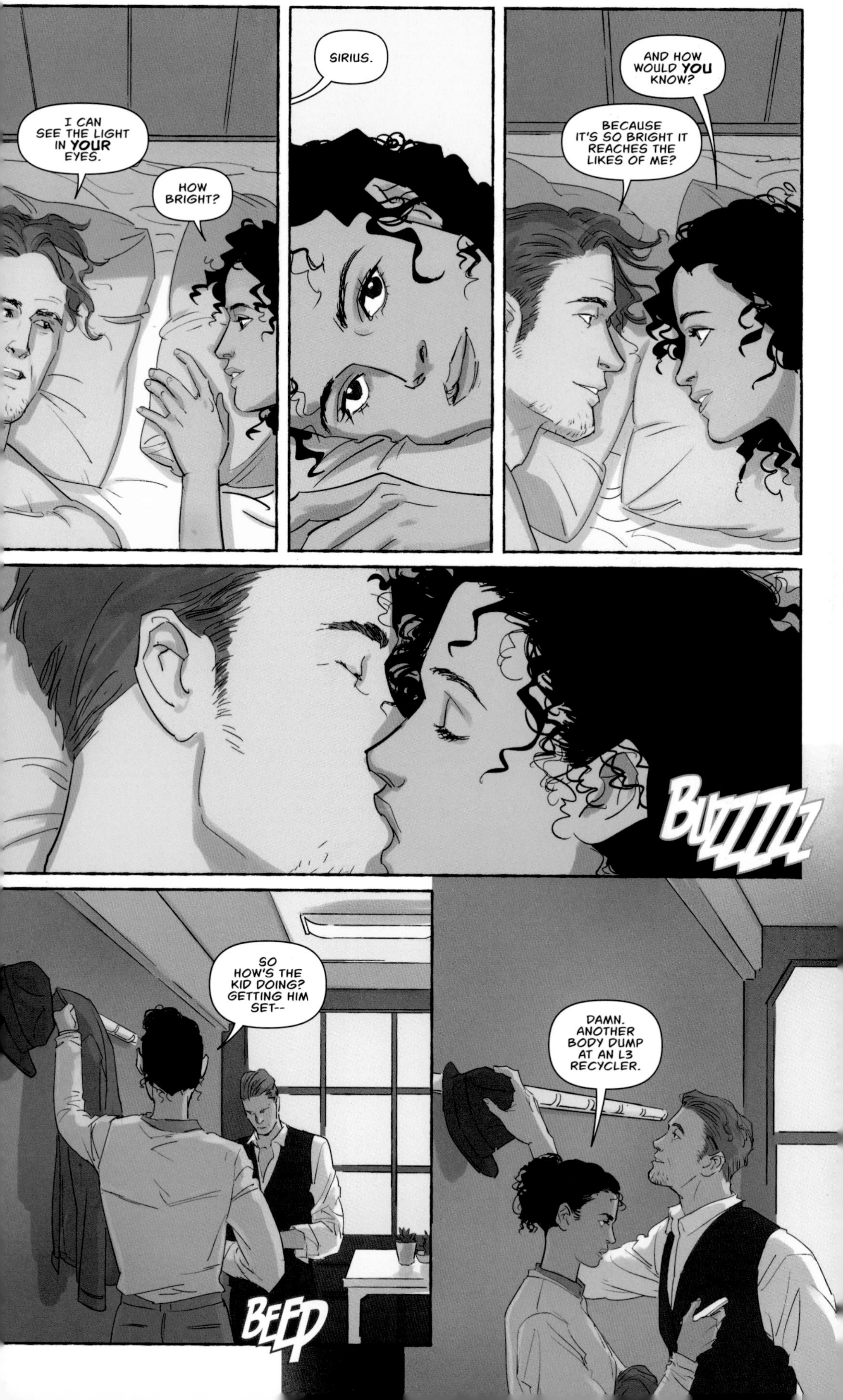
I CAN SEE THE LIGHT IN YOUR EYES.
HOW BRIGHT?
SIRIUS.
AND HOW WOULD YOU KNOW?
BECAUSE IT'S SO BRIGHT IT REACHES THE LIKES OF ME?
BUZZZZZ
SO HOW'S THE KID DOING? GETTING HIM SET--
BEEP
DAMN. ANOTHER BODY DUMP AT AN L3 RECYCLER.

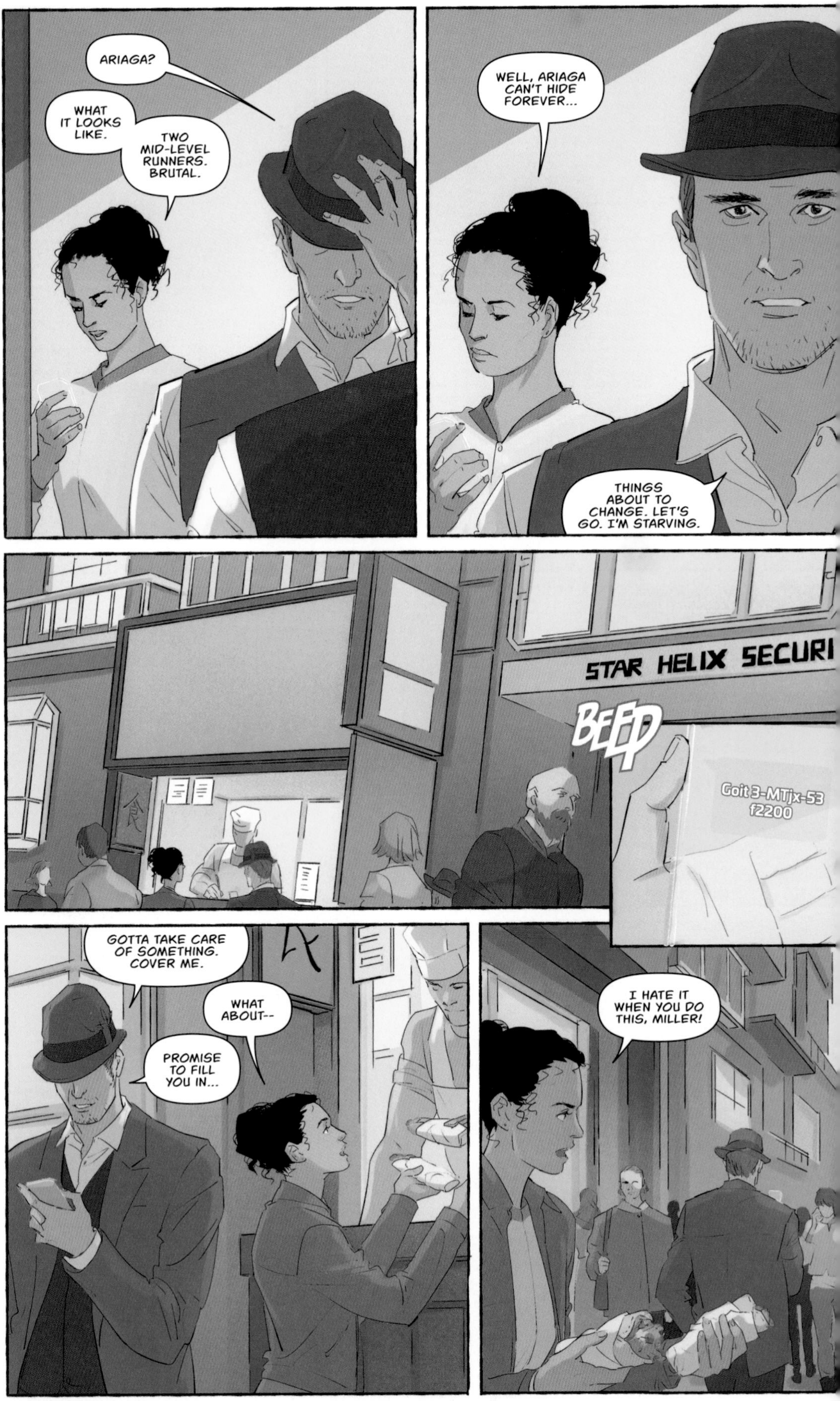
ARIAGA?
WHAT IT LOOKS LIKE.
TWO MID-LEVEL RUNNERS. BRUTAL.
WELL, ARIAGA CAN'T HIDE FOREVER...
THINGS ABOUT TO CHANGE. LET'S GO. I'M STARVING.
STAR HELIX SECURI
BEEP
Goit 3-MTjx-53 f2200
GOTTA TAKE CARE OF SOMETHING. COVER ME.
WHAT ABOUT--
PROMISE TO FILL YOU IN...
I HATE IT WHEN YOU DO THIS, MILLER!

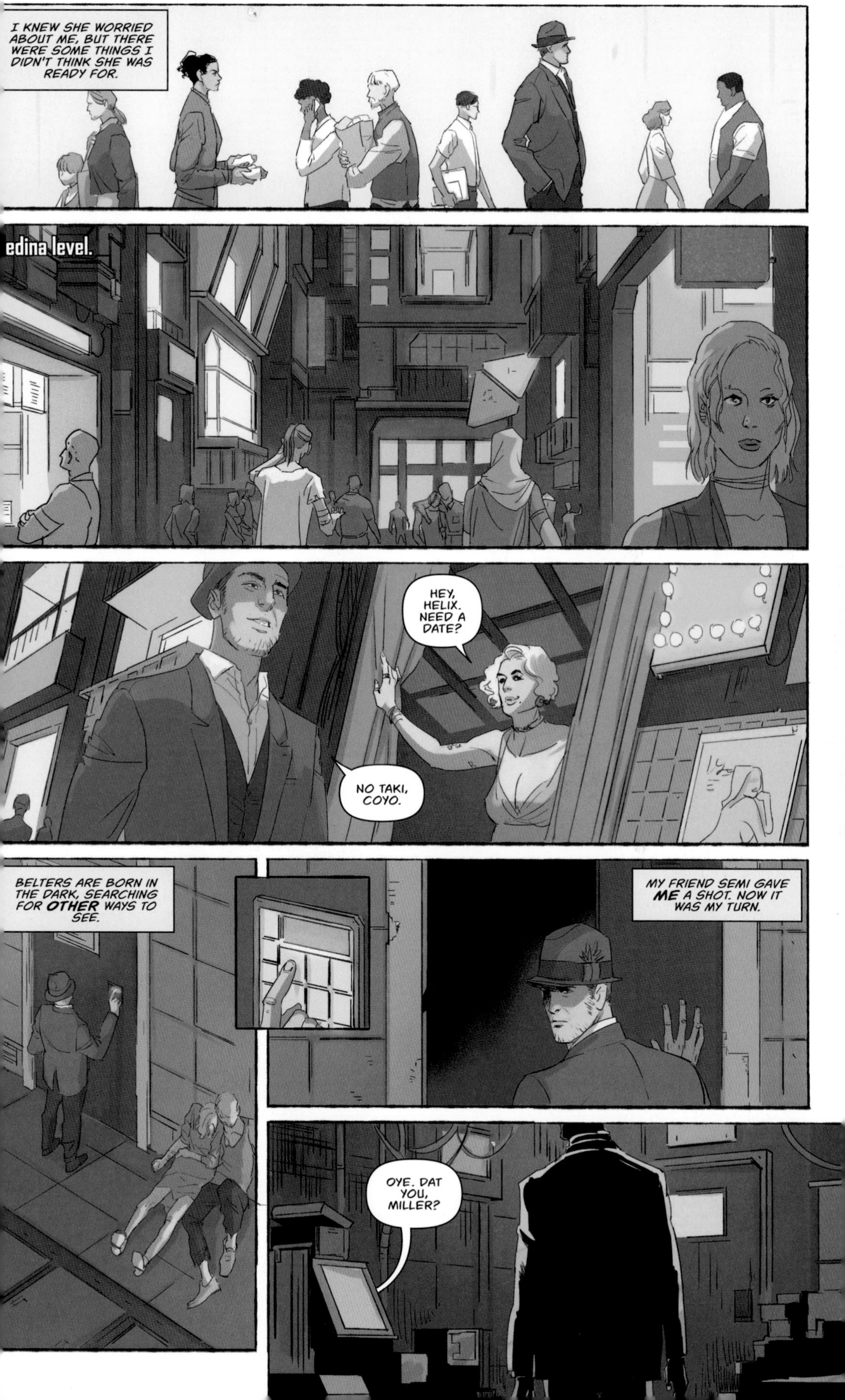
I KNEW SHE WORRIED ABOUT ME, BUT THERE WERE SOME THINGS I DIDN'T THINK SHE WAS READY FOR.
edina level.
HEY, HELIX. NEED A DATE?
NO TAKI, COYO.
BELTERS ARE BORN IN THE DARK, SEARCHING FOR OTHER WAYS TO SEE.
MY FRIEND SEMI GAVE ME A SHOT. NOW IT WAS MY TURN.
OYE. DAT YOU, MILLER?

YOU GOT IT?

JAX HAD GUTS. HE SOUGHT ME OUT...

...WANTED TO BE STAR HELIX. SO WE MADE A DEAL.

THIS'LL GET YOU THROUGH INNER DOORS SA SA...

MOST IMPORTANT, FREIGHT 31 WHERE THEY'RE BEING HELD.

WHAT'S THE LOAD?

SEVEN KIDS AND NINETY KILOS ARE GOING TO BUYER SHIPPING IN TONIGHT AT 2300.

THE KIDS ARE IN ROUGH SHAPE...

JAX WOULD HELP ME TAKE DOWN THESE SEX TRAFFICKING SCUM, AND I'D GET HIM A ROOKIE SPOT.

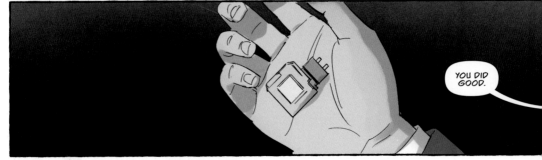

YOU DID GOOD.

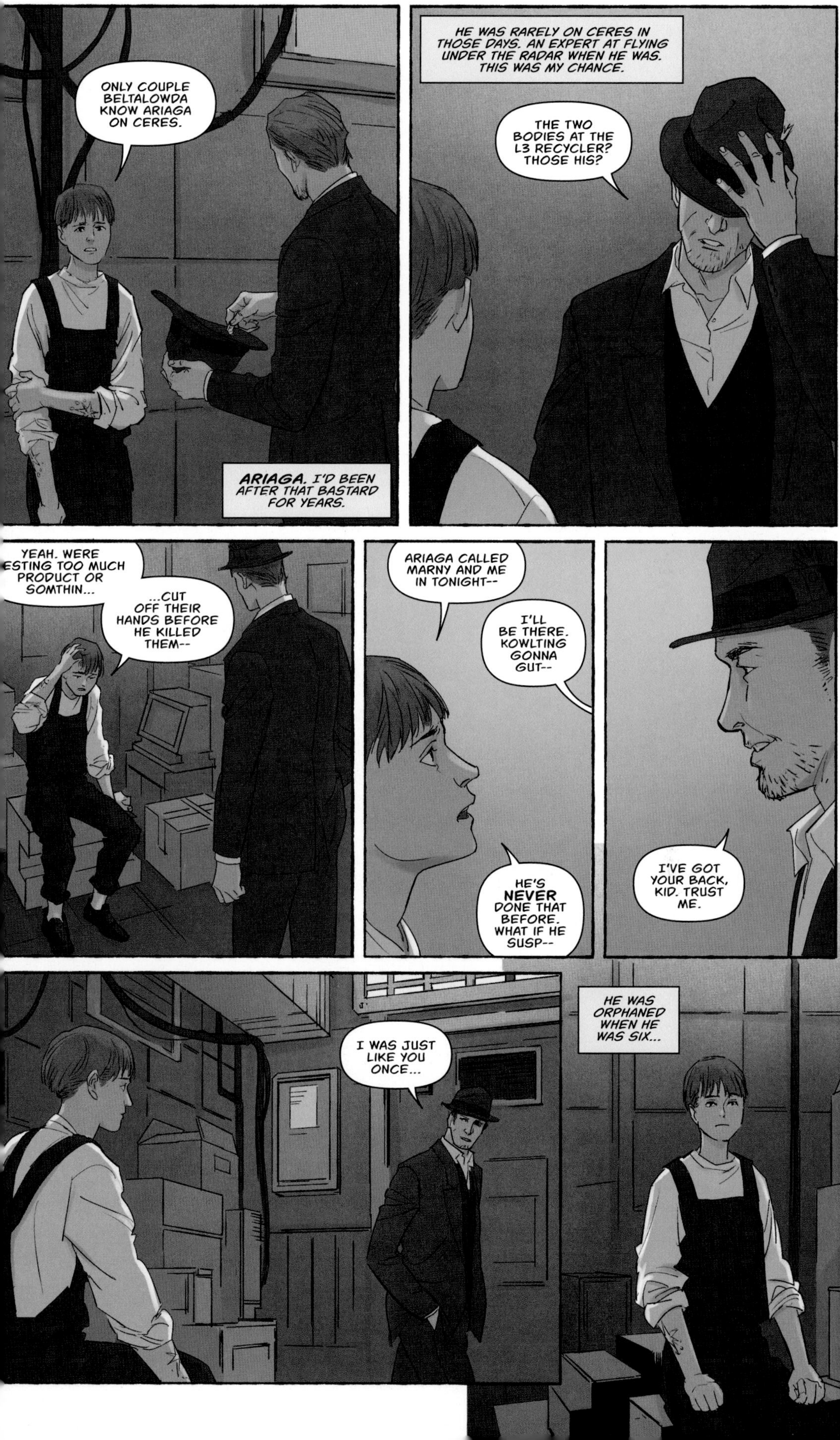
ONLY COUPLE BELTALOWDA KNOW ARIAGA ON CERES.
ARIAGA. I'D BEEN AFTER THAT BASTARD FOR YEARS.
HE WAS RARELY ON CERES IN THOSE DAYS. AN EXPERT AT FLYING UNDER THE RADAR WHEN HE WAS. THIS WAS MY CHANCE.
THE TWO BODIES AT THE L3 RECYCLER? THOSE HIS?
YEAH. WERE ESTING TOO MUCH PRODUCT OR SOMTHIN...
...CUT OFF THEIR HANDS BEFORE HE KILLED THEM--
ARIAGA CALLED MARNY AND ME IN TONIGHT--
I'LL BE THERE. KOWLTING GONNA GUT--
HE'S NEVER DONE THAT BEFORE. WHAT IF HE SUSP--
I'VE GOT YOUR BACK, KID. TRUST ME.
I WAS JUST LIKE YOU ONCE...
HE WAS ORPHANED WHEN HE WAS SIX...

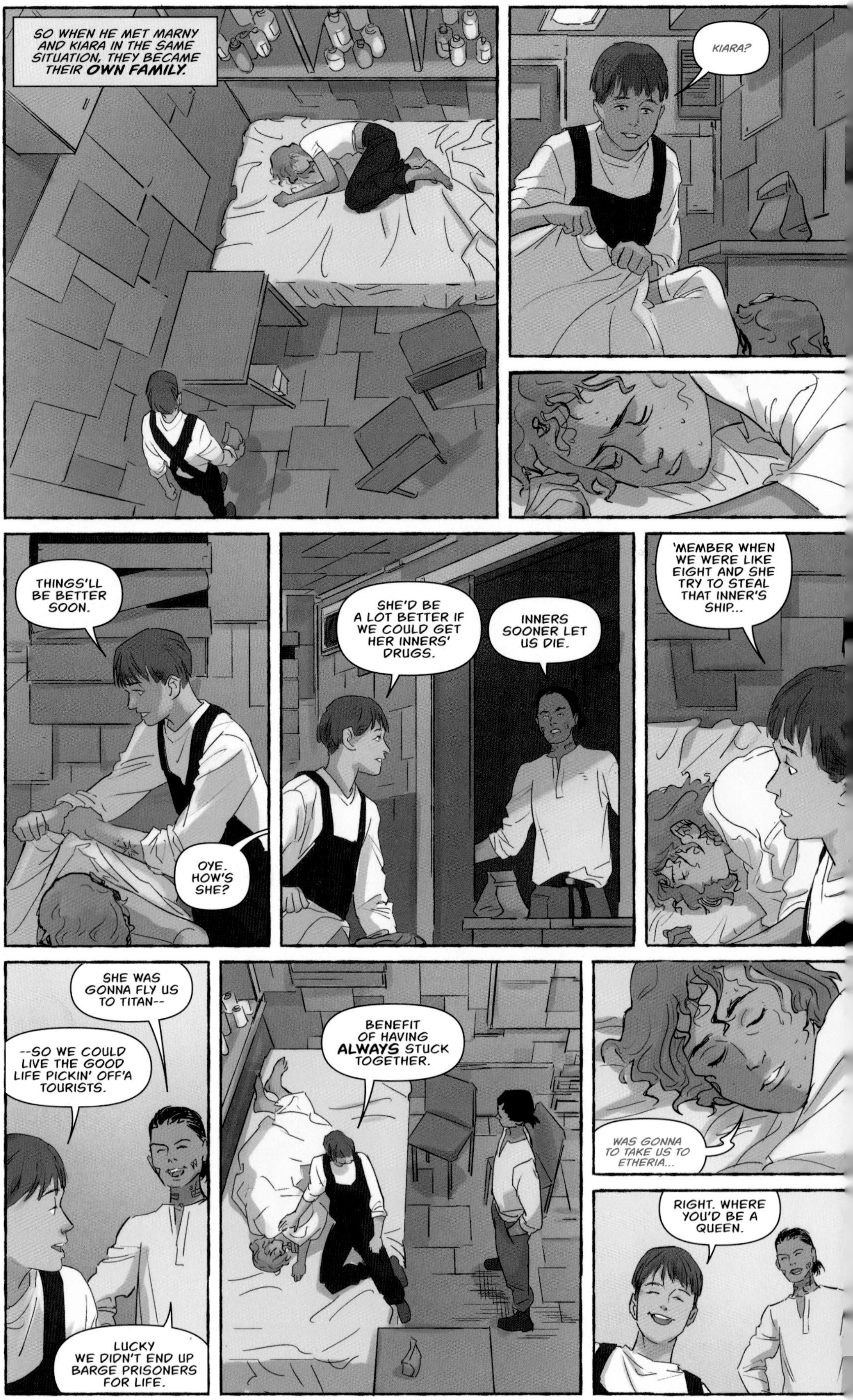
SO WHEN HE MET MARNY AND KIARA IN THE SAME SITUATION, THEY BECAME THEIR **OWN FAMILY.**
KIARA?
THINGS'LL BE BETTER SOON.
OYE. HOW'S SHE?
SHE'D BE A LOT BETTER IF WE COULD GET HER INNERS' DRUGS.
INNERS SOONER LET US DIE.
'MEMBER WHEN WE WERE LIKE EIGHT AND SHE TRY TO STEAL THAT INNER'S SHIP...
SHE WAS GONNA FLY US TO TITAN--
--SO WE COULD LIVE THE GOOD LIFE PICKIN' OFF'A TOURISTS.
LUCKY WE DIDN'T END UP BARGE PRISONERS FOR LIFE.
BENEFIT OF HAVING **ALWAYS** STUCK TOGETHER.
WAS GONNA TO TAKE US TO ETHERIA...
RIGHT. WHERE YOU'D BE A QUEEN.

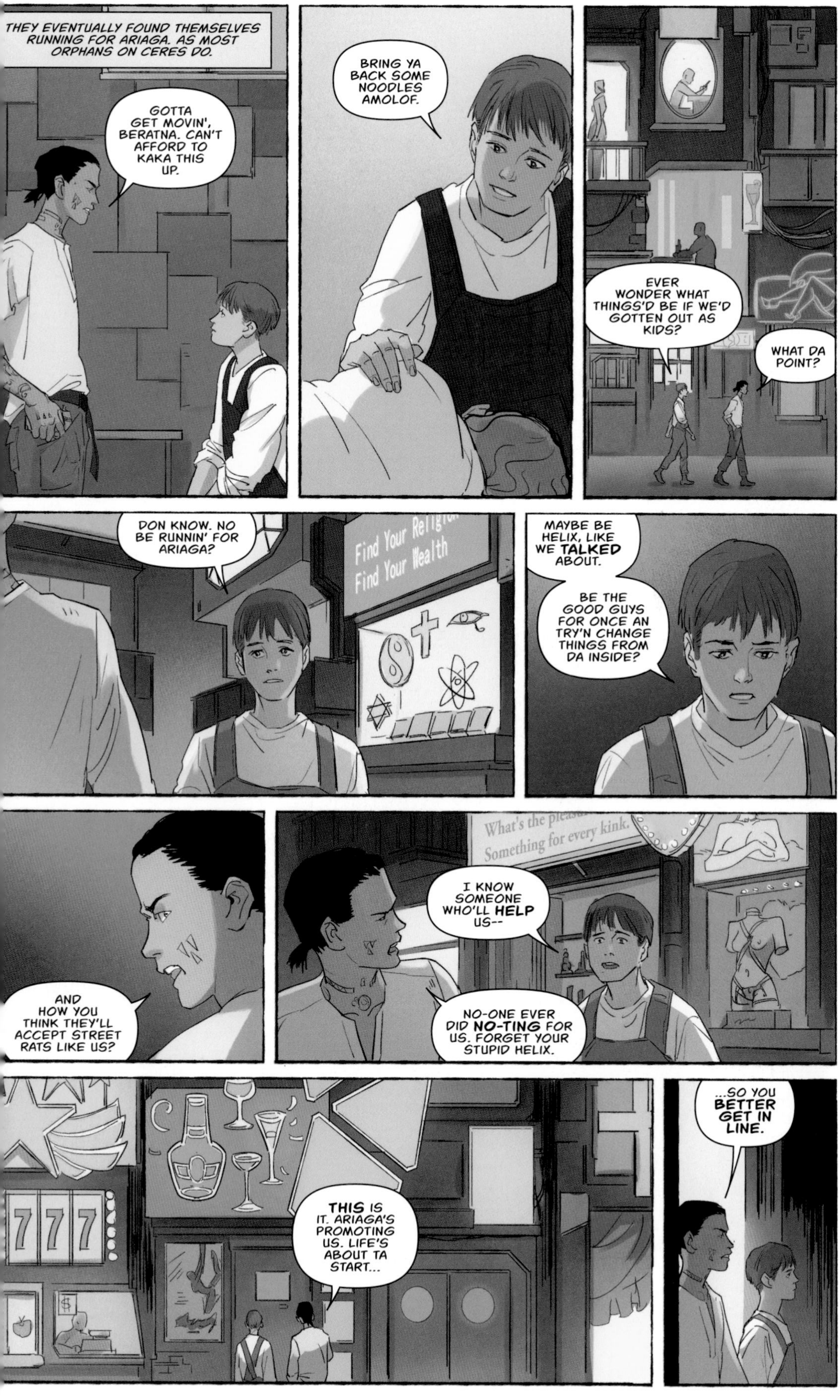
THEY EVENTUALLY FOUND THEMSELVES RUNNING FOR ARIAGA. AS MOST ORPHANS ON CERES DO.
GOTTA GET MOVIN', BERATNA. CAN'T AFFORD TO KAKA THIS UP.
BRING YA BACK SOME NOODLES AMOLOF.
EVER WONDER WHAT THINGS'D BE IF WE'D GOTTEN OUT AS KIDS?
WHAT DA POINT?
DON KNOW. NO BE RUNNIN' FOR ARIAGA?
Find Your Wealth
MAYBE BE HELIX, LIKE WE **TALKED** ABOUT.
BE THE GOOD GUYS FOR ONCE AN TRY'N CHANGE THINGS FROM DA INSIDE?
AND HOW YOU THINK THEY'LL ACCEPT STREET RATS LIKE US?
Something for every kink.
I KNOW SOMEONE WHO'LL **HELP** US--
NO-ONE EVER DID **NO-TING** FOR US. FORGET YOUR STUPID HELIX.
777
THIS IS IT. ARIAGA'S PROMOTING US. LIFE'S ABOUT TA START...
...SO YOU **BETTER GET IN LINE.**

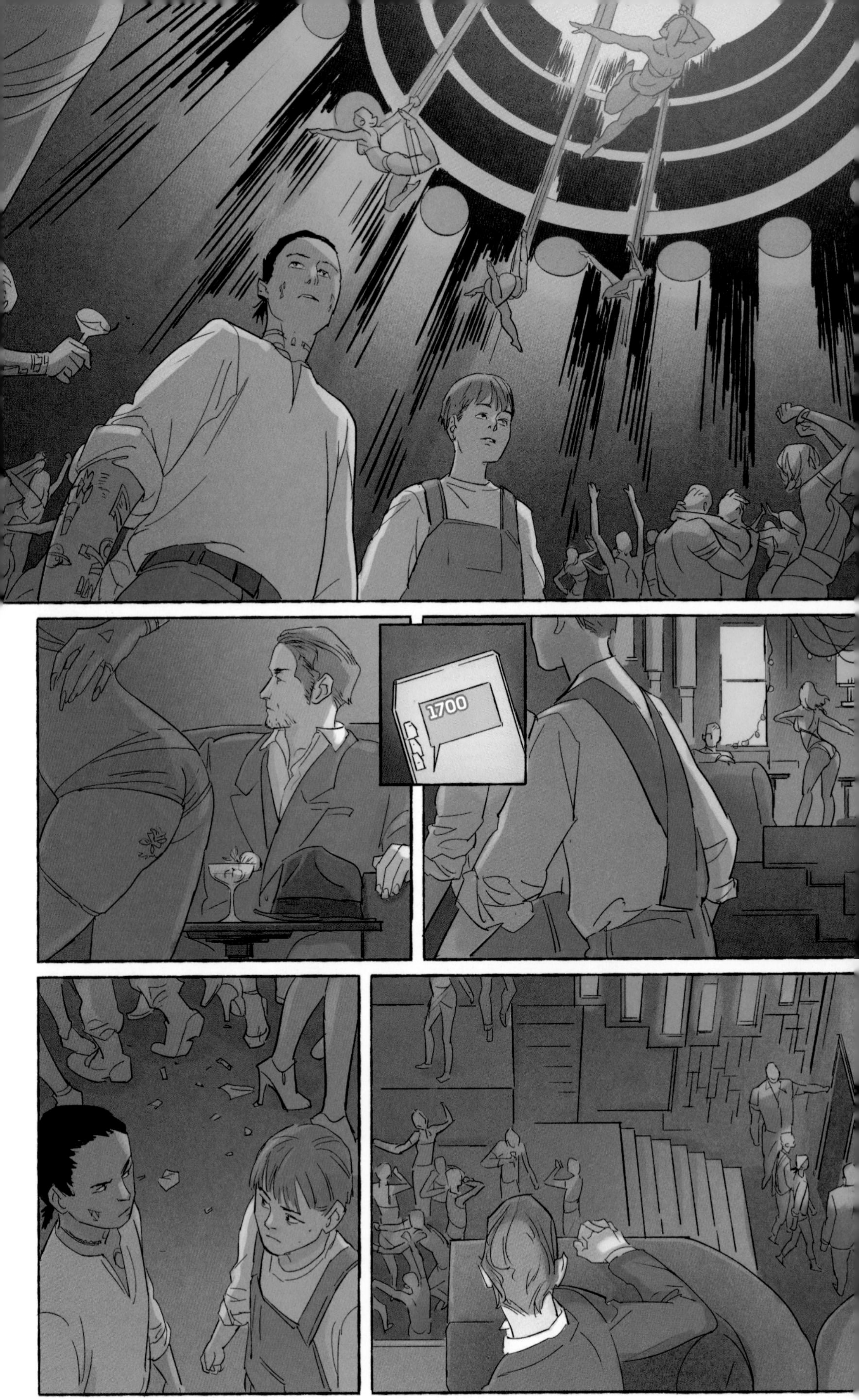
1700

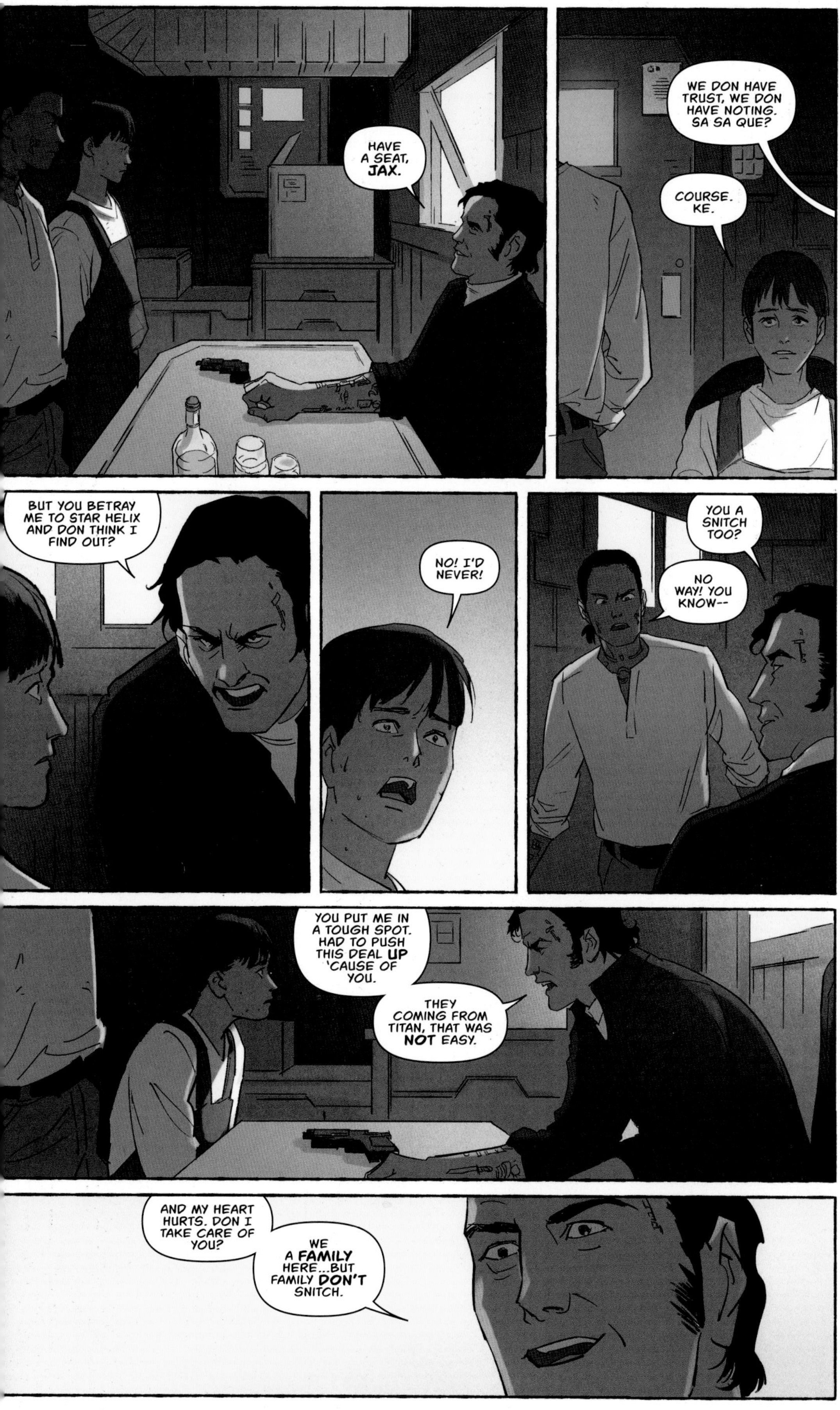
HAVE A SEAT, JAX.
WE DON HAVE TRUST, WE DON HAVE NOTING. SA SA QUE?
COURSE. KE.
BUT YOU BETRAY ME TO STAR HELIX AND DON THINK I FIND OUT?
NO! I'D NEVER!
YOU A SNITCH TOO?
NO WAY! YOU KNOW--
YOU PUT ME IN A TOUGH SPOT. HAD TO PUSH THIS DEAL UP 'CAUSE OF YOU.
THEY COMING FROM TITAN, THAT WAS NOT EASY.
AND MY HEART HURTS. DON I TAKE CARE OF YOU?
WE A FAMILY HERE...BUT FAMILY DON'T SNITCH.

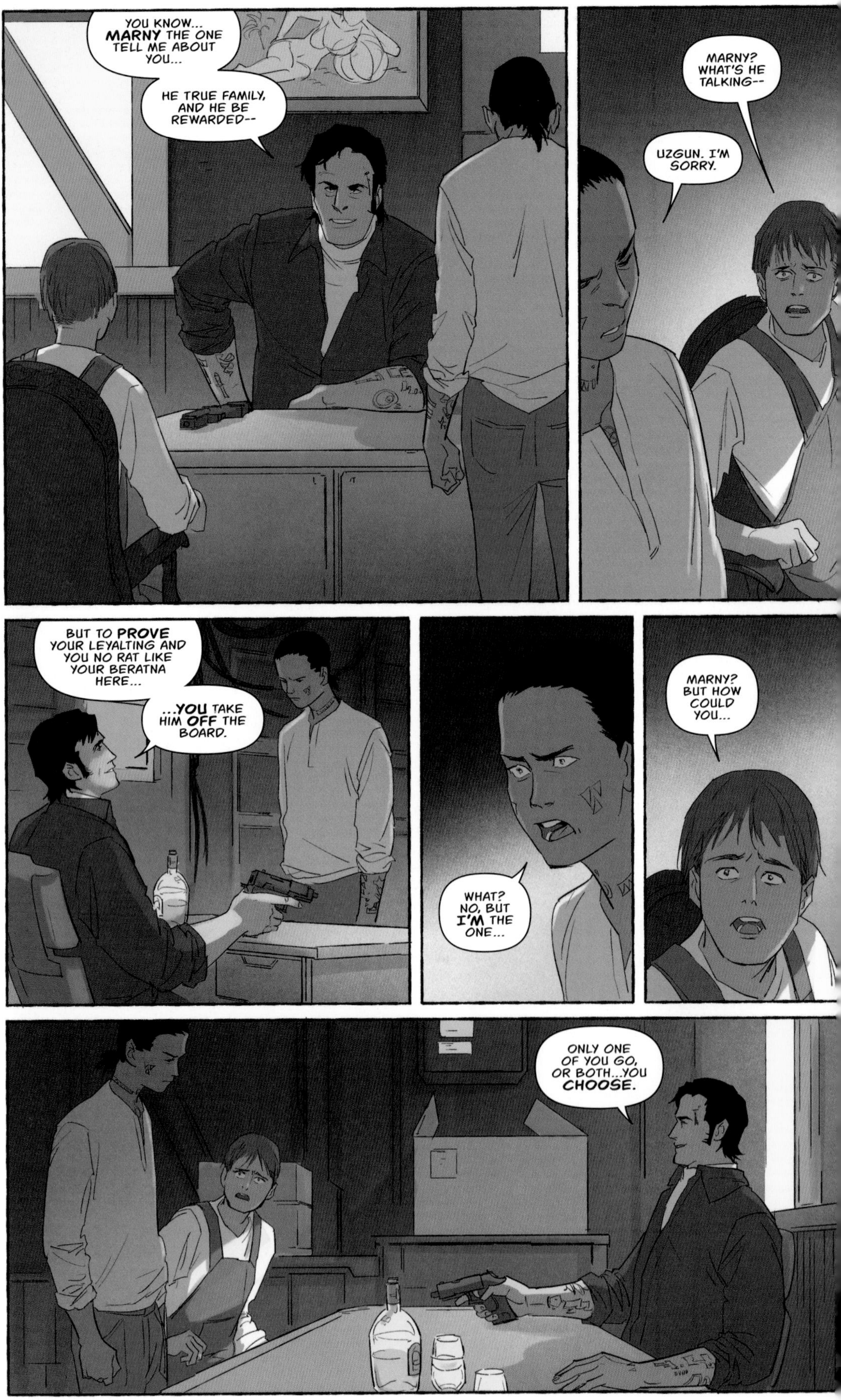
YOU KNOW... MARNY THE ONE TELL ME ABOUT YOU...
HE TRUE FAMILY, AND HE BE REWARDED--
MARNY? WHAT'S HE TALKING--
UZGUN. I'M SORRY.
BUT TO PROVE YOUR LEYALTING AND YOU NO RAT LIKE YOUR BERATNA HERE...
...YOU TAKE HIM OFF THE BOARD.
WHAT? NO, BUT I'M THE ONE...
MARNY? BUT HOW COULD YOU...
ONLY ONE OF YOU GO, OR BOTH...YOU CHOOSE.

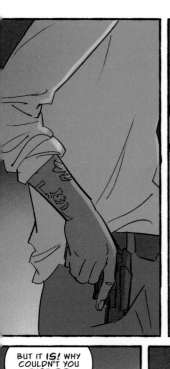

FODAGUT! MARNY, IT'S ME, YOUR BERATNA.

WHAT ABOUT KIARA?

AND ETHERIA--

YOU STUPID TA THINK WE COULD'A BE SOMTIN' ELSE--

IT'S NOT TOO LATE--

BUT IT IS! WHY COULDN'T YOU JUST GO ALONG?

THIS ISN'T YOU--

YES IT IS. DESH TIM DENIM MANG IM MOWSH LEVA SIF XOX.

SORRY BERATNA, DID'N WAN IT'D COME TO THIS--

BANG

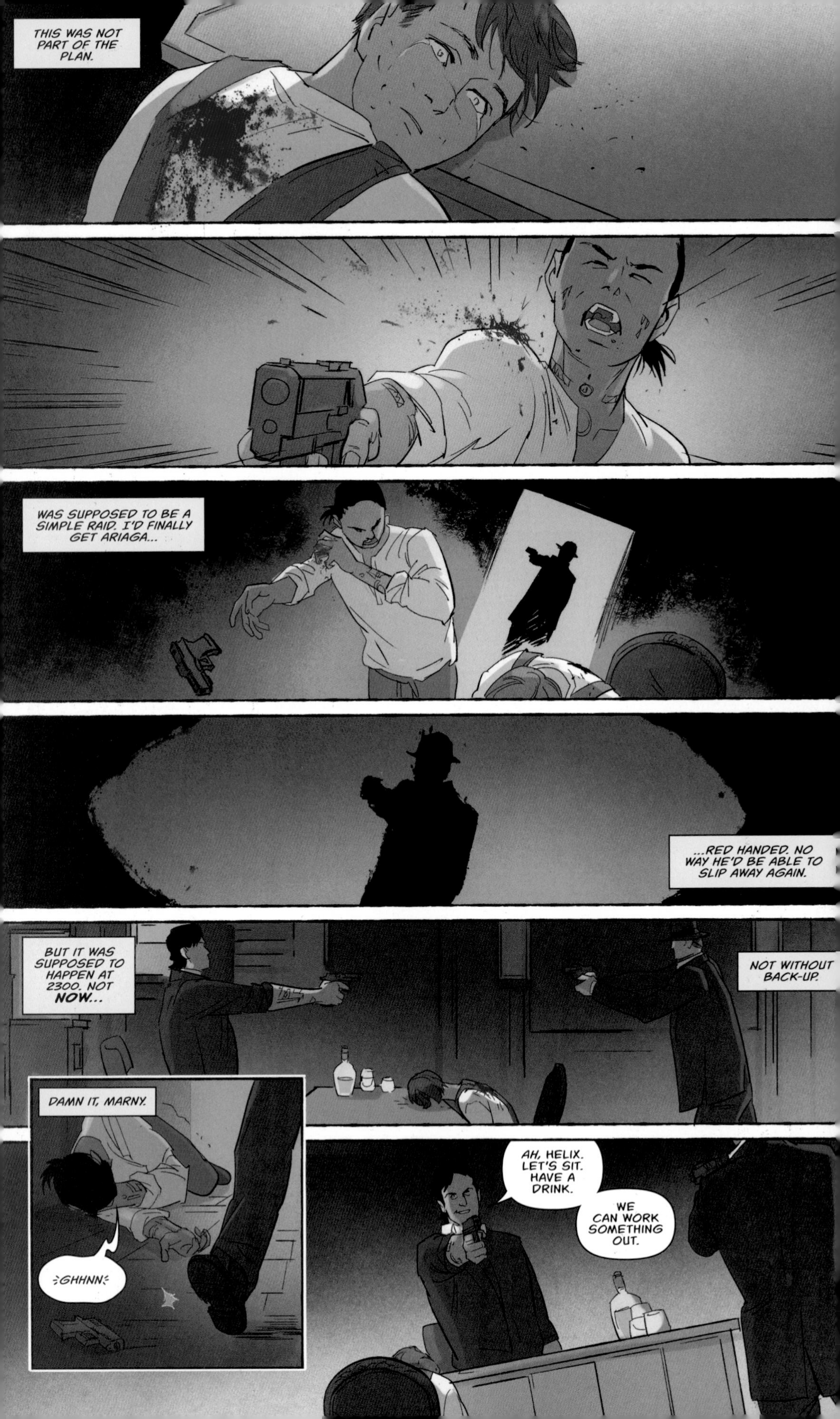
THIS WAS NOT PART OF THE PLAN.
WAS SUPPOSED TO BE A SIMPLE RAID. I'D FINALLY GET ARIAGA...
...RED HANDED. NO WAY HE'D BE ABLE TO SLIP AWAY AGAIN.
BUT IT WAS SUPPOSED TO HAPPEN AT 2300. NOT NOW...
NOT WITHOUT BACK-UP.
DAMN IT, MARNY.
GHHNN
AH, HELIX. LET'S SIT. HAVE A DRINK.
WE CAN WORK SOMETHING OUT.

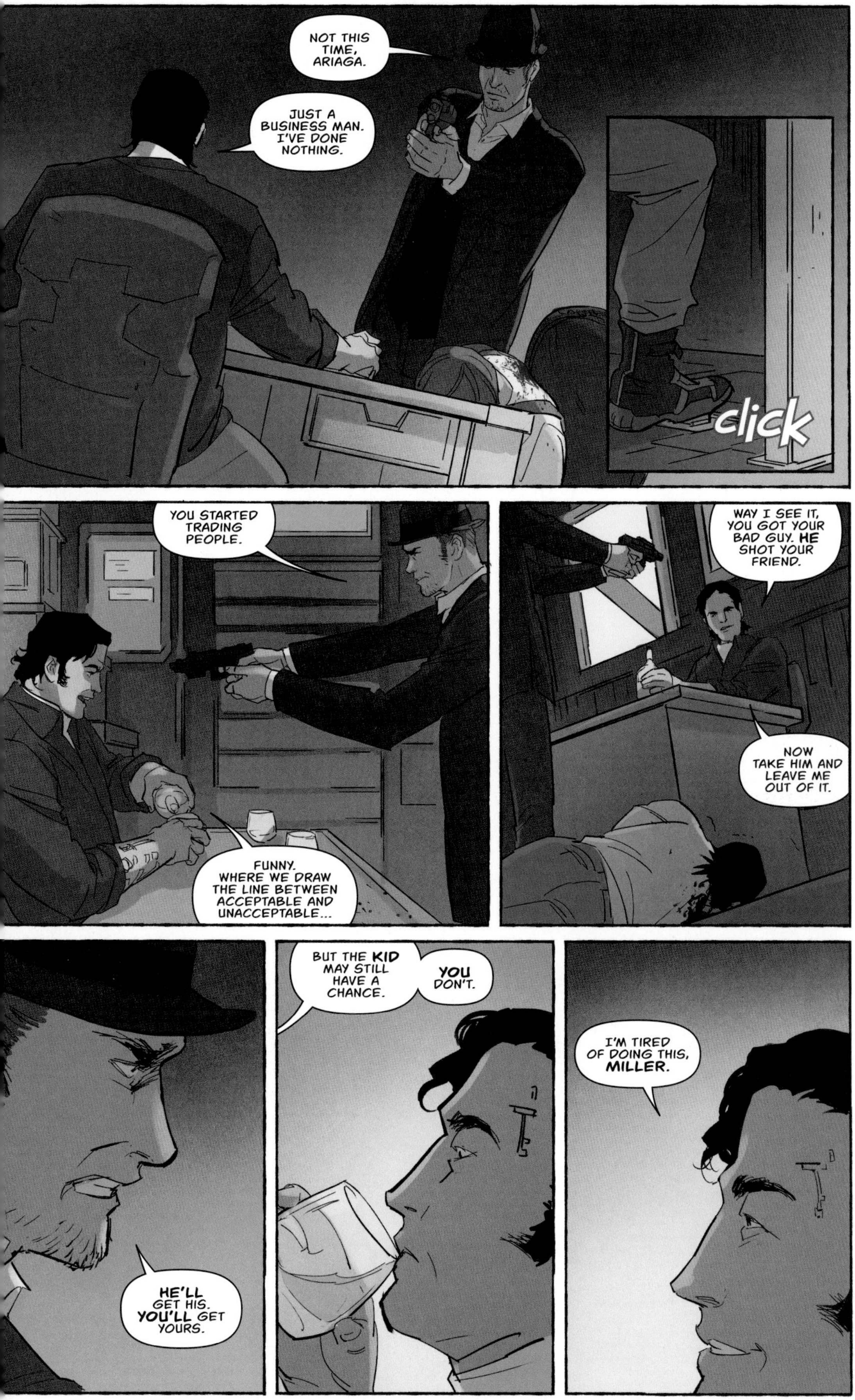
NOT THIS TIME, ARIAGA.
JUST A BUSINESS MAN. I'VE DONE NOTHING.
click
YOU STARTED TRADING PEOPLE.
FUNNY. WHERE WE DRAW THE LINE BETWEEN ACCEPTABLE AND UNACCEPTABLE...
WAY I SEE IT, YOU GOT YOUR BAD GUY. HE SHOT YOUR FRIEND.
NOW TAKE HIM AND LEAVE ME OUT OF IT.
HE'LL GET HIS. YOU'LL GET YOURS.
BUT THE KID MAY STILL HAVE A CHANCE.
YOU DON'T.
I'M TIRED OF DOING THIS, MILLER.

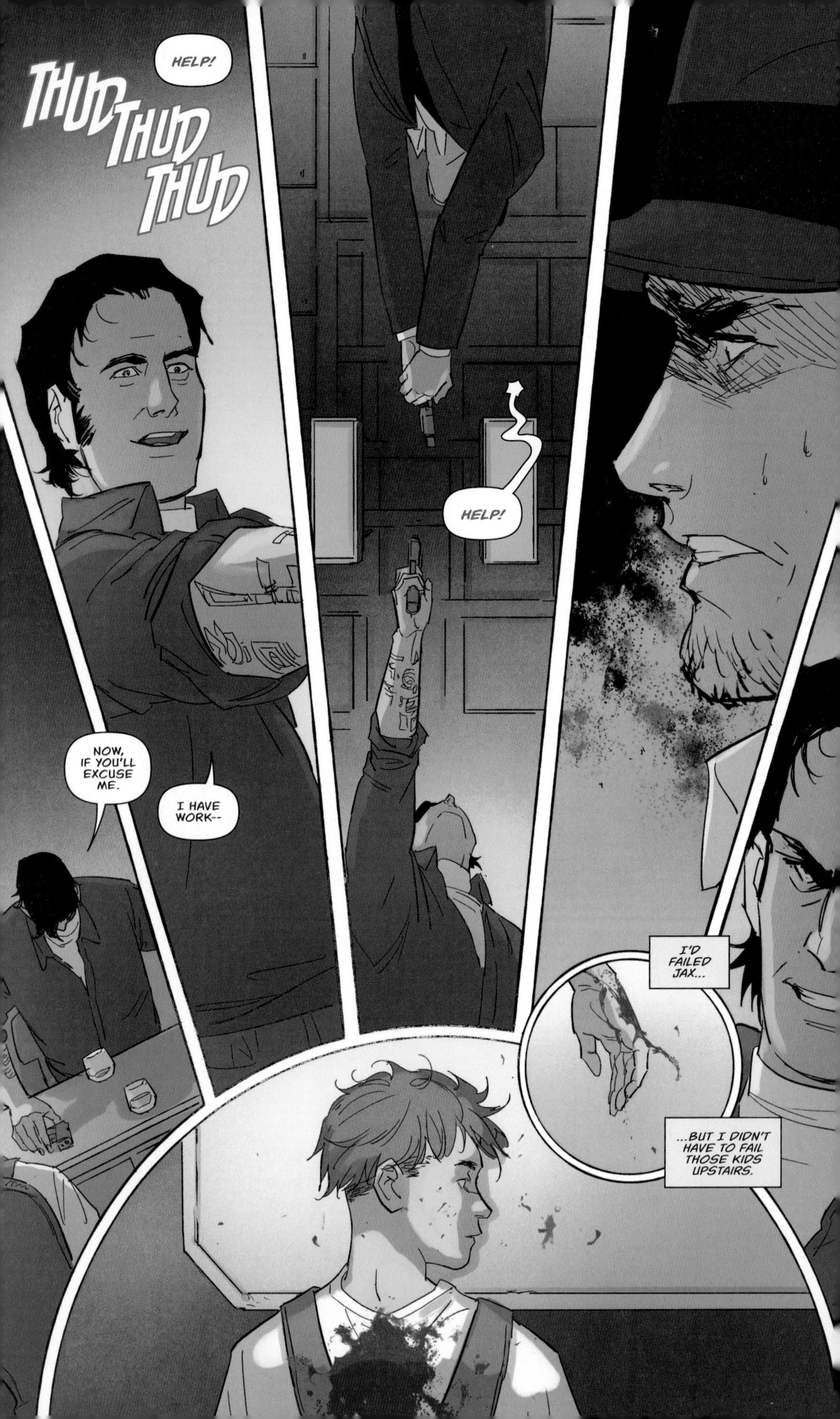
HELP!
THUD THUD THUD
NOW, IF YOU'LL EXCUSE ME.
I HAVE WORK--
HELP!
I'D FAILED JAX...
...BUT I DIDN'T HAVE TO FAIL THOSE KIDS UPSTAIRS.

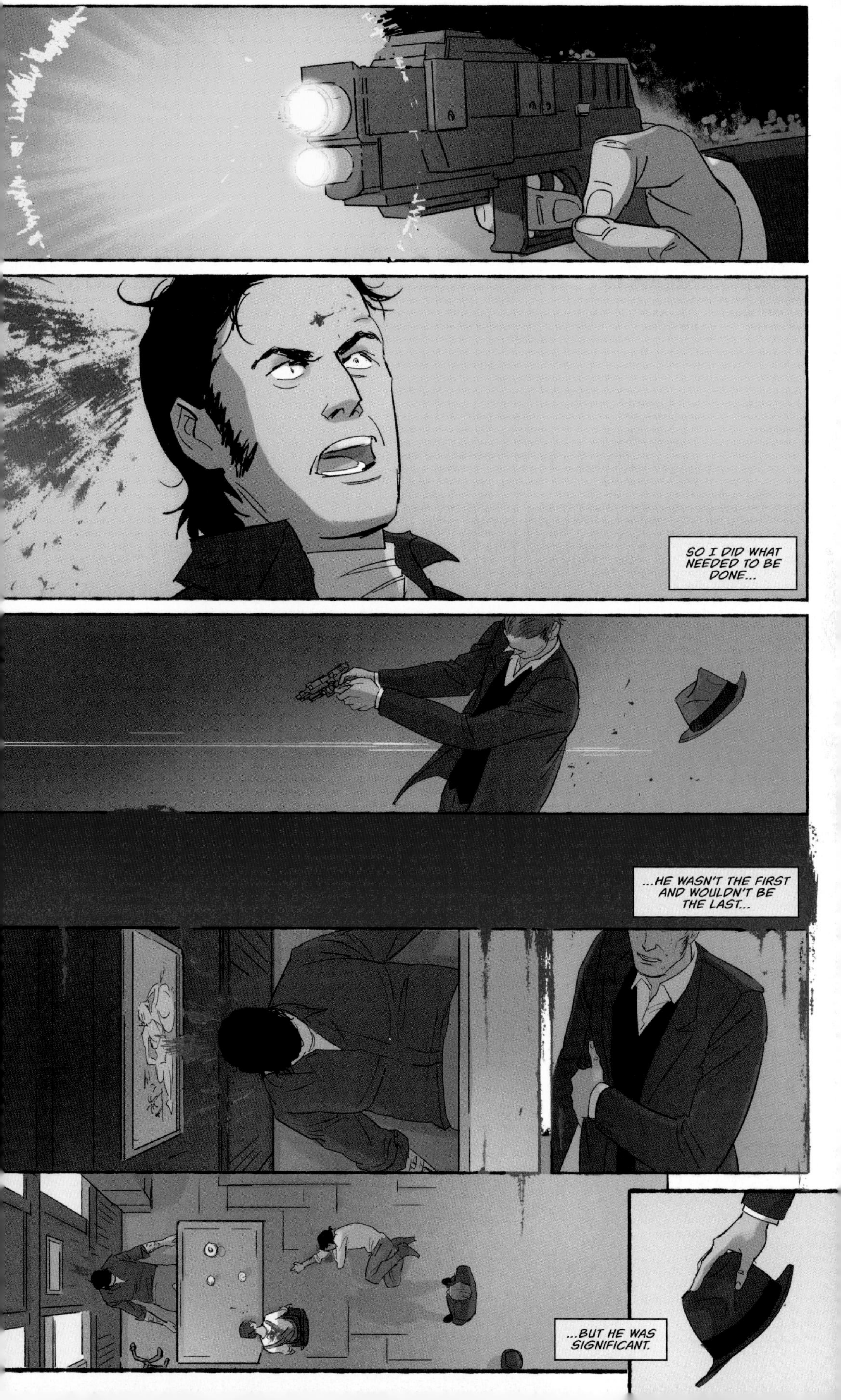
SO I DID WHAT NEEDED TO BE DONE...
...HE WASN'T THE FIRST AND WOULDN'T BE THE LAST...
...BUT HE WAS SIGNIFICANT.

HELP...

ARIAGA'S BIG FISH HAD GOTTEN AWAY WITH MOST OF THE DRUGS...

...AND THREE OF THE KIDS.

DON'T SHOOT. PLEASE.

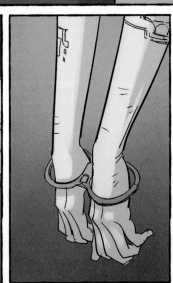

CRAZY THING...

...THESE KIDS ARE THE LUCKY ONES.

I'D FINALLY GOTTEN ARIAGA, BUT FELT LIKE I'D LOST.

MUSS. I NEED YOU.

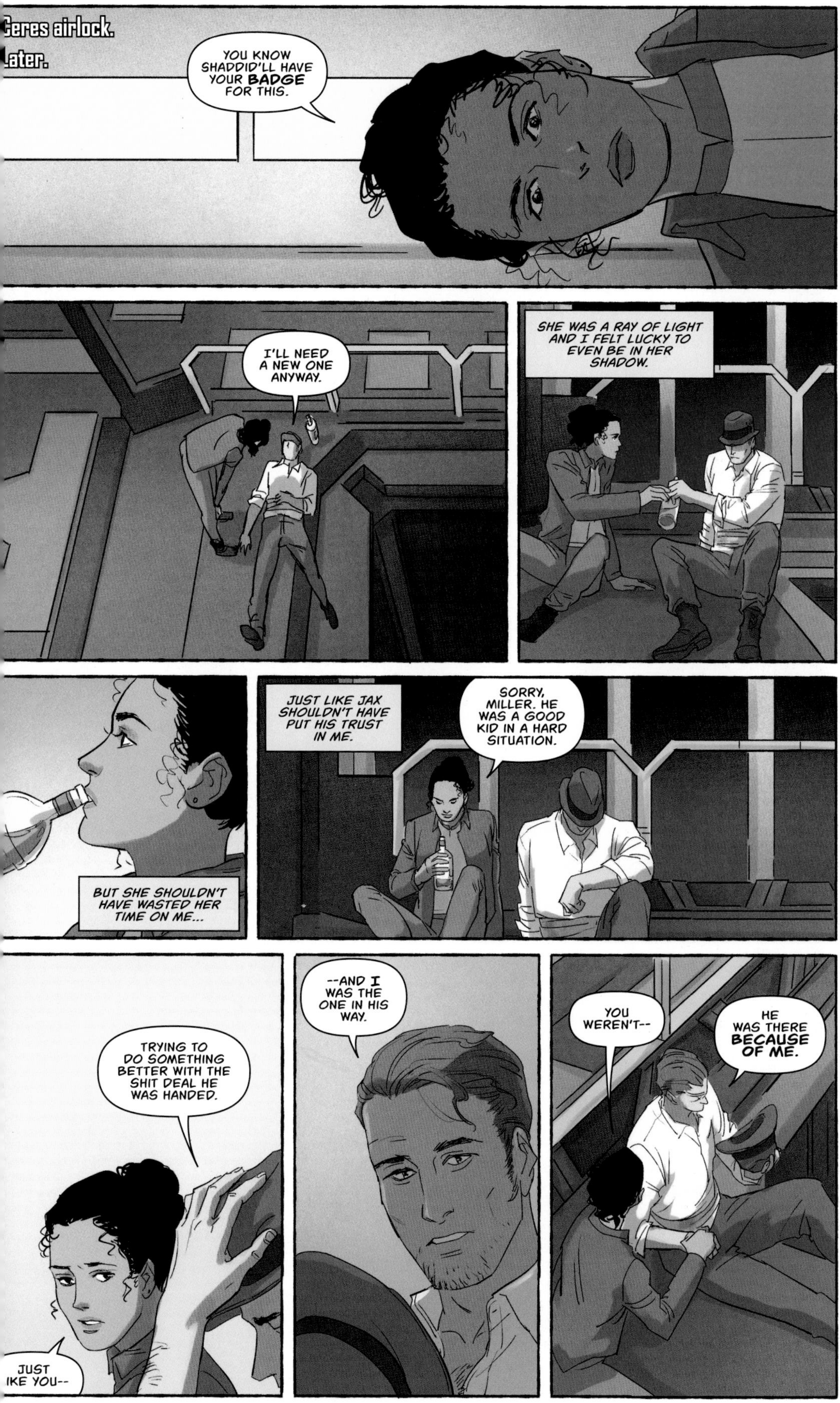

Ceres airlock.
Later.
YOU KNOW SHADDID'LL HAVE YOUR BADGE FOR THIS.
I'LL NEED A NEW ONE ANYWAY.
SHE WAS A RAY OF LIGHT AND I FELT LUCKY TO EVEN BE IN HER SHADOW.
BUT SHE SHOULDN'T HAVE WASTED HER TIME ON ME...
JUST LIKE JAX SHOULDN'T HAVE PUT HIS TRUST IN ME.
SORRY, MILLER. HE WAS A GOOD KID IN A HARD SITUATION.
TRYING TO DO SOMETHING BETTER WITH THE SHIT DEAL HE WAS HANDED.
JUST IKE YOU--
--AND I WAS THE ONE IN HIS WAY.
YOU WEREN'T--
HE WAS THERE BECAUSE OF ME.

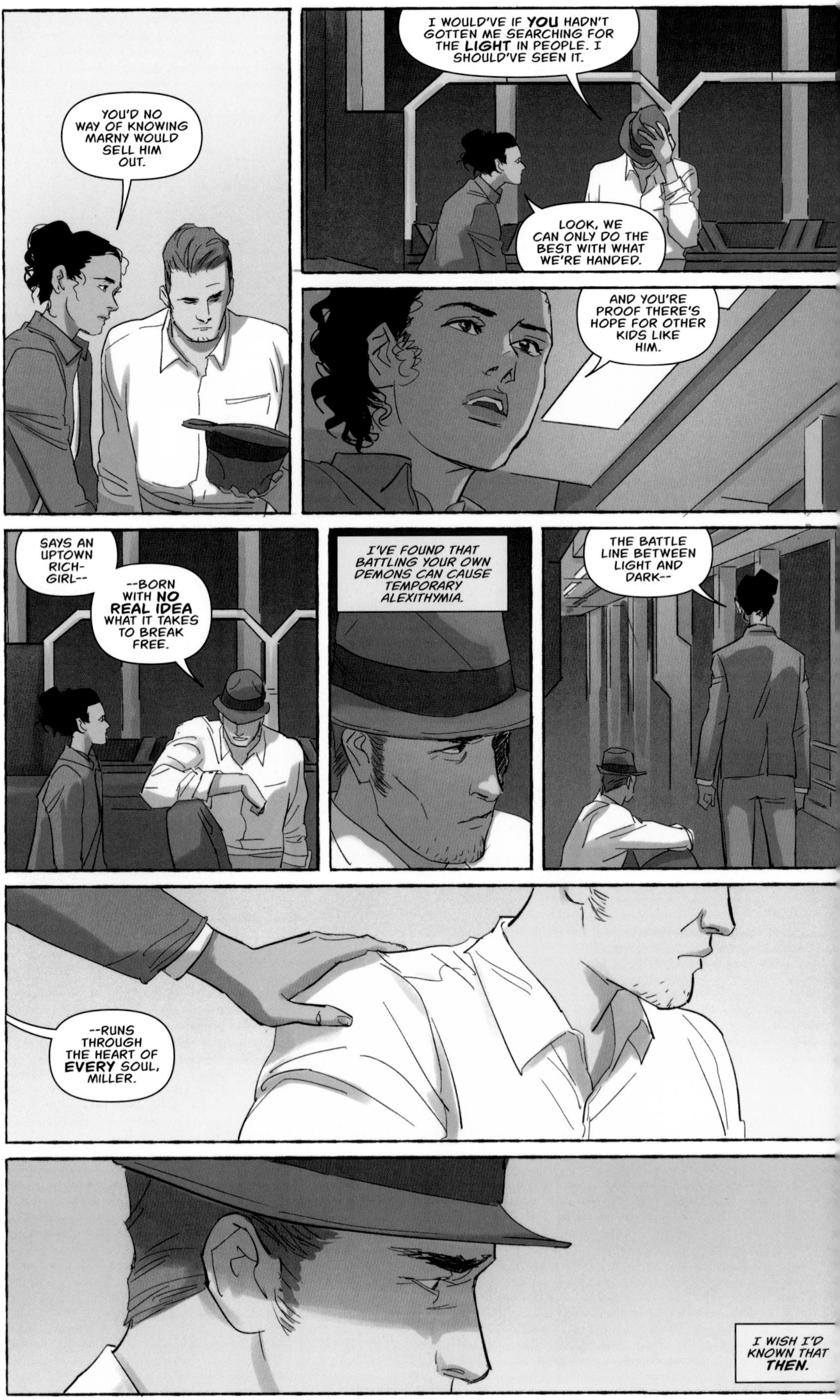
YOU'D NO WAY OF KNOWING MARNY WOULD SELL HIM OUT.
I WOULD'VE IF YOU HADN'T GOTTEN ME SEARCHING FOR THE LIGHT IN PEOPLE. I SHOULD'VE SEEN IT.
LOOK, WE CAN ONLY DO THE BEST WITH WHAT WE'RE HANDED.
AND YOU'RE PROOF THERE'S HOPE FOR OTHER KIDS LIKE HIM.
SAYS AN UPTOWN RICH-GIRL--
--BORN WITH NO REAL IDEA WHAT IT TAKES TO BREAK FREE.
I'VE FOUND THAT BATTLING YOUR OWN DEMONS CAN CAUSE TEMPORARY ALEXITHYMIA.
THE BATTLE LINE BETWEEN LIGHT AND DARK--
--RUNS THROUGH THE HEART OF EVERY SOUL, MILLER.
I WISH I'D KNOWN THAT THEN.

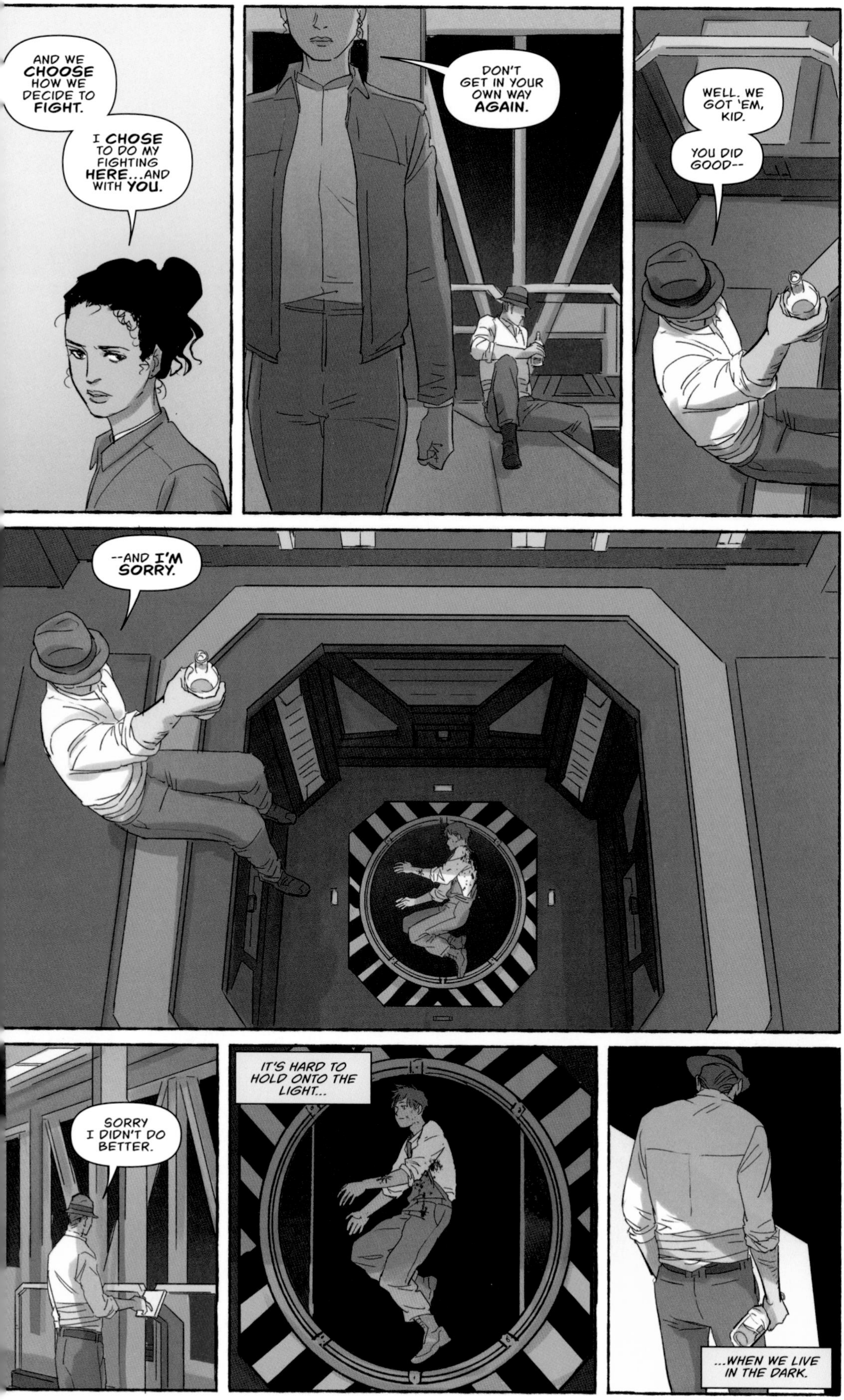

AND WE CHOOSE HOW WE DECIDE TO FIGHT.
I CHOSE TO DO MY FIGHTING HERE...AND WITH YOU.
DON'T GET IN YOUR OWN WAY AGAIN.
WELL. WE GOT 'EM, KID.
YOU DID GOOD--
--AND I'M SORRY.
SORRY I DIDN'T DO BETTER.
IT'S HARD TO HOLD ONTO THE LIGHT...
...WHEN WE LIVE IN THE DARK.

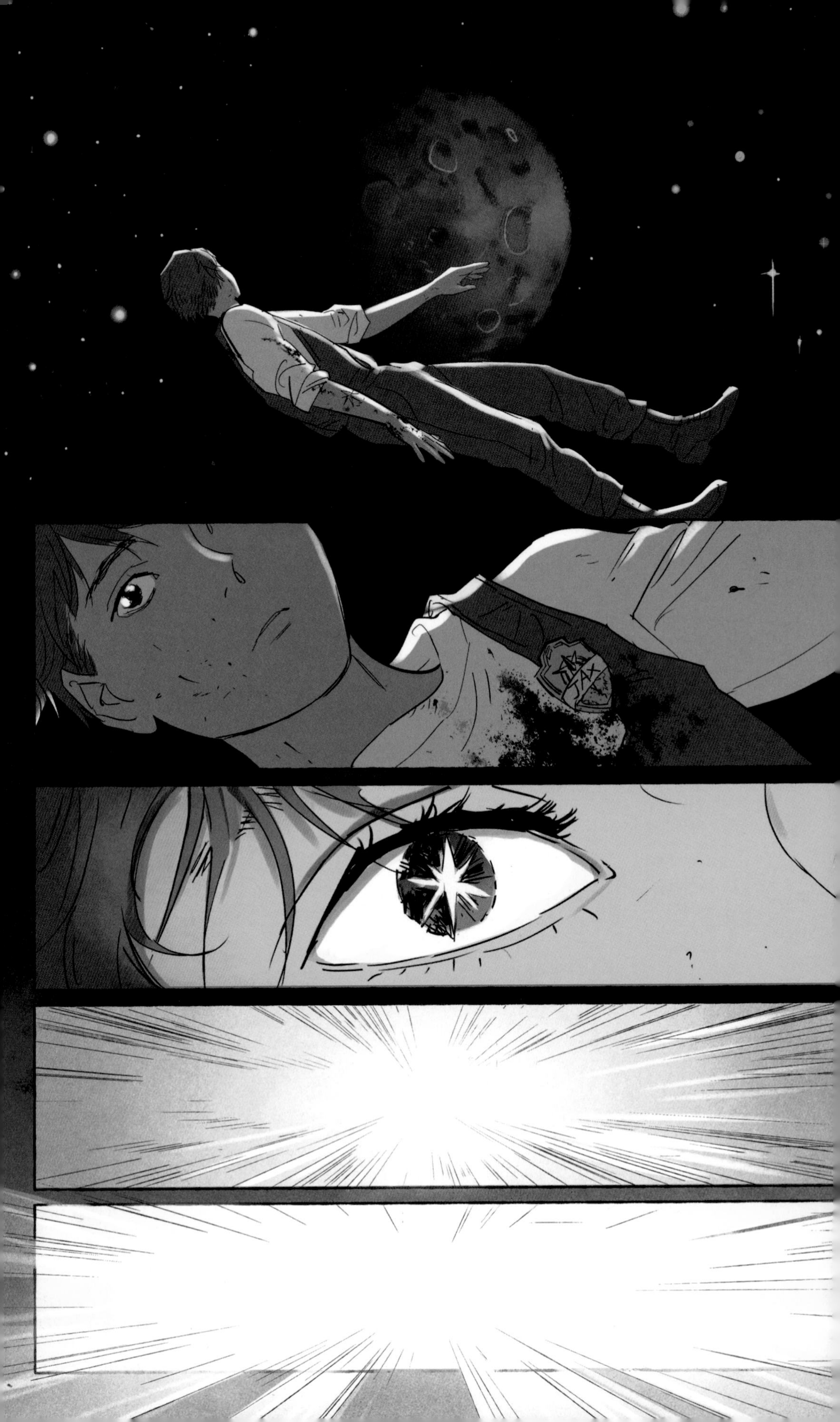

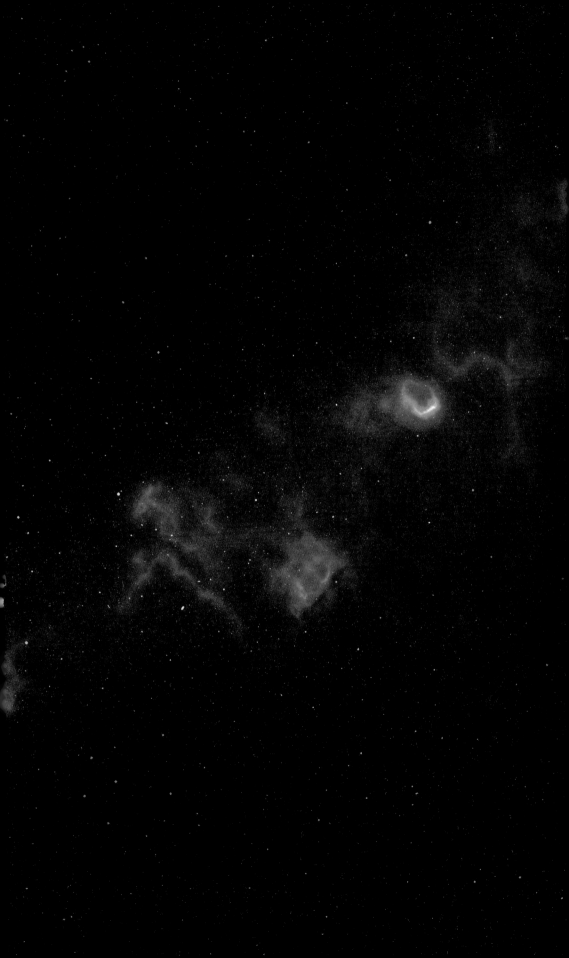

ADDITIONAL ARTWORK BY **SCOTT NEWMAN**

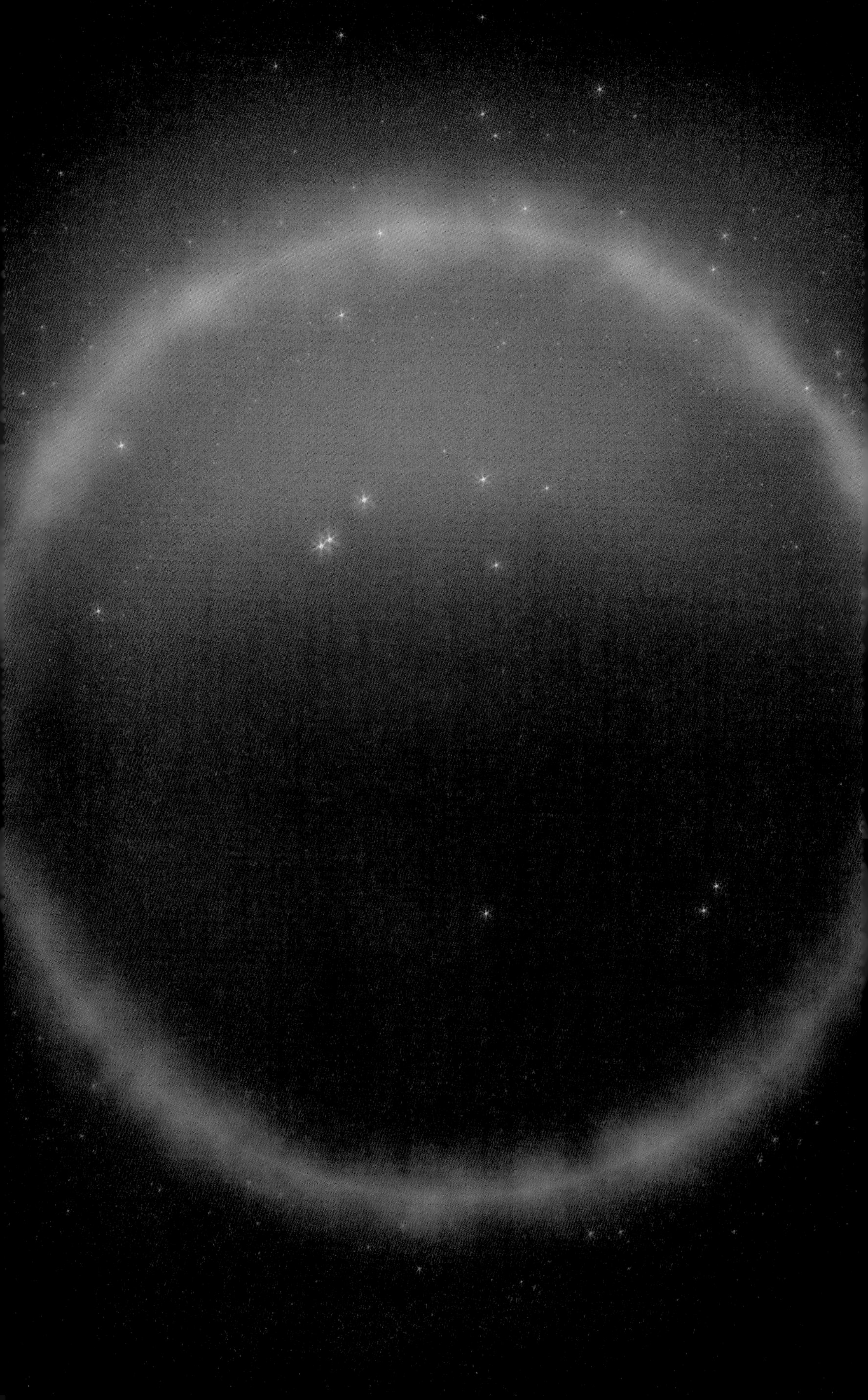

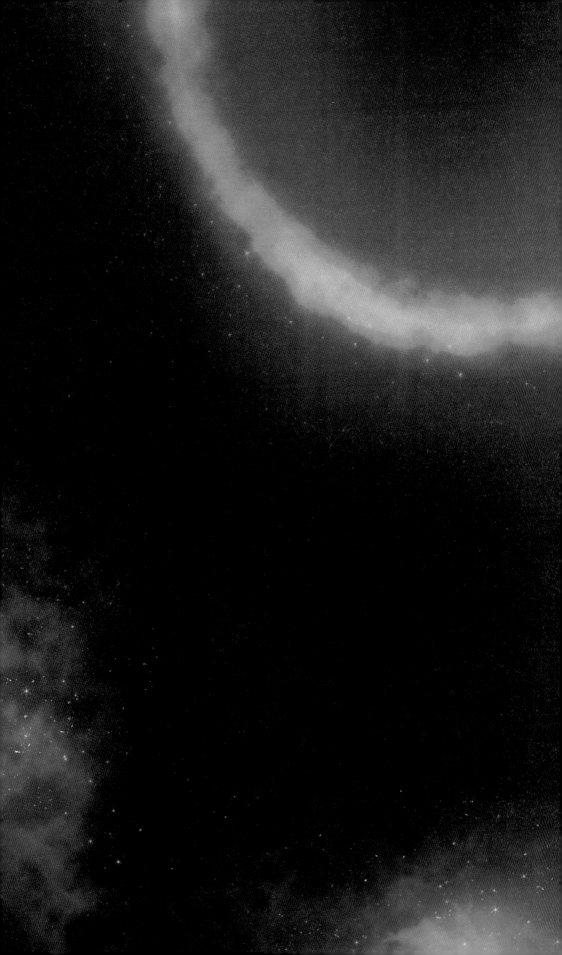

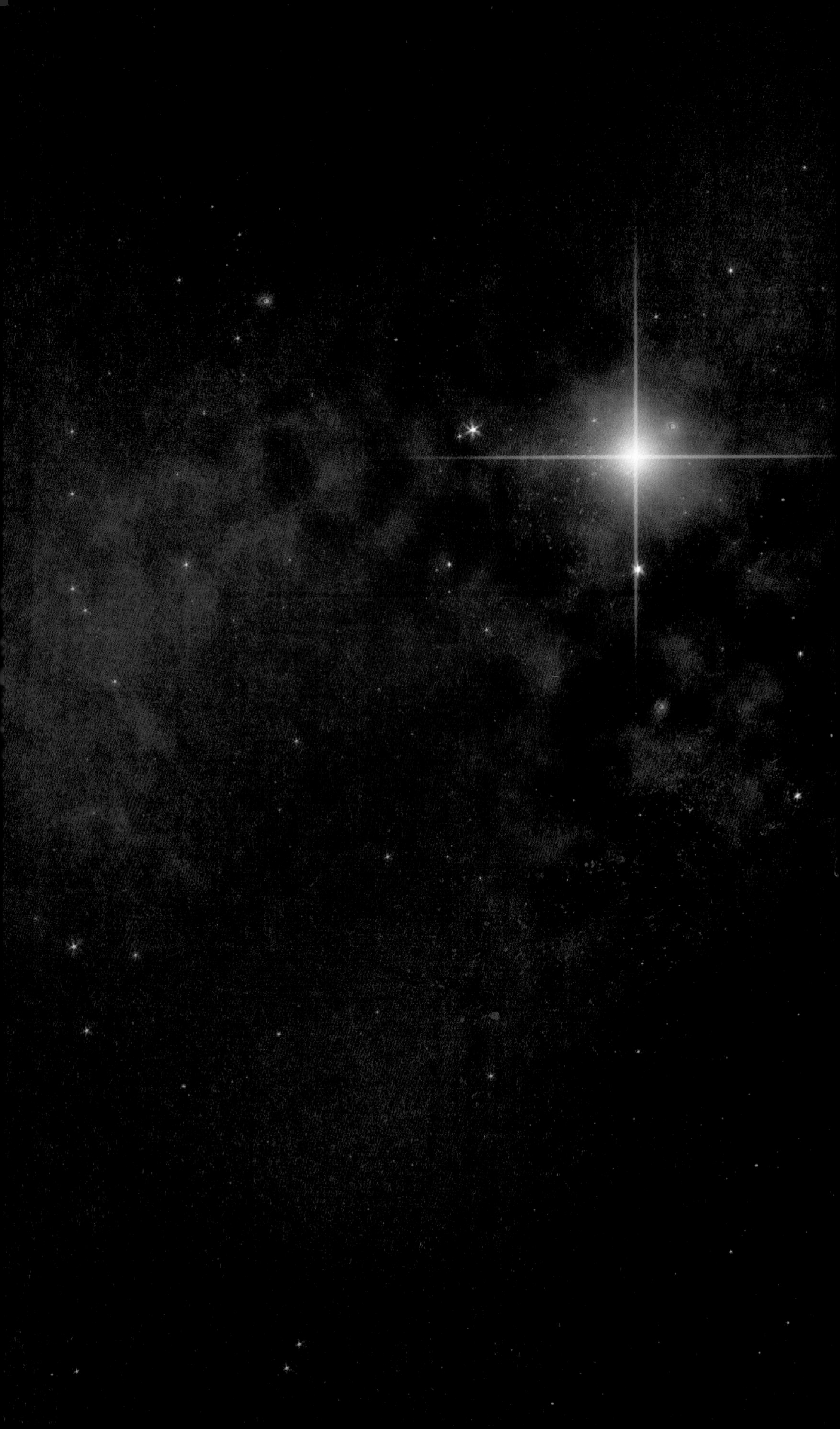

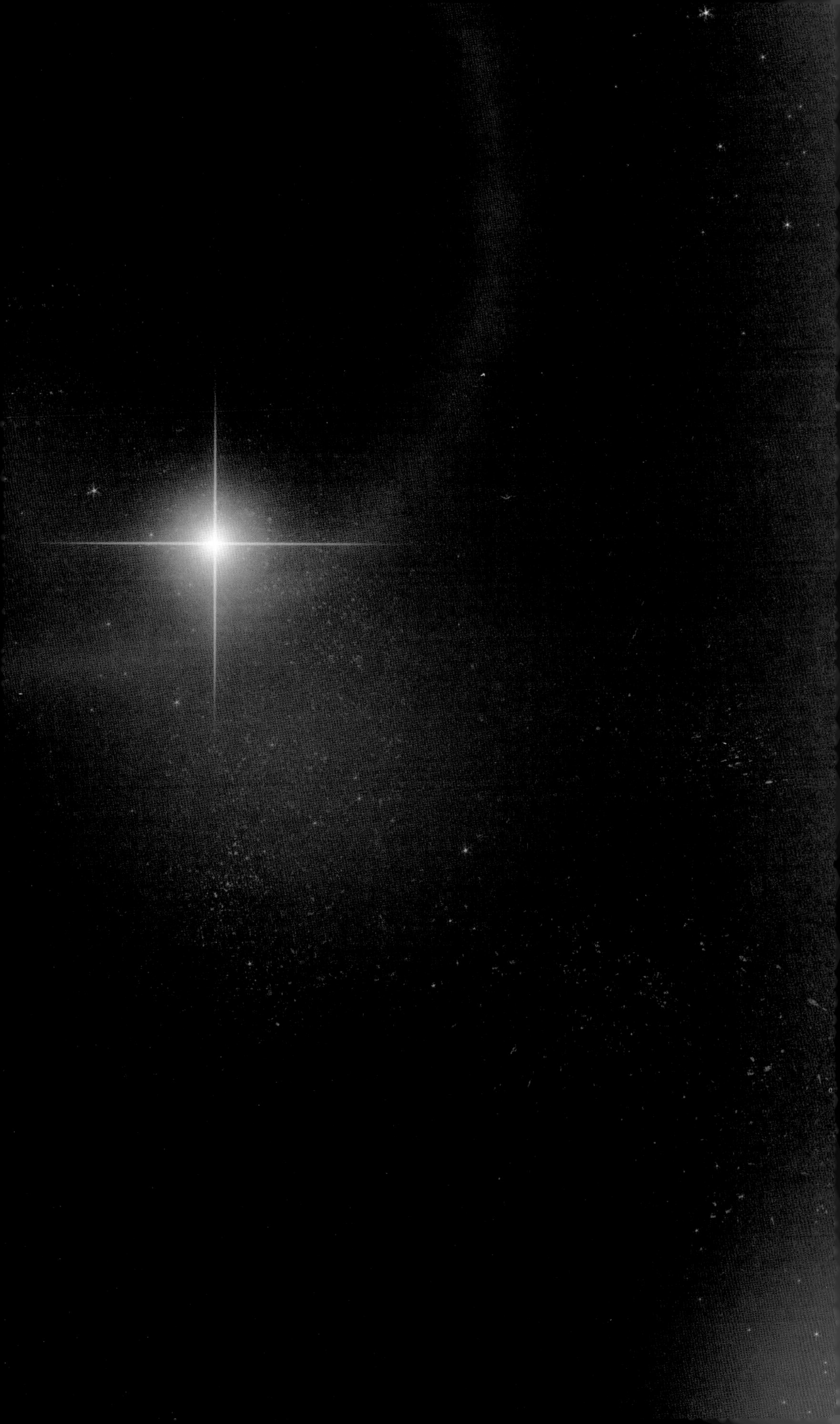

DISCOVER
VISIONARY CREATORS

THE WOODS
JAMES TYNION IV • MICHAEL DIALYNAS
VOL. 1
THE ARROW

"The Spire is fantastic! My kind of genre free-for-all."
—BRIAN K. VAUGHAN (Saga)
THE SPIRE
SIMON SPURRIER
JEFF STOKELY
ANDRÉ MAY

MARK WAID · PETER KRAUSE
IRREDEEMABLE
AFTERWORD BY GRANT MORRISON

J.G. JONES
MARK WAID
STRANGE FRUIT
Foreword by
ELVIS MITCHELL

MICHAEL ALAN NELSON
DAN MORA
GABRIEL CASSATA
HEXED
THE HARLOT & THE THIEF VOLUME ONE

ABNETT & CULBARD
WILD'S END
FIRST LIGHT
"IT'S REALLY GREAT"
JEFF LEMIRE

BOOM! STUDIOS

AVAILABLE AT YOUR LOCAL COMICS SHOP AND BOOKSTORE

To find a comics shop in your area, call 1-888-266-4226

WWW.**BOOM-STUDIOS**.COM

James Tynion IV

The Woods

Volume 1
ISBN: 978-1-60886-454-6 | $9.99 US
Volume 2
ISBN: 978-1-60886-495-9 | $14.99 US
Volume 3
ISBN: 978-1-60886-773-8 | $14.99 US

The Backstagers

Volume 1
ISBN: 978-1-60886-993-0 | $14.99 US

Simon Spurrier

Six-Gun Gorilla

ISBN: 978-1-60886-390-7 | $19.99 US

The Spire

ISBN: 978-1-60886-913-8 | $29.99 US

Weavers

ISBN: 978-1-60886-963-3 | $19.99 US

Mark Waid

Irredeemable

Volume 1
ISBN: 978-1-93450-690-5 | $16.99 US
Volume 2
ISBN: 978-1-60886-000-5 | $16.99 US

Incorruptible

Volume 1
ISBN: 978-1-60886-015-9 | $16.99 US
Volume 2
ISBN: 978-1-60886-028-9 | $16.99 US

Strange Fruit

ISBN: 978-1-60886-872-8 | $24.99 US

Michael Alan Nelson

Hexed The Harlot & The Thief

Volume 1
ISBN: 978-1-60886-718-9 | $14.99 US
Volume 2
ISBN: 978-1-60886-816-2 | $14.99 US

Day Men

Volume 1
ISBN: 978-1-60886-393-8 | $9.99 US
Volume 2
ISBN: 978-1-60886-852-0 | $9.99 US

Dan Abnett

Wild's End

Volume 1: First Light
ISBN: 978-1-60886-735-6 | $19.99 US
Volume 2: The Enemy Within
ISBN: 978-1-60886-877-3 | $19.99 US

Hypernaturals

Volume 1
ISBN: 978-1-60886-298-6 | $16.99 US
Volume 2
ISBN: 978-1-60886-319-8 | $19.99 US

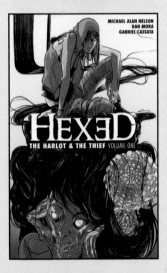